Desert Rock

Wall Street to the San Rafael Swell

Eric Bjørnstad

Graphics by Chris Becker

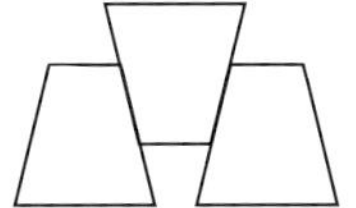

CHOCKSTONE PRESS, INC.
Conifer, Colorado

Desert Rock: Wall Street to the San Rafael Swell

Send all corrections and new route information to Eric Bjørnstad, PO Box 790, Moab, UT 84532 or call (801)259-7516. For information on the Colorado Plateau not covered in these volumes, you may contact the author at the above address.

Desert Rock Series ISBN 1-57540-010-3
Desert Rock: Rock Climbs in the National Parks ISBN 0-934641-92-7
Desert Rock: Wall Street to the San Rafael Swell ISBN 0-57540-004-9

Desert Rock works in progress:
Desert Rock: Kane Creek to Colorado National Monument (1998)
Desert Rock: Indian Creek and Isolated Areas (1999)

Published and distributed by:

Chockstone Press, Inc.
P.O. Box 1269
Conifer, Colorado 80433

Front cover photo: Colorado River and Wall Street, photo by Bill Godschalx.

Back cover photo: Factory Butte, photo courtesy of Tom Till Photography PO Box 337, Moab, UT 84532 (801) 259-5327

WARNING: CLIMBING IS A SPORT WHERE YOU MAY BE SERIOUSLY INJURED OR DIE.

READ THIS BEFORE YOU USE THIS BOOK.

This guidebook is a compilation of unverified information gathered from many different climbers. The author cannot assure the accuracy of any of the information in this book, including the topos and route descriptions, the difficulty ratings, and the protection ratings. These may be incorrect or misleading and it is impossible for any one author to climb all the routes to confirm the information about each route. Also, ratings of climbing difficulty and danger are always subjective and depend on the physical characteristics (for example, height), experience, technical ability, confidence and physical fitness of the climber who supplied the rating. Additionally, climbers who achieve first ascents sometimes underrate the difficulty or danger of the climbing route out of fear of being ridiculed if a climb is later down-rated by subsequent ascents. Therefore, be warned that you must exercise your own judgment on where a climbing route goes, its difficulty and your ability to safely protect yourself from the risks of rock climbing. Examples of some of these risks are: falling due to technical difficulty or due to natural hazards such as holds breaking, falling rock, climbing equipment dropped by other climbers, hazards of weather and lightning, your own equipment failure, and failure or absence of fixed protection.

You should not depend on any information gleaned from this book for your personal safety; your safety depends on your own good judgment, based on experience and a realistic assessment of your climbing ability. If you have any doubt as to your ability to safely climb a route described in this book, do not attempt it.

The following are some ways to make your use of this book safer:

1. **CONSULTATION:** You should consult with other climbers about the difficulty and danger of a particular climb prior to attempting it. Most local climbers are glad to give advice on routes in their area and we suggest that you contact locals to confirm ratings and safety of particular routes and to obtain first-hand information about a route chosen from this book.
2. **INSTRUCTION:** Most climbing areas have local climbing instructors and guides available. We recommend that you engage an instructor or guide to learn safety techniques and to become familiar with the routes and hazards of the areas described in this book. Even after you are proficient in climbing safely, occasional use of a guide is a safe way to raise your climbing standard and learn advanced techniques.
3. **FIXED PROTECTION:** Many of the routes in this book use bolts and pitons which are permanently placed in the rock. Because of variances in the manner of placement, weathering, metal fatigue, the quality of the metal used, and many other factors, these fixed protection pieces should always be considered suspect and should always be backed up by equipment that you place yourself. Never depend for your safety on a single piece of fixed protection because you never can tell whether it will hold weight, and in some cases, fixed protection may have been removed or is now absent.

Be aware of the following specific potential hazards which could arise in using this book:

1. **MISDESCRIPTIONS OF ROUTES:** If you climb a route and you have a doubt as to where the route may go, you should not go on unless you are sure that you can go that way safely. Route descriptions and topos in this book may be inaccurate or misleading.
2. **INCORRECT DIFFICULTY RATING:** A route may, in fact, be more difficult than the rating indicates. Do not be lulled into a false sense of security by the difficulty rating.
3. **INCORRECT PROTECTION RATING:** If you climb a route and you are unable to arrange adequate protection from the risk of falling through the use of fixed pitons or bolts and by placing your own protection devices, do not assume that there is adequate protection available higher just because the route protection rating indicates the route is not an "X" or an "R" rating. Every route is potentially an "X" (a fall may be deadly), due to the inherent hazards of climbing – including, for example, failure or absence of fixed protection, your own equipment's failure, or improper use of climbing equipment.

THERE ARE NO WARRANTIES, WHETHER EXPRESS OR IMPLIED, THAT THIS GUIDEBOOK IS ACCURATE OR THAT THE INFORMATION CONTAINED IN IT IS RELIABLE. THERE ARE NO WARRANTIES OF FITNESS FOR A PARTICULAR PURPOSE OR THAT THIS GUIDE IS MERCHANTABLE. YOUR USE OF THIS BOOK INDICATES YOUR ASSUMPTION OF THE RISK THAT IT MAY CONTAIN ERRORS AND IS AN ACKNOWLEDGMENT OF YOUR OWN SOLE RESPONSIBILITY FOR YOUR CLIMBING SAFETY.

Dedication

Dedicated to Jim Beyer, whose astoundingly bold routes have set a new standard of excellence in sandstone climbing. Jim's extreme solo ascents are works of art, delicately balancing aesthetics of line and quality of execution. His climbs are generations ahead of their time. Accolades to this dancer of the vertical.

Table of Contents

Foreword

It has been well over a half century since I journeyed with three climbing comrades from my alternate home, the Sierra, to the unknown, harsh, and desolate land of the southwest for the first ascent of Shiprock. Twelve failed attempts had made it the number one climbing challenge on our continent.

We were among the few outsiders to come in 1939. Information about desert climbing was virtually nonexistent. The few maps were sketchy and often misleading. Roads tried to see how unfriendly they could be. But we had photographs, a hand lens to suggest a possible route, the idea of adding expansion bolts to make our belays safer, and from our first high bivouac, we began to appreciate the pristine beauty of the southwest.

The desert remained remote and largely inaccessible, with only a handful of climbs established, until the uranium boom of the '50s. Prospectors brought bulldozers and four-wheel-drive vehicles. Roads were blazed in canyon after canyon, giving access to many difficult-to-reach locations. We didn't like that, but we were glad to see our old hemp ropes upgraded. State of the art Goldline arrived later, and stiff Goldline metamorphosed into strong, pliable Perlon. The modern climber's lifeline can now hold a 14-wheeler falling from a 100-foot cliff. Our hemp may have held a 10-foot fall.

In the '60s the number of routes grew into dozens, and impact on the desert escalated dramatically. In 1963 "Lake Powell" began to supersede what had been the magnificent Glen Canyon. Happily, 1996 found the Sierra Club advocating that Powell be drained and Glen Canyon restored.

In 1967 Fred Beckey, Eric Bjørnstad, Alex Bertulis, and Harvey T. Carter came to Shiprock and established a second line to its remote summit. The '70s ushered in the technology of lightweight camming devices, and articles about desert climbing began to appear in magazines. People came in increasing numbers with each passing decade.

By the '80s the southwest had experienced a surge of jeepers, ORVs, river runners in power boats, rappel-bolters, mountain bikers, jet skiers, couch potatoes in houseboats, and whatever mass recreation required least effort. In the '90s climbing has grown exponentially. Visitors are coming to the desert by the thousands each year. If I were 80 again, I'd be tempted to join them–but not their mechanical garbage.

There was too little consciousness of ecology in years past. The land, like youth, seemed untrashable. We never stopped to think about the impact of the bold climber's boot on the fragile cryptogamic soil, or the scars of bolts and pitons on rock.

When Eric's first *Desert Rock* was published in1988, the Colorado Plateau was in the wake of the mining boom. Interest in desert climbing was coming of age, and it became increasingly important to think of caring for the land. The new *Desert Rock* series asks for "the kindling of a new consciousness," and a willingness to preserve and restore our heritage, one of the planet's unique places.

David R. Brower
Berkeley, CA
February 3, 1997

ACKNOWLEDGMENTS

The monumental task of collecting, sorting, and researching the countless details of sandstone climbs on the Colorado Plateau–a vast area nearly the size of California–has been possible only through collaboration with hundreds of climbers. Many contributed not only topos and details of their climbs but also gave slides and reviewed information on other areas they had climbed.

Those providing slides are credited with their photographs. Size limitations for these new *Desert Rock* volumes have prevented the use of many photos I would like to have included.

The following are gratefully thanked for their time, support and contributions:

Jeff Achey, Tom Addison, Jon Allen, Steve Allen, Dave Anderson, Jay Anderson, Steve Anderton, Chris Andrews, Steve Angelini, Jim Angione, Mark Austin, Jonathan Averbach, Christie Babalis, Benny Bach, Fran Bagenal, Jed Ballas, Mike Baker, Brad Barlage, Fran Barnes, Dave Barnett, Steve "Crusher" Bartlett, Alen Bartlette, Fred Beckey, Christine Beekman, Chris Begue, George Bell, Mark Bennett, Bobbi Bensman, Mary Laurence Bevington, Jim Beyer, John Blumental, Jim Bodenhamer, Brad Bond, Jake Bos, Titoune Bouchard, George Bracksieck, Paul Brien, Cameron Burns, Ralph Burns, John Butler, Keen Butterworth, Doug Byerly, John Byrnes, Tony Calderone, Kitty Calhoun, Chip Chace, Les Choy, Erick Christianson, Ben Clower, Tim Coats, Drizzt Cook, Darren Cope, Kyle Copeland, Torm Cotter, Jeff Crystal, John Culberson, Carolyn Dailey, Perry Davis, Steph Davis, Eric Decaria, Carl Diedrich, Topher Donahue, Rick Donnelly, Bill Duncan, Glenn Dunmire, Jimmy Dunn, Teri Ebel, Warren Egbert, Al Engelbach, Greg Epperson, Blain Erickson, Dave Evans, Paul Evans, Jeff Fassett, Randy Falk, Matt Fetbrod, Joe Fitschan, Bill Flemming, Bill Forrest, Charlie Fowler, Craig Francois, Mike Fredrichs, Elaine Frederick, Graham Frontella, Doug Frost, Andrew Fry, James Funsten, Cindy Furman, Paul Gagner, Peter Gallagher, Bego Gerhart, Julie Gilje, John Glaze, David Gloudemans, Jim Goldberg, David Goldstein, Paul Gonzales, Todd Gordon, Stewart Green, Tony Grenko, Patience Gribble, Ken Guza, Chris Haaland, Lisa Hathaway, Jorma Hayes, Leslie Henderson, Mark Hesse, Stanley Hill, Kris Hjelle, Ryan Hokanson, Peter Holcombe, Jeff Hollenbaugh, Steve Hong, Paul Horton, Jim Howe, Tommie Howe, Galen Howell, Rodger "Strappo" Hughs, Al Hunt, Bruce Hunter, Ray Huntzinger, George Hurley, Dave Insley, Eric Johnson, Steve Johnson, Chris Kalous, Teri Kane, Pete Keane, Todd Kearns, Jason Keith, Tobin Kelley, Max Kendall, Craig Kenyon, Aaron Kitscher, Fred Knapp, Robert Kooken, Jon Krakauer, Eric Kraut, Chuck Kroger, Luke Laeser, Matt Laggis, Rollie Lamberson, Jim Langdon, Mark Lassiter, Dave Levine, John Lewis, Davin Lindy, Young Hee Lowrie, Craig Luebben, the late Keith Maas, Dougald MacDonald, Glen Mann, John Merkel, Mel Macdonell, Kishen Mangat, Andrew Marquardt, Scott Martin, Bonnie McElhinny, Rob McKeracher, Betsi McKittrick, Patrick A. Mcloney, Kelly McMenamen, Doug McQueen, Steve Mesdough, Chris "Renegade" Meyer, Paul Midkiff, David Mondeau, Sasha Montagu, Matt Moore, Martha Morris, Melisa Morrow, Sherry Needich, Karen Newman, Bob Novellino, Mike O'Donnel, Tom and Laurie O'Keeffe, Jim Olsen, Michele Olsen, Greg Olson, Lin Ottinger, Bob Palais, Dava Parr, Sonja Paspal, Simon Peck, Mike Pennings, Rich Perch, Andy Petefish, Andy Pitas, Wendy Pitas, Linus Platt, Ferdl Ploerer, Hanni Ploerer, David Pollari, Jack Pope, Steve Porcella, Jason Predock, Brad Quinn, Steve Quinlin, Duane Raleigh, Glenn Randall, Alf Fandell, Eric Rasmussen, Keith Reynolds, Fred Rice, Scott Riley, Stu Ritchie, Mike Ritter, Christopher Roberts, Jack Roberts, Ann Robertson, Bill Rothstin, Bill Russel, Chuch Santagati, Antoino Savelli, Joede Schoeberlein, Sallie Shatz, Joseph Sheader, Tom Sherman, Walt Shipley, John Shireman, Rick Showalter, Paul Sibley, Paul Seibert, Eric Siefer, Ken Sims, Jeff Singer,

Doug Sinor, Geoff Sluyter, Jo Smith, Rick Smith, Doug Snively, Kirby Spangler, Merlin Spiller, Carrie Sood, Alan Stephenson, Tracy Sternburg, Andrea Stoughton, Brett Sutteer, Mary Sutton, John Sweeley, Pete Takeda, Brian Takei, Eve Tallman, Ramsey Thomas, Tom Thomas, Mel Thorsen, Reed Tindall, Tim Toula, Jake Tratiak, Paul Turecki, Mark Vogel, Ray Vought, Barry Ward, Robert Warren, Darren Watson, Cristie Wayment, Randall Weekley, Ed Webster, Frosty Weller, David Whidden, Mark Whiton, Dawn Widden, Earl Wiggins, Chad Wiggle, Ron Wiggle, Chip Wilson, Tony Wilson, Mike Wood.

I have been very fortunate being given permission to use the photos of nationally acclaimed photographers Ed Cooper (my climbing partner in the early 1960s), Bill Hatcher, Frank Mendonca, Dan Norris, and Tom Till. Michelle Goldstein was liberal with her professional photo work. Bill Godschalx has given freely of time and expense, telephotographing Wall Street then developing and enlarging the shots into an 8x10 format. These volumes would lack much in quality without his generous contribution.

Chris Becker took time from teaching and house building to accompany me on weekends to Zion National Park with John Middendorf, Colorado National Monument with K.C. Baum, Indian Creek with Steve Petro, Bret Ruckman and Marco Cornacchione, the San Rafael Swell with Cris Coffey and Rene and Warren Newman, as well as numerous other infield jaunts. Chris' meticulously drawn topos have set a standard for detail, accuracy and artistic excellence. I am profoundly indebted to him.

James Garrett and his wife Dr. Franziska Garrett camped with me in the San Rafael and James was tireless in his collaboration on routes there. James also wrote the "Brief history of Climbing in the San Rafael." Mike Friedrichs gave generously of his vast knowledge not only of Dylan Wall, but much of the north San Rafael. The late Doug Hall (killed in an avalanche in 1997) drew the excellent topos for Bottleneck Peak and was a frequent visitor to Moab, always with new route information for me.

Jeff Lowe gave his time and his knowledge of Zion and Capitol Reef National Parks and kindly wrote the Foreword to the National Parks volume. John Middendorf made possible the selection of climbs in Zion and also contributed the Zion climbing history profile. K.C. Baum made the Colorado National Monument chapter possible, with his time and principle contributions, as well as the climbs in the Unaweep area, and wrote the climbing history for Colorado National Monument and the Unaweep area. Steve Petro made available his file on Indian Creek and drove a couple hundred miles to meet me there and hike to the climbs. Bret Ruckman and Marco Cornacchione's support and help with Indian Creek climbs has been invaluable, and they also provided much help with areas west of the Colorado River.

David Brower kindly wrote the poignant and humorous foreword to the present volume. The Latitude 40-degrees Company who produce the excellent Moab West and Moab East maps continues to add numerous climbing designations and landform names to their popular four-wheel-drive and mountain bike maps, making them as valuable to climbers as to other recreationists.

Charlie Fowler was inadvertently omitted from the acknowledgments section of the National Parks volume. He was of inestimable help with both the Arches and Canyonlands National Parks chapters, and gave freely of his excellent photographic expertise.

The Potash Road and popular Wall Street were reviewed by numerous climbers including Dan Batwanis, Jim Beyer, Kevin Chase, Kyle Copeland, Jimmy Dunn, Tom Gilje, Lisa Hathaway, Jorma Hayes, Dan McRoberts, Dave Medara, Bob Novellino, and Peter Verchick. Many of these climbers also helped with the Potash Road Side Canyons and other areas of these guides.

A.J. Moll traveled many miles with me mapping areas west of the Colorado, and Jorna Hayes and Bill Godschalx on separate occasions provided me with the four-wheel-drive approach into Tusher Canyon and Courthouse Pasture and were valuable in helping ferret out the numerous routes there. The late Rob Slater (killed in an avalanche on K2 in 1995) was a frequent visitor and provider of detailed topos of the Moab region, especially the Fisher Towers.

Jay Smith and Kitty Calhoun hiked Offwidth City at Long Canyon with me, and provided a vehicle able to take us over treacherous snow-packed and quagmire-laden four-wheel roads down the steep switchbacks to routes along the Green River north of Canyonlands National Park, and up to Hellroaring Canyon under winter conditions. Jay Smith also has provided information on Indian Creek and Castle Valley, and accompanied Chris Becker and me on research outings along the River Road.

Kevin Chase of Moab Adventure Outfitters reviewed many parts of Moab West climbs and provided the paraphernalia size comparison chart on page 10.

Bob Van Belle, park administrator at Capitol Reef, and his wife Joslin, provided bed and vittles and guidance to the routes.

Canyonlands Natural History Association, together with a host of park personnel, edited or in one way or another were helpful with the Canyonlands chapter. They are Jim Braggs, Nancy Coulam, Paul Cowan, Larry Fredricks, Galen Howell, Wendy Hurlbert, Mary Beth Maynard, Char Oberg, Sonja Paspal, Steve Swanke, Cynthia Williams, and Tara Williams. Noel Poe, superintendent at Arches, together with Paul Cowan and Diane Allen, reviewed the Arches chapter.

Jeff Widen wrote the "Environmental Considerations" section of the Introduction, as well as contributing numerous slides for consideration, and reviewed many chapters with an eye for detail and accuracy.

Finally, the keystone to bringing these volumes to fruition, Cris Coffey, who contributed the majority of the editing on the original *Desert Rock* (Chockstone, 1988) has, with her critical eye, sharpened and helped clarify these new *Desert Rock* volumes, bringing them from the dark ages to literacy.

Eric Bjørnstad
Moab, 1997

Desert Rock: Wall Street to the San Rafael Swell

Overview Map

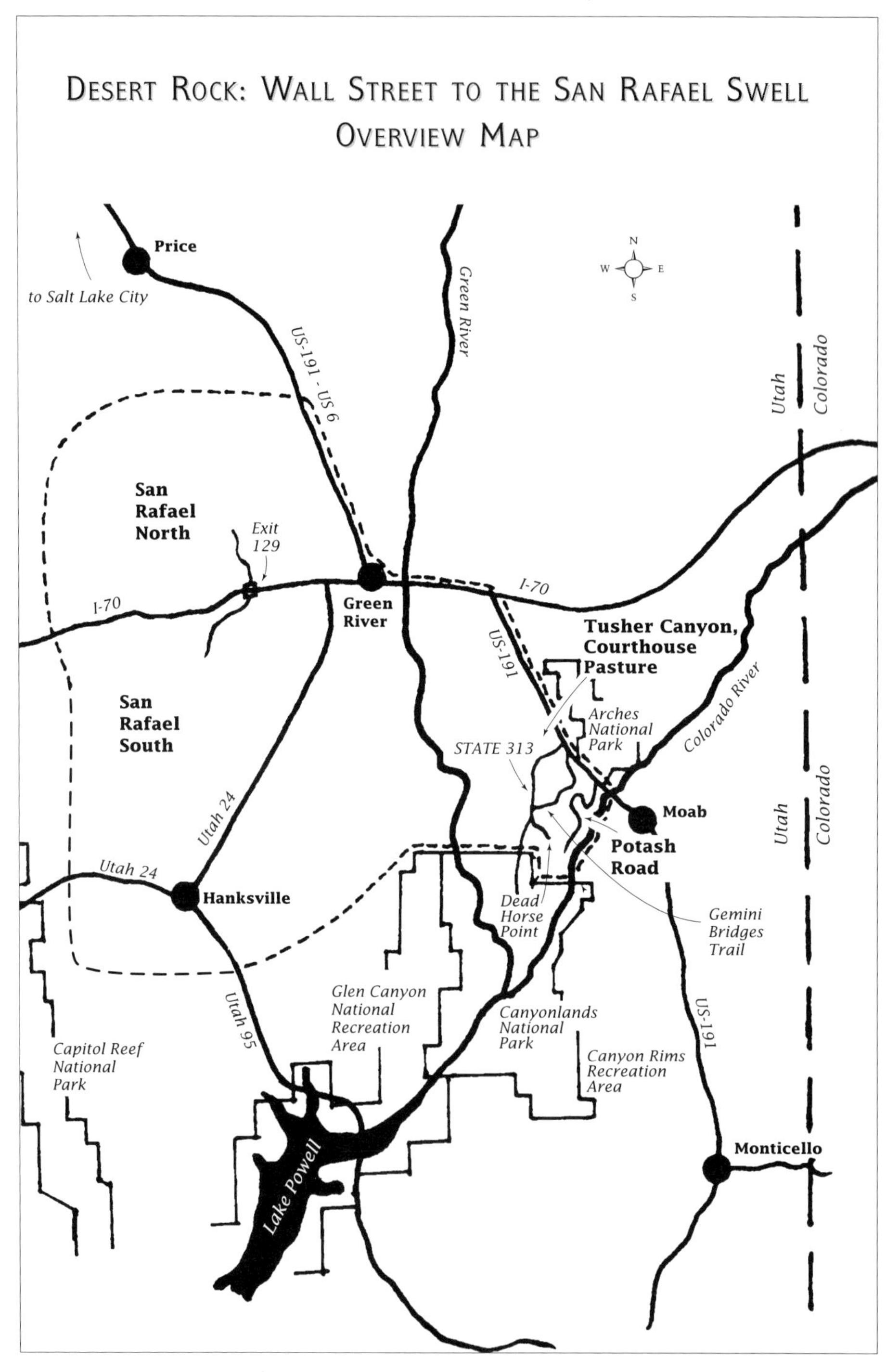

INTRODUCTION

The sandstone canyon walls, mesas, buttes and spires of the Colorado Plateau are the focus of this new *Desert Rock* series.

The Colorado Plateau is a physiographic province lying north and east of the Basin and Range province and south and west of the Rocky Mountain province. It covers approximately 160,000 square miles (nearly the size of California) in Utah, Arizona, New Mexico, and Colorado. Within its vast reaches of sedimentary sandstone lie the greatest potential for crack climbing in the world. It is a sector of North America with thousands of miles of vertically fractured Wingate Sandstone walls. Although thousands of climbs have been established, this is only a fraction of the potential on the Plateau. The majority of routes lie within the higher registry of difficulty, but there remains a large selection of excellent climbs below the 5.10 level, and all within the incomparable canyon country of the high southwest desert.

Stephen Trimble in *The Bright Edge* says, "Time ticks slowly for the Canyon Country. A year means nothing, a human lifetime sees arroyos deepened a bit, the collapse of an arch or cliff here and there, the creation of a new window or two. A millennium scarcely changes the landscape. Only in tens of thousands of years does the land see much change. And even then, a hundred thousand years is a fraction of an instant in the millions and billions of years of the earth's history. On this time scale the Plateau itself becomes a temporary phenomenon, a passing fancy of an earth with a restless skin of drifting, dynamic continents."

The Plateau contains eight national parks–Zion, Bryce, Capitol Reef, Arches, and Canyonlands in Utah; Mesa Verde, Grand Canyon, and Petrified Forest outside Utah, in addition to 20 other regions managed by the National Park Service–the greatest concentration of national parks and wilderness areas outside Alaska.

The Colorado River is the principle artery of the Plateau, giving its name to and draining 90% of canyon country. Each year the river transports approximately three cubic miles of sandstone sediment to the impounded waters behind Glen Canyon Dam. Like the branches of a tree, the Colorado is fed by a network of tributaries, with countless arroyos further contributing during periods of storm. It is a land of haunting beauty, a region without parallel on earth, and its fragile ecosystem is in grave danger.

What has changed in the years since *Desert Rock* was first published early in 1988 are the escalating numbers discovering and frequenting the desert. Each season attendance records

Rock Strata Sequence Chart

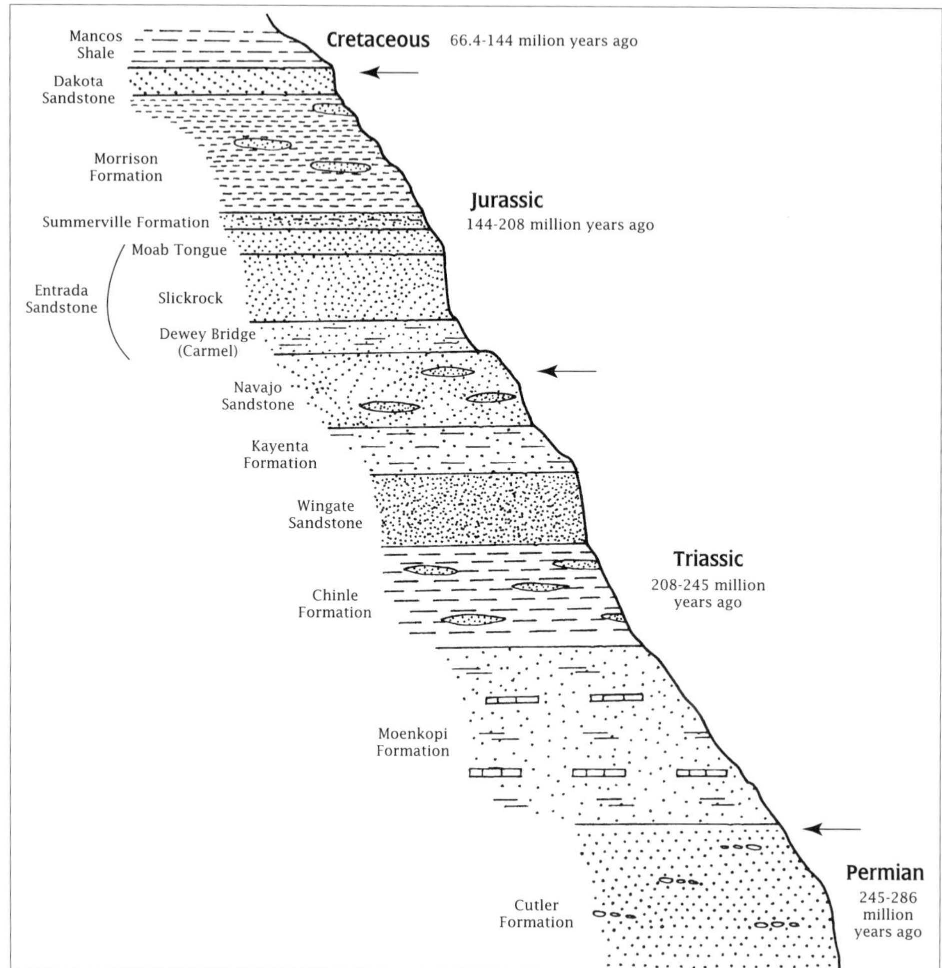

are routinely broken at Canyonlands National Park, Natural Bridges National Monument, and Dead Horse Point State Park. Visitation at Zion National Park exceeds two million and Arches National Park now approaches one million per year. Recreationists of every disposition now make the desert their vacation destination. The gamut runs from mountain bikers, river runners, climbers, four-wheel drivers, to hikers, campers, artists, photographers, mystics, and nature enthusiasts. The challenge becomes balancing their enjoyment with preserving what they have come to enjoy.

It has long been assumed that the desert is a tough, indestructible land, indifferent to human impact. In other regions of the country moisture promotes a bacterial breakdown–trees rot, litter (with time) dissolves, new growth covers scars. But here the desert is so dry and growth so slow that the land is like another planet where time has stopped. Our appearance has been dramatic and caustic. The dry air mummifies our castaways. Orange peels, egg shells, and other material tossed to the land do not biodegrade. Discards become permanent monuments to our sloth.

Cryptobiotic soil is eminent to the health of the desert. Without the aid of this vulnerable crust the majority of indigenous flowers and other shrubs would simply not exist. Once the soil is impacted by tire or foot, such prints remain visible for decades. Recovery is estimated to take up to 250 years. If we are to preserve this island of earth, it is most important that we walk only on slickrock (rock devoid of soil or vegetation), in drainages, or on a trail. Direct cross-country travel is unconscionable.

The indelible print of our seemingly benign inroads to the desert are not readily apparent from our state-of-the-art vehicles equipped with the emblems of our sybaritic society. With us we bring not only quickdraws, spaceship alloy light cams, freeze dried foods, and satellite maps but also an invincible confidence in our superiority as a species. We have a long history of annihilating the land as we reshape it to suit us. I implore all who visit the unique canyon country to be responsible not only for our present love of the desert, but for the generations yet to be thrilled by this magical place.

Perhaps now, with the kindling of a new consciousness, we are on the threshold of a new direction not previously traveled. We may now value and protect the wild regions of the planet not for the short-term plunder of the past, but as the very root of our survival.

Please visit with prudence, responsibility, and love.

Eric Bjørnstad
January 1996
Moab, Utah

About the new Desert Rock series

Desert Rock (1988) attempted to document the known climbs established throughout the sandstone formations of the Colorado Plateau. Not included were hundreds of ascents up the buttes, towers, and walls of the Grand Canyon and Zion National Parks. The first volume of the new series included a subjective selection of the best of Zion but left the 280-mile-long Grand Canyon to future writers.

A technical rock climbing guide is necessarily an assemblage of material from a great many sources. This is especially true regarding the vast deserts of the Colorado Plateau. Unlike most areas, where routes are established mainly by resident climbers and route detail is easily accessible, here resident climbers are comparatively few and the majority of sources for route information are scattered across the country and overseas. Although the three years and 8,000 hours of research which went into *Desert Rock* (1988) has provided a solid foundation for the present series of guides, the succeeding years have brought additional contacts with hundreds of climbers and racked up an astonishing number of research hours. I have climbed on the desert for over 30 years and for many years made canyon country my home. This series of guides is the product of a long love affair with the desert.

This new *Desert Rock* series covers the Colorado Plateau from Colorado National Monument east to Zion National Park west, from San Rafael and Moab south to Indian Creek and Valley of the Gods.

Desert Rock: Rock Climbs in the National Parks includes a subjective selection of routes in Arches and Zion National Parks and the known routes of Capitol Reef and Canyonlands National Parks. It also includes the adjacent Glen Canyon National Recreational Area and Green River area just outside the park boundary of Canyonlands.

Desert Rock: Wall Street to the San Rafael Swell is a definitive guide exploring the diversity of ascents established along the Colorado River corridor west of Moab, the dramatic drainages of Culvert, Day, and Long Canyons, the incomparable landscape of the Green River north of Canyonlands National Park, Island-in-the-Sky, and the magic and splendor of the remote San Rafael.

Desert Rock: Kane Creek to Colorado National Monument covers climbs east of the Colorado River in the Moab area. Included are Kane Creek, the River Road (Scenic Byway 128), Castle Valley, Fisher Towers, and the Colorado National Monument.

Desert Rock: Indian Creek and Isolated Areas is a definitive coverage of Indian Creek, Valley of the Gods, Tooth Rock, Arch and Texas Canyons, and other isolated regions of the Colorado Plateau.

Though the Navajoland was documented in *Desert Rock* (1988) from a historic point of view (equipment lists and other pertinent ascent information excluded), the present volumes do not include the climbs on the reservation. There is still a climbing ban imposed by the Navajo Tribal Council although there have been numerous new routes clandestinely established since *Desert Rock*. There have been reports of windshields broken on anglo-owned vehicles left unattended, as well as climbing equipment confiscated and stiff fines imposed on those disregarding the climbing ban. On the other hand, reports have also surfaced regarding numerous climbs accomplished on the reservation with the permission of the neighboring Navajo residents. If permission cannot be obtained, please respect tribal limits. After all, there is more than a lifetime of legal and spectacular buttes, towers, spires, and canyon walls to climb on the Colorado Plateau.

E. B.

Environmental Considerations of Desert Rock Climbing by Jeff Widen

The Colorado Plateau is a stunning and magical arena in which to climb. After experiencing the desert world, many climbers have written about the need to slow down, take in the desert's aura and walk more softly. Indeed, just being within this incredible landscape is a major part of any climbing trip. The starkness of the earth's bare bones, along with the extremes of heat, cold, wind, and weather, are all part of the desert climbing experience. As harsh as the desert may be in many ways, though, it is also an extremely fragile place. Plants and animals carry out a tentative existence and are easily disturbed. The visual scars left by careless activity are extremely slow to heal. The desert needs extra care, a lighter touch.

There is another compelling reason to tread lightly in the desert. The extractive industries of mining, timber cutting, ranching and water development have long been criticized for their abuse of public lands. Damaging climbing practices threaten to put climbers in the same category, at least in the eyes of environmental organizations if not the general public. Land managing agencies increasingly view climbing as an activity with real impacts and also one that can be dealt with fairly easily, meaning increased regulation. One has only to look at recent attempts at bolt bans by various agencies to understand the seriousness of the threat. Climbers can go a long way toward staving off overly harsh regulation by acting responsibly. Although the debates over climbing styles rage endlessly, nearly all climbers agree on the importance of protecting the climbing environment. The desert contains some of the most radical and outrageous crack climbs on Earth. It's up to everyone climbing there to help protect access to these climbs–and to protect the rock and land itself.

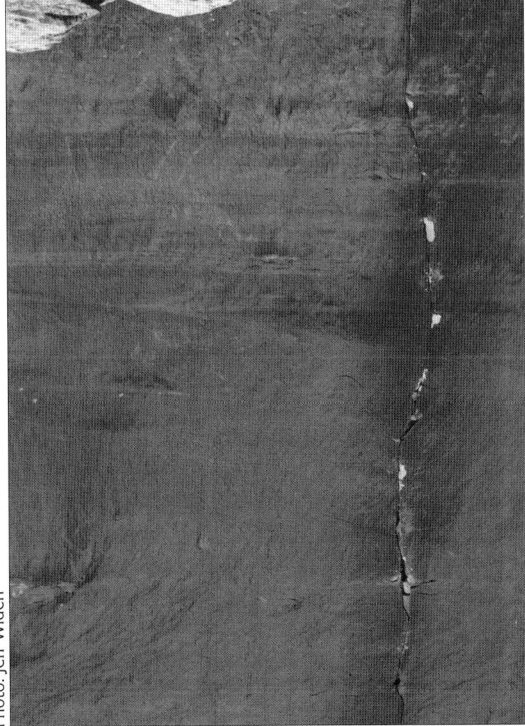
Photo: Jeff Widen

Pin scars

Climbing impacts in the desert center around all aspects of a climb, from multiple trails to rock damage to trash. The desert environment requires extra care at each turn.

Approaches: Check out approach routes in advance. For the driving portion of the approach–a major part of many desert climbs–stay on established roads. If you are unlike most desert climbers and own some beefy four-wheel drive with real clearance, resist the urge to get a few hundred yards closer to the route by driving off road. On foot, follow established approach paths wherever possible. Take an extra minute to see if there is a common route up to a climb. Take special care not to walk over areas of cryptobiotic soil (you can recognize this unique desert plant assemblage by its appearance as black, crusty soil). It is critical for prevention of erosion in the desert, takes hundreds of years to form, and is destroyed instantly when crushed. To avoid cryptobiotic soil and other plants and animals, walk in washes and over slickrock and boulders whenever possible. Approaching climbs in this way will also prevent the all-too-visible trashing of the desert's surface.

Protection: Using clean pro is perhaps most important in the desert–the rock simply can't take the abuse of piton placement. Free routes don't present much of a problem, since desert cracks are tailor-made for camming devices. On aid routes, however, there are too many examples where cracks have been nailed that could have been climbed with clean hardware (see "Pitons" section). It's true that you need a huge stock of cam devices to climb desert routes, but that's part of the game. People often go in groups and pool their gear to do these routes. When retreating or rapping off, leave gear, webbing, etc. of neutral colors–brown, black, or tan are the best.

Bolts: Nothing raises the ire of land managers more than over-bolting, whether real or perceived. If there is one thing climbers can do to prevent excessive regulation, it is to minimize bolt use. This doesn't mean bolt placement elimination, for indeed the nature of

Photo: Linottinger

Petroglyphs

desert climbing–vertical walls and towers without natural rappel anchors–makes bolt placement a necessity. But climbers should keep the number to a minimum. The days of long bolt ladders in the desert are long gone. Short ladders are sometimes necessary to reach the crackless summits of towers, but when the route is a predominantly bolt-clipping ascent, the formation is better left unclimbed.

Bolts placed next to cracks would seem anathema to most climbers, yet a disturbing number of bolts can be found next to bomber cam placements. If you don't have the gear, go hit up your friends and come back later. When bolts are placed, they should be placed well, whether to give you the extra courage to do a few more free moves or to prevent the eventual formation of an ugly and unusable hole when the bolt comes out.

The standard desert bolt has long been a ½" angle piton pounded into a ⅜" hole drilled at a slight downward angle. Some of the newer ½" expansion bolts are now being used–check out recent reviews in various climbing publications to see which ones are best for soft rock.

Power drills have no place in the desert. Not only can holes be quickly hand-drilled in sandstone, but a major part of the desert climbing experience is the feeling of quiet and vast open spaces, and the sense of high adventure. The use of power drills not only runs counter to this sense, but leads quickly to over-bolting.

Pitons: Climbers should adopt an attitude of minimization when nailing in the desert. Pin scars are more visible in sandstone and nailing routes here get beat out faster than on any other rock type. Minimizing piton damage includes reducing the number of pin placements as much as possible, looking for alternative routes and perhaps stopping to ask yourself whether a formation with existing routes really needs a new nail-up. Devices such as Lowe ball nuts and Tri-cams, Rock and Rollers and small camming devices can often substitute for pins down to Lost Arrow size. Using clean gear can also have the desirable effect of upping the fear factor of an aid route.

If you must nail, use constructive scarring techniques. This involves favoring upward blows to the pin when cleaning so the eventual hole will accept a nut or other clean pro.

Chipping/Gluing: These are destructive practices that are indefensible anywhere, especially in the desert.

Chalk: Many desert pioneers and early locals climbed without it, but most modern climbers use chalk. White chalk is especially visible and obnoxious on red rock. If you use chalk, use colored chalk–dark brown or dark red are the best colors. Most of the national parks already require colored chalk.

Archaeological Sites: The Colorado Plateau is rich in Native American archaeological resources. Special care must be taken to avoid these areas, whether ruins, rock art panels or areas with pot shards, tool fragments or other ancient artifacts. Stealing artifacts is a federal crime. Avoid climbing near any of these archaeological sites–you can bet there is another perfect crack around the corner.

Human Waste: Desert areas are booming in popularity and human waste is becoming an increasing problem. It is critical to take the extra couple of minutes to do it right. Go at least 300 feet (91m) from major washes and other watercourses. Although land managers are looking at the viability of surface disposal, the currently accepted method for dealing with excrement is still to dig a small hole six-to-eight inches deep and bury the waste. Used toilet paper should be packed out in Ziploc-like bags and disposed of. There are also reports of increasing human waste near the bases of popular towers–climbers should treat the base of towers as a stream and go several hundred feet away to do their business. It goes without saying that all other trash, tape, old slings, etc. should be carried out.

Wildlife: It is important to respect wildlife closures, usually imposed to protect nesting raptors or other species. Closures are posted at visitor centers or land manager's headquarters.

Attitude: No climbing is totally without impact. But in this desert land–with its special qualities of fragility, beauty and silence–it is essential to adopt an attitude of reducing our impact. We must walk and climb a bit more lightly. The self-interest issue of preventing over-regulation is crucial. But there is also a much bigger issue–it is the right thing to do and makes the incredible experience of climbing in this place all the richer.

About This Book

Each chapter has the same format. Shaded areas title the general location of the climbs and are followed with a written description of the area's location. Route names are followed by grade, free climbing difficulty, aid rating, number of pitches, length of route or height of the landform measured from its longest side, followed by a star rating where available. First ascent particulars are followed by location and access of the climb. Paraphernalia is followed by descent information. Example below:

Wall Street

61 SUMMIT CHIMNEY III, 5.9, 4 pitches, 410 feet (125m)

First Ascent: Jim Beyer, solo, March 1991.

Location and Access: *Summit Chimney* is two crack systems, or 31 feet (9.4m) left of *Mystery Route* and climbs to the top of the rimrock.

Pitch 1: The crux, 5.9 offwidth.

Pitch 2: Climb a 5.9 handcrack.

Pitch 3: Continue up a 5.8 offwidth chimney.

Pitch 4: Finish up a 5.7 chimney.

Paraphernalia: Up to 5" protection; cams and nuts.

Descent: Third class down and right to a rib right of a chimney/gully. Rappel from a single bolt 40 feet (12m) to the top of Drop Out. Continue down the route with double 150 foot (46m) ropes.

Rating System

Each climb is given a grade of I through VI:

Grade I	One to two hours of climbing
Grade II	Less than half a day
Grade III	Half a day climb
Grade IV	Full day climb
Grade V	Two day climb
Grade VI	Multi-day ascent

Free climbing difficulty on a scale 1 through 6 with 5 broken down from 5.0 through 5.13+ free climbing and 6 broken down to A1 through A5 of aid climbing.

1	Trail
2	Cross-country hiking
3	Scrambling
4	Exposed scrambling usually with rope for protection
5	Free climbing
6	Aid climbing

Free climbing difficulty 5.0 through 5.13+
Aid climbing difficulty A1 through A5– C1, C2, A0

A0	Aid points fixed.
A1	Easy secure placements.
A2	More awkward placement which will hold less weight than A1.
A3	Still more difficult placement and less secure. Will hold only a short fall.
A4	Difficult placement, not secure enough for a fall. Will hold body weight only.
A5	Multiple A4 placements. A fall would result in injury or death.
C1, C2	Ratings for clean, hammerless aid of increasing difficulty

Star Rating

Ratings are based on a scale of 1 to 5 stars of increasing aesthetics and with few exceptions are the consensus of those who have climbed the routes. The absence of a star rating on a climb is only an indication that this information was not available as we go to press.

Paraphernalia

A standard desert climbing rack for free climbs includes two sets of Friends, one set of TCUs, one set of stoppers and quickdraws with 25-inch slings for multiple pitch climbs.

The following chart is designed to assist the climber in assembling and borrowing gear necessary for desert climbing. It gives a general idea of size comparisons between brands. Measurements are from the manufacturer or distributor but in no way are guaranteed to be accurate. Provided courtesy of Moab Adventure Outfitters, 550 North Main, Moab, Utah 84532, (801)259-2725.

Paraphernalia Size Comparison Chart

Colorado Custom Hardware Aliens

Measurements are manufacturer's fully closed to fully open. Cams are not strong fully open.

.33	3/8	1/2	3/4	1	1 1/2	2	2 1/2
.33–.38	.38–.65	.53–.87	.6–1.06	.76–1.34	1.03–1.63	1.2–1.95	1.4–2.35
black	blue	green	yellow	red	orange	violet	silver

Wired Bliss TCU and FCU

Measurements are manufacturer's list of "range."

.4	.5	.75	1.0	1.5	2.0	2.5	3.0
.4–.6	.5–.8	.6–.9	.8–1.3	.9–1.4	1.2–1.9	1.4–2.2	1.8–2.8
blue	yellow	red	purple	silver	black	green	pink

Wild Country Friends and Flexible Friends

Measurements are manufacturer's list of "range."

.0	1/2	1	1 1/2	2	2 1/2	3	3 1/2	4
.52–.76	.60–.96	.76–1.16	.92–1.40	1.16–1.76	1.32–2.20	1.72–2.64	2.08–3.24	2.56–4.00
	orange	yellow	silver	pink	lt. blue	blue	purple	black

Metolius TCU and FCU

Measurements are manufacturer's list of "range."

00	0	1	2	3	4	5	6	7	8	9	10
.35–.40	.40–.60	.50–.75	.60–.90	.75–1.10	1.90–1.35	1.10–1.70	1.28–1.9	1.65–2.25	2.0–2.75	2.2–3.3	2.8–4.2
gray	purple	blue	yellow	red	black	green					

Hugh Banner (HB) Quadcams and Micromates

Manufacturer's measurement of "crack size."

00	0	.5	1	1.5	2	2.5	3	3.8	5
.42–.66	.52–.76	.60–.92	.76–1.16	.80–1.45	1.12–1.76	1.40–2.20	1.80–2.76	2.36–3.72	3.40–5.08
red	orange	yellow	lt. blue						

Black Diamond Camalot and Camalot Jr.

Manufacturer's measurements of "size range." Old style Camalots are slightly larger in sizes 1 through 4.

.5	.75	1	2	3	3.5	4	4.5	5
.8–1.3	1.0–1.6	1.2–2.0	1.5–2.5	2.0–3.4	2.56–4.0	2.9–4.8	3.74–6.0	4.2–7.0
purple	green	red	gold	blue	gray	purple	red	green

Sidewinder Protection Big Bros.

Manufacturer's measurements of "expansion range."

1	2	3	4
3.2–4.4	4.0–5.8	5.2–8.0	7.3–12.0
blue	green	blue	green

Lowe Balls

Actual minimum and maximum size "functional size is less."

1	2	3
3mm–6mm	4.5mm–9mm	6mm–12mm
yellow	red	blue

Yates Big Dudes

Manufacturer's stated "camming range."

1	2
3.74–6.0	4.5–7.0
black	blue

Wall Street to Green River

Cultural History

The Fremont Indian culture lived generally west and the Anasazi east of the Colorado River (650–1250 years ago). In the Moab area they established few permanent dwellings but are thought to have traveled through the region trading, hunting, and foraging. The region west of the river is rich in rock art, both petrographs (pecked into stone) and pictographs (painting on stone). There are hundreds of rock art panels along the Colorado River corridor west of Moab and the land of the Island-in-the-Sky mesa. The panel 5 miles (1.5km) down the Potash Road is one of the largest and finest in the area. In a few locations there are also found the much older Barrier Canyon pictograph rock art and Desert Archaic petroglyph art dating to before the time of Christ.

Flora and Fauna

The region surrounding Moab and the Island-in-the-Sky mesa, and in particular Long Canyon, is home to desert bighorn sheep. The Colorado River corridor is also the home of golden and bald eagles. At the Nature Conservancy-owned Scott M. Matheson Wetland Preserve (across the river from the Potash Road) over 180 species of birds live or stop over on their migratory flights. During the season Great Blue Heron are often seen fishing along the banks of the Colorado, and red-tailed hawks and turkey vultures are a common sight, soaring on summer updrafts. Along the Potash Road mud nests of swallows can be seen. The sweet, descending notes of the canyon wren and the plaintive call of the mourning dove are frequently heard. Found throughout the mesa and canyons is the playful raven, said to have the intelligence of a canine. Averaging up to 27 inches in length, with a wingspan of four feet (1.2m) or more, the raven is the largest member of the crow family. They mate for life and share in the raising of their nestlings. As they fly overhead ravens can be distinguished from crows by their V-shaped tail–crow's tails are rounded.

When hiking the high deserts west of the Colorado River one should always be wary of the pygmy rattlesnake. Also found in the area but less common are the Great Basin rattler, sidewinder, and the largest rattler of the southwest, the 7-foot (1.5m) diamondback. A variety of lizards are ubiquitous, especially western fence, whiptail, and the amazing collared lizard (member of the iguana family), distinguished by a prominent black band around its neck and on females in estrus, bright red and orange streaks on their sides until eggs are laid. The collared lizard has been clocked at 17 mph, ranking it among the fastest of reptiles. It runs on all four legs until reaching maximum speed, at which point it stands upright and continues running on its hind legs, looking much like a miniature dinosaur. Be on the lookout for black widow spiders hidden in rock cracks and scorpions (the arachnid who gives birth rather than laying eggs) who live in the bark of trees or hide beneath clumps of dry wood (or sleeping bags).

Generally during the latter part of April and the first week or two of May the deserts west of the Colorado River are ablaze with an astonishing variety of wildflowers, including prickly pear, fishhook, and claret cup cacti. Along the Potash Road are numerous patches of poison ivy which sometimes guard the approach to climbs. At Wall Street I recently saw a reclining desert neophyte happily taking refuge from 100-degree heat in the inviting leaves of poison ivy while belaying his partner. Remember "Leaves of three, let it be." Also abundant along the Potash Road are rabbit brush and willow, tamarisk, serviceberry, and hackberry trees which will not sting you. Beside the roadway are sweet smelling bell-shaped blooms of the deadly jimson weed (aka datura or moonflower), said to be a psychedelic drug used in the past by Indians.

Cryptobiotic Soil: On the Colorado Plateau the vulnerable ecosystem of the desert is being dramatically affected by an exponential surge in visitation. Cryptobiotic soil crust is the critically fragile skin upon which the health of this unique ecosystem depends. It is the product of a symbiotic relationship between moss, lichen, fungus, and algae. It traps nutrients, fixes nitrogen, and is crucial to the development of vascular plants. Without the aid of cryptobiotic soil the majority of indigenous flowers and shrubs on the desert would not exist. Not only is the black, crusty cryptobiotic soil to be avoided, but its fledgling form, a reddish or light brown crust know as cyanobacteria soil (nearly invisible in early stages) must also be preserved for the health of the desert.

If we are to preserve this beautiful land, it is most important to walk only on slickrock (rock devoid of soil or vegetation), in drainages, or on an established trail. If this is not possible, it is important to keep impact at a minimum by not walking abreast but following single file in companions' footsteps. Direct cross-country travel is unconscionable. See "Environmental Considerations of Desert Rock Climbing" by Jeff Widen at the beginning of this book, page 4.

Potholes: Whether dry or filled with rainwater, potholes are vulnerable to degradation by the uninformed visitor. Although they appear to be inviting pools maintained for the hot, weary traveler, they are actually home to a variety of organisms which may be destroyed by pollution from human contact (sunscreen, sweat, insect repellents, pets and other foreign materials). Numerous creatures have adapted to the desert's wet and dry cycle, including crustaceans, insects, tadpoles, frogs, and snails. Many aestivate, hibernate, or are dormant during dry periods and awaken to intense life when moisture returns. It is important for the health of the desert that we do not disturb these fragile islands of life. Unless it is a medical emergency, it is crucial we do not bathe in, swim in, or trample wet or dry potholes. Please be a responsible visitor in this very special land.

Climate

Throughout the Colorado Plateau spring and autumn are the most pleasant months for visits. In the spring, however, relentless winds are common. Although summer temperatures during June, July, and August are often in the 100-degree range, days are much less unpleasant than in humid areas. Thundershowers can be expected spring, summer, and fall, and are especially dangerous. There have been a number of deaths from lightning strikes throughout the years, including a fatality to a climber on Castleton Tower in 1995. A few precautions: If lightning occurs, avoid high ground, tall trees, moist regions such as alcoves or drainages. If possible, stay in your vehicle until the storm passes, or crouch on the ground, preferably on something dry to insulate the body. Do not become a lightning rod by bunching together with your comrades. Mountain bikes and climbing hardware can also be natural lightning rods.

Flash floods are another real hazard. They can appear from nowhere and are frequently powerful enough to dislodge large boulders, uproot trees, and tumble vehicles like weightless toys. Avoid washes and dry arroyos, even though a storm seems distant. On the positive side, summer thunderstorms produce spectacular waterfalls cascading from slickrock canyon rims. Locals frequently jam the River Road (Scenic Byway 128 east of Moab) during cloudbursts to view more than a dozen major waterfalls within the first mile (1.6km). Numerous waterfalls also add drama along the Potash Road.

Geology

For additional detail of the layers of sedimentary rock found west of the Colorado River, see the geology section of the San Rafael Swell chapter, page 183.

Presented in descending order of age:

Entrada Sandstone composes the landforms along State Highway 313 (except Heat Wave which is Wingate), Tombstone Rock, and the climbs at Tusher Canyon and Courthouse Pasture. It is also the dominant rock of Arches National Park north of Moab. The rock is not as dense as Wingate, and although in many areas it fractures vertically, it often breaks conchoidally or along curves, producing rounded arch forms which are not the most desirable features to climb.

Below the Entrada is **Navajo Sandstone**. Most routes on this relatively softer rock are found at Zion National Park and Wall Street. Like the Wingate, it is of aeolian (wind) deposition, fine grained, and often white to buff.

Kayenta forms a bench between the two cliff-forming layers of Navajo and Wingate. It is the stream deposited base rock of Dead Horse Point, Island-in-the-Sky, and Colorado National Monument. It is the protective caprock of most desert towers.

Wingate Sandstone is the predominant rock upon which climbs are established west of the Colorado River. It is also the stratum composing the well-known Castleton Tower, Moses, the walls of Indian Creek, and the climbs of Colorado National Monument. Wingate is unique in that it erodes slowly, fracturing along straight vertical planes. It is angular in appearance, often with chimneys and crack systems remaining the same size for a hundred feet (30m) or more. Wingate rock is sometimes confused with Navajo Sandstone. When erosion has removed its Kayenta caprock and its form has changed from russet to lighter-colored rounded domes, the rock will be extremely soft and nearly impossible for placement of belay or rappel anchors. Examples are The Bride west of the Colorado River and the Coke Ovens in Colorado National Monument.

Below Wingate Sandstone are the slope-forming **Chinle** (no climbs established) and the red-to-maroon **Moenkopi** of mudflat deposition. The Moenkopi is the most recognizable stratum of rock on the Colorado Plateau. It resembles a chocolate layer cake and often appears with thin horizontal bands of light green (organic deposition). At the time of deposition, the Moenkopi Formation was a 200-mile (322km) flood plain which stretched from present-day western Colorado to western Utah. Few climbs exist on Moenkopi, although it is the caprock of the Fisher Towers east of Moab. Both Chinle and Moenkopi appear dramatically in Long Canyon.

The Cutler Formation rests below the Moenkopi, often a deep bright red in color and resembling Wingate in density. Because it tends to fracture horizontally and bears a soft stucco of decomposing mud, it is loose and dangerous to climb. Cutler is the rock of Powerline Crag beside U.S. 191 and the Aiguille du Putterman cliffs north of Moab.

Colorado and Green Rivers

One of Major John Wesely Powell's men christened the Colorado River "The Dragon." Above its confluence with the Green it sleeps, but south of the confluence it is formidable, roaring ferociously through Cataract Canyon, a challenging and sometimes even deadly stretch.

As the Green and Colorado carved the canyonlands, these same rivers will inevitably return them to level land. They rasp their way through layer after layer of rock, creating a gorge no wider than the river itself. Canyon walls are undercut and succumb to the laws of gravity. Big rocks are reduced to little rocks and little rocks to particles of sand washed to the (temporarily) impounded waters behind the dam at Lake Powell, then in time to the Gulf of California in Mexico. Canyons are formed from the original river gorge, and by a complicated network of tributaries. The system resembles branches of a tree, smaller and more numerous as they move further from the main trunk. Occasional flash floods contribute enormously to this endless erosion, sweeping debris from the high land to the river. Geologists estimate the Colorado River washes away three cubic miles of rock each century.

From the town of Green River, the Green glides at the base of deep canyon walls through Labyrinth and Stillwater canyons to confluence with the Colorado River 120 miles (193km) below. The Colorado River runs 64 miles (103km) from Moab to reach the confluence–47 miles (75.6km) downriver from the potash mine off Scenic Byway 279.

Above the confluence of the Green and Colorado Rivers, layers of rock dip slightly northward, so that the rivers flow against the texture of the rock. Consequently the rivers are braked, and glide at gentler grades. The Green drops less than a foot per mile (1.6km) through Labyrinth and Stillwater, and the Colorado meanders smoothly through its canyons at a similar rate. The flow is so lazy that the Green makes a double loop at Bowknot Bend and the Colorado slides back upon itself in a great circle at the Goose Necks below Dead Horse Point and further downstream at the Loop.

Below the confluence the river flows with the texture of the rock. The grade steepens dramatically to a point where, throughout Cataract Canyon , it drops an average of 8 feet (2.4km) per mile, exceeding the gradient in the Grand Canyon. At Big Drop, the river plunges thirty feet (9m) in one mile (1.6km). There were 52 rapids before Lake Powell inundated Lower Cataract Canyon in the early 1960s, now only 26 remain. No dams restrict the flow of the Green and Colorado Rivers for hundreds of miles upstream from Cataract Canyon, and since the flow of the lower Colorado beyond this point is now programmed from Glen Canyon Dam, Cataract Canyon is a unique remnant of the untamed river of Major Powell's acquaintance.

For information on the rivers of the San Rafael see "River Gorges" in the San Rafael chapter, page 182.

Visitor Information

Moab Information Center–The multi-agency Moab Information Center is at the corner of Main and Center Streets and houses representatives of the Forest Service, Bureau of Land Management, Travel Council, National Park System and Canyonlands Natural History Association. At the center are public restrooms, drinking water, local events bulletin board, and hundreds of free brochures relating to the nearby rivers, mountain, parks, and canyon country. Its 72-seat auditorium is a cool and comfortable haven where educational videos on the area may be viewed.

Canyonlands Natural History Association–There are 64 non-profit Natural History Associations working in partnership with National Park Service areas throughout the U.S. In the Moab area the Canyonlands Natural History Association is the concessionaire at the Moab Information Center and nearby Arches National park, Canyonlands National Park, and Natural Bridges National Monument. The association offers an excellent selection books, maps, slides, postcards, et cetera. The organization's professional staff publishes brochures, books, and maps (many are free to visitors) and produces numerous educational programs.

Campgrounds

Moab provides a dozen or more fully equipped campgrounds, or one may camp at Bureau of Land Management (public land) sites along the river corridor. Camping is permitted only at improved recreation sites such as the Jaycee Campground on the Potash Road (with facilities managed for overnight use) and at designated undeveloped campsites. Camping at all locations is limited to 14 days within a 30-day period. After 14 days, the next camp must be more than 30 miles (48km) from the previous camp. Improved campsites contain tables, fire rings, and toilets and are obtained on a "first come, first served" basis. Designated undeveloped campsites are identified by posts with a tent symbol and require a portable toilet system. Ground fires are permitted in existing campfire rings, but one must burn only driftwood or wood obtained from outside the river corridor. Making ground fires and new fire rings at unestablished sites is not permitted. Vehicles (including mountain bikes) are allowed only on exiting roads. Please be responsible.

Maps

The Moab West map is waterproof and tear resistant (published by Latitude 40-degrees, Inc. P.O. 4086 Boulder, Colorado 80306) and is most useful for climbs west of the Colorado River (except for the San Rafael). It was compiled from 7.5-minute USGS maps field checked between 1984 and 1990 using aerial photographs. This excellent map gives a "For Your Information" section on its reverse side. Included are map-reading basics, land use, camping etiquette, archeological and historic sites, environmental considerations, personal considerations, canyon country photography, weather statistics for Moab, desert ecology, elevation profiles, and a list of nearby agencies and organizations. Also included are names given by climbers to numerous landforms.

The Moab West map is available from bookstores, cycle shops, Moab Adventure Outfitters, and Moab Information Center as well as park visitor centers.

Photo: Harvey T. Carter

Point of Moab (aka Frog on a Lily Pad)

THE POTASH ROAD AREA

To me there is an enchantment in these dry canyons that once roared with water and still sometimes do, that absorbed the voices of those who came before, something of massive dignity about sandstone beds that tell of a past long before human breathing, that bear the patterns of ancient winds and water in their crossbeddings . . . . Here I find something of necessity. Were I to discover that I could not walk here again, something essential would be missing from my life.

Ann Zwinger, *Wind in the Rock*

When I wake up to eternity I'd prefer it to be just like this: under a venerable cottonwood just leafing out, sunlight sliding down the canyon wall, the soft rustle of dried cottonwood leaves on the ground, a canyon wren caroling, and then the silence of an April morning.

Ann Zwinger, *Wind in the Rock*

The Potash Road (Scenic Byway 279) is a south turn from U.S. Highway 191, 1.3 miles north (2km) of the bridge over the Colorado River (north of Moab), or 1 mile south (1.6km) of the entrance to Arches National Park. Two and seven-tenths miles (4.3km) from U.S. Highway 191 is The Portal, where the river passes into the canyon. High on the walls across the river are rounded domes of Navajo Sandstone (petrified sand dunes) and a massive syncline where the strata dips sharply downward. In less than a mile (1.6km) the syncline will have dropped the Navajo layer to river level, and a short distance beyond, Wall Street begins. Two miles south (3.2km) of 191 the road parallels the river for 17 miles (27km), then at the BLM river put-in for Cataract Canyon the road becomes dirt and veers west from the river gorge, 1 mile (1.6km) beyond the potash mine. Potash (potassium chloride or KCl) is used primarily as a chemical fertilizer and is mined along with sodium chloride (NaCl, halite, or common salt) and processed at the plant for water softener compound.

Three and nine-tenths miles (6.2km) down the Potash Road from U.S. 191 is the Jaycee Campground, with restrooms, tables, and campfire rings. A $5 per night fee is charged for overnight stays. If not camping in a developed campground, one must carry a portable toilet system or be subject to a $50 fine. A sign at the campground reads "Portal Overlook 1.5–Poison Spider Mesa 2.5." This hiking trail leads to the top of the rimrock and is highly recommended for its views of Arches National Park, Moab valley, and the land east and west of the Colorado River. Upriver from the campground 0.2 mile (0.3km) is an excellent bouldering area.

Several spectacular canyons drain into the river from the right (west) as one travels down the Potash Road. See locator map page 18 and Potash Road Side Canyons chapter for their location and established climbs.

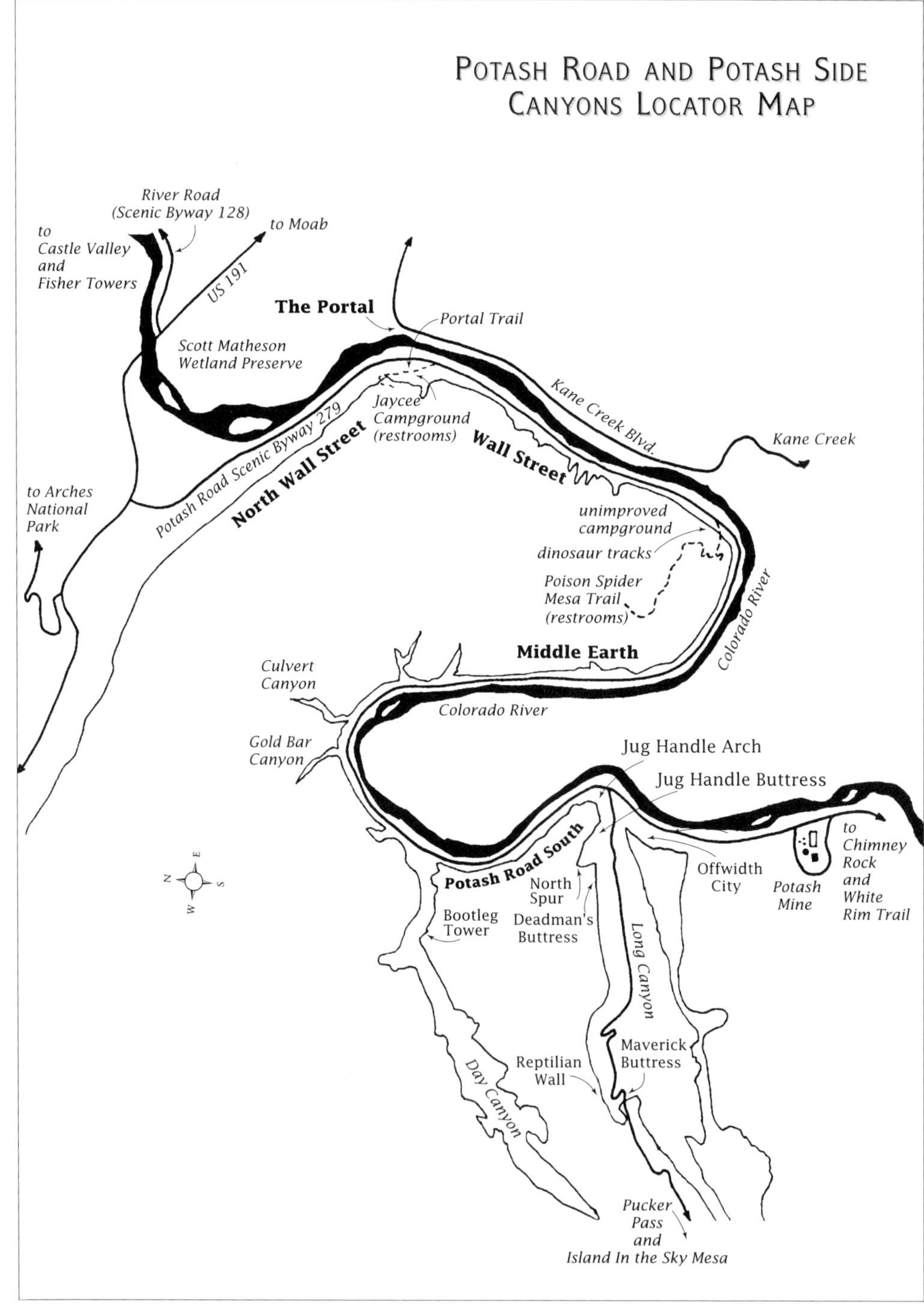
Potash Road and Potash Side Canyons Locator Map
River Road (Scenic Byway 128)
to Castle Valley and Fisher Towers
to Moab
US 191
The Portal
Portal Trail
Scott Matheson Wetland Preserve
Jaycee Campground (restrooms)
Kane Creek Blvd.
Kane Creek
Potash Road Scenic Byway 279
North Wall Street
Wall Street
to Arches National Park
unimproved campground
dinosaur tracks
Poison Spider Mesa Trail (restrooms)
Colorado River
Middle Earth
Culvert Canyon
Colorado River
Gold Bar Canyon
Jug Handle Arch
Jug Handle Buttress
to Chimney Rock and White Rim Trail
Potash Road South
North Spur
Offwidth City
Potash Mine
Bootleg Tower
Deadman's Buttress
Long Canyon
Maverick Buttress
Reptilian Wall
Day Canyon
Pucker Pass and Island In the Sky Mesa

Physical History

The 16-mile-long (26km) Potash Road was built in 1960 to service the plant at the site of the largest deposit of potash in North America. In 1964 an underground gas explosion at the mine killed 18 people. Shortly after the disaster the plant converted to "solution" mining–480 gallons of water per minute are pumped from the Colorado River into the mine's 340 miles of shafts and drifts, which range in depth from 2,000 to 3,000 feet (610–914m). After approximately a year the water (heavily in solution with potash and salts) is pumped out of the mine and into one of 24 settling ponds covering 400 acres of ground. A blue dye is added to increase the speed of evaporation (the rate of solar heat absorption). Months later when the water has evaporated leaving the white residues of potash and salts, they are bulldozed, slurried to the main plant, then submerged in a pond and aerated. The salts float to the top, are skimmed off, dried, bagged, and shipped throughout the U.S. to be sold as a water softner compound. The remaining potash is shipped in bulk by truck and rail to fertilizer markets from Canada to Mexico.

With the building of the road to the mine several rock slopes extending to the river were cut away. As a result, at the "Indian Writing" sign 5 miles downriver (8km), a 100-foot-long (30m) Fremont and Anasazi petroglyph panel is preserved out of reach-free from mutilation or graffiti. Defacement by vandals of rock art is often not malicious, but most often it shows ignorance of this nonreplaceable heritage belonging to all people. Even touching or outlining in chalk for photographing is damaging to these delicate rock canvases.

Geology

Rock along Wall Street is Navajo Sandstone. As one approaches the side canyons of Potash Road an anticline exposes the older strata of Kayenta, Wingate, Chinle, and Moenkopi. See their descriptions in this book's introductory geology section, and the San Rafael Swell chapter, on pages 9 and 183.

Wall Street North

This is the area upriver from Mile Post 11 on the Potash Road (Scenic Byway 279). Routes are listed right to left as one drives downriver from the Portal.

MORNING THUNDER I, 5.5, 2 pitches, 100 feet (30m)

First Ascent: Bill Lowther, Tim Kemple.

Location and Access: *Morning Thunder* is difficult to see because of its position high above the roadway. It is a collapsed-looking pinnacle 100 yards (91m) past the transmission lines crossing the Potash Road as one enters the Portal 2.7 miles downriver (4.3km) from U.S. Highway 191. The route begins at the farthest downhill point of the landform, or the first 30 feet (9m) may be bypassed by traversing onto the route from a shelf on the tower's right side. It may also be climbed by traversing onto the route from high up the left gully. Approach up the scree slope to the right of the tower in a line directly below the leftmost guy-wire of the transmission line, then traverse left to the tower. A single bolt is visible at the top of Pitch 1, 60 feet (18m) up the route.

Pitch 1: If beginning at the landform's lowest point climb to a belay ledge protected by a bolt, 60 feet (18m).

Pitch 2: Face climb past the bolt to rappel anchors not visible from below.

Paraphernalia: Small units; (1) quickdraw.

Descent: Single-rope rappel to the notch between the tower and the wall behind.

POSITRONIC I, 5.11, 1 pitch, 50 feet (15m), ★★★

First Ascent: Kyle Copeland, Paul Frank, June 1991.

Location and Access: *Positronic* is fifty feet (15m) upriver from Mile Post 12 on dark varnished rock 3 feet (0.9m) from the roadway. Face climb past two pitons, then two bolts to triple rappel anchors above and right of an overhang. Good route with many rests.

Paraphernalia: Four quickdraws.

Descent: Rappel the route.

NOTE: There is a ruin in a small cave across the river from Mile Post 12. It is identified by a few stacked rocks which are the remains of an Anasazi grainery.

Point of Moab (aka Frog on a Lily Pad)

The following two routes are located on Point of Moab which is obvious when looking west at the portal through which the Colorado River leaves Moab valley. It is visible from Moab but not visible from the Potash Road. Approach from the Portal Overlook Trail which begins at the Jaycee Campground 3.9 miles (6.2km) down the Potash Road from U.S. 191. The monolith forms part of the Navajo rimrock bordering Poison Spider Mesa.

DEAD SEA ROUTE III, 5.10, A1+, 4 pitches, 440 feet (134m)

First Ascent: Harvey T. Carter, Tim Jennings, 9 November 1967, 5.8, A2. One bivouac, 19 bolts, 27 pitons.

Location and Access: The route ascends the tower from the southeast up a crack system directly below the right-hand saddle.

Pitch 1: Climb a bolt ladder to a rotten crack. Continue past a make-shift belay to a large ledge with bolt anchors, 150 feet (46m).

Pitch 2: Free climb a thin corner to thin hands (5.10), then up to the notch, 70 feet (21m).

Pitch 3: Walk around to the back (west) side, 4th class, and climb a crack through a roof (on clean aid) to a bolt ladder. Belay from a ledge at the top of the ladder, 150 feet (46m).

Pitch 4: Climb a short pitch past two bolts to the top.

Paraphernalia: Double set of cams to 3.5"; TCUs; a few sawed off 0.5"–1" angles for Pitch 1; quickdraws.

Descent: Downclimb to solid rock, then double-rope rappel to the notch. Two more double-rope rappels reach the ground.

ANOTHER WIDE ONE III, 5.11+, 3 pitches, 440 feet (134m)

First Ascent: Earl Wiggins, Sonja Paspal, Spring 1991.

Location and Access: *Another Wide One* begins left of *Dead Sea Route*.

Pitch 1: Climb a right-facing (offwidth) dihedral which narrows to a handcrack and ends at a ledge.

Pitch 2: Traverse up and right over loose rock to the chimney of the original route, 25 feet (7.6m).

Pitch 3: Follow *Dead Sea Route* to the summit.

Paraphernalia: Standard desert rack with units up to 6".

Descent: Rappel to the notch, then to the ground.

P.F. FLYER III, 5.11, 4 pitches, 315 feet (96m)

First Ascent: Kyle Copeland, Paul Frank, 28-29 October 1990.

Location and Access: *P.F. Flyer* is 0.5 mile upriver (0.8km) from the Jaycee Campground. To the right of the route Little Arch is barely discernable high on the cliff when viewing from the river side of the roadway. Approach from the Portal Overlook Trail beginning at the campground.

Pitch 1: Climb 5.11 up 80-degree, then 90-degree rock past seven fixed anchors to a double-anchor belay station, 90 feet (27m).

Pitch 2: Traverse third class 300 feet (91m) left.

Pitch 3: Climb rotten rock 75 feet (23m)) to double anchors.

Pitch 4: Continue up a 4-inch (10cm) crack to double anchors, 150 feet (46m).

Paraphernalia: Friends (2) sets with many large pieces; (7) quickdraws.

Descent: Rappel the route.

UNKNOWN SPLITTER Rating unknown

There are rappel anchors at the top of a splitter crack on a smooth dark varnished wall 0.2 mile upriver (0.3km) from Jaycee Campground, above the bouldering area. Further information is unknown.

MORMON TEA I, 5.9, 1 pitch, 95 feet (29m)

First Ascent: Warren Egbert, Mattias Holiday, Kevin Holiday, May 1992.

Location and Access: *Mormon Tea* is 500 feet (152m) upriver from the Jaycee Campground. It climbs the right most of three prominent right-facing dihedrals. Begin up a chimney with the crux at its top, right of a right-facing corner (5.9), then climb the corner at 5.7 past two bolts.

Double rappel anchors are between two horizontal cracks at the top and right of the dihedral. They may be difficult to see from the road with binoculars but are clear with a spotting scope.

Paraphernalia: Friends #2, #3, #4.

Descent: One double-rope rappel from bolts right of the corner.

CAUTION: As with *30 Seconds Over Potash* (#69) there is an imminent bomb above the route. In the case of *Mormon Tea* the guillotine is a curved blade of rock tenuously attached to the wall above the route. Kyle Copeland: "Can it last 5 minutes or 5 million years?"

MORMON TEA DIRECT (Top-rope) I, 5.10b, 1 pitch, 95 feet (29m)

First Ascent: Warren Egbert, Mattias Holiday, Kevin Holiday, May 1992.

Location and Access: Top-rope the wall right of *Morman Tea.*

Paraphernalia: Top-rope.

Descent: Rappel *Mormon Tea.*

MUSK MUSTARD I, 5.9, 1 pitch, 80 feet (24m)

First Ascent: Warren Egbert, Mattias Holiday, May 1992.

Location and Access: *Musk Mustard* climbs the center of three prominent right-facing dihedrals upriver from the Jaycee Campground, the next dihedral left of *Mormon Tea.* Climb 5.9 into a lieback past three bolts to double rappel anchors on the wall right of the top of the crack system.

Paraphernalia: In ascending order: Friends #3; Camalot #4, #3, #2; (3) quickdraws.

Descent: Rappel the route with a single rope from double bolts.

KING'S HAND RIGHT II, 5.10, 4 pitches, 375 feet (114m)

First Ascent: Tony Valdes, Paul Frank, Bob Milton, 8 September 1987.

Location and Access: *King's Hand* is obvious high on the wall directly above the turn into the Jaycee Campground. This is 3.9 miles (6.2km) down the Potash Road from State Highway 191. A short hike to the beginning of the climb begins 0.33 mile downriver (0.5km) from where the landform can first be seen from the Potash Road. The route shares the first pitch with *King's Hand Left* and is characterized by much face climbing.

Pitch 1: Climb straight up past one drilled angle to a belay stance, 5.8, 150 feet (46m).

Pitch 2: Traverse up and right, then climb 85 feet (26m) to a two bolt, one piton belay station, 5.10.

Pitch 3: Ascend up, then diagonally left to join *King's Hand Left* again. This is a point at a loose chimney where the route climbs between the tips of two finger formations.

Pitch 4: Traverse to the back side of the landform and to a rappel point behind the summit block. The pitch is shared with *King's Hand Left.*

Paraphernalia: Small Friends; TCUs; (1) set Lowe Balls; (2) knifeblades.

Descent: Three double-rope rappels down the route.

KING'S HAND LEFT II, 5.9, 4 pitches, 375 feet (114m)

First Ascent: Bego Gerhart, Barry Miller, 8 September 1987.

Location and Access: Begin as for *Hand Right.*

Pitch 1: Climb straight up past one drilled angle to a belay stance, 5.8, 150 feet (46m). The pitch is shared with *King's Hand Right.*

Pitch 2: Traverse left before climbing 85 feet (26m) past two pockets to a belay station, 5.9.

Pitch 3: Ascend diagonally right to join the *King's Hand Right* route again. At this point a loose chimney is encountered and the route climbs between the tips of two finger formations.

Pitch 4: Shared with *King's Hand Right* which traverses to the back side of the landform and a rappel point behind the summit block.

Paraphernalia: Small Friends; TCUs; (1) quickdraw.

Descent: Rappel *King's Hand Right.*

KING'S HAND SUMMIT BLOCK II, A0

First Ascent: Peter Gallagher.

Location and Access: The summit block of the King's Hand was first climbed with a belay from a rope thrown over its top.

Photo: Lin Ottinger

Rappelling Wall Street

Wall Street

CAUTION: Many of the routes along Wall Street begin only a few feet from the 55 mph Potash Road, which is busy with gawking tourists, mountain bikers, and speeding trucks hauling salt and potash from the mine. For obvious safety reasons and to not endanger future access to this spectacular climbing area, it is important to keep the roadway clear and respect all other users. This includes keeping the decibels low on the boombox, pets under control, and other courtesies to co-existence. Please use restrooms at Jaycee Campground at the north end of Wall Street or at the parking lot at the dinosaur tracks 0.8 mile downriver (1.2km) from the Indian Writing sign at the southern end of Wall Street.

"Wall Street routes were put in ground up, the honorable way to establish new lines in an area dominated by ground up routes. If one wants to rappel bolt routes, it is important to go to a crag dominated by that type of route." Jim Beyer.

Finding the Routes

Wall Street begins at Mile Post 11, 4.2 miles downriver (6.7km) from U.S. Highway 191, or 0.3 miles downriver (0.48km) from the Jaycee Campground. The distance between routes was measured with a hip-chain by Eric Bjørnstad and BLM civil engineer John Lewis. Distances are noted in the "Location and Access" section of each climb and are identified either in feet

WALL STREET INDEX: Routes listed by Route Number

1 Another Pussy Bolt Route 5.12
2 Face Off 5.11a
3 Let's Go to Pluto 5.10
4 Gonad the Barbarian 5.11b
5 Kokopelli Seam 5.10

REFLECTOR POST #1
6 Scratch and Sniff 5.11
7 Seibernetics 5.8+
8 Seibernetics Direct 5.10-
9 Unemployment Line 5.10+
10 Unemployment Line Variation
11 Seam As It Ever Was 5.11b/c
12 Rude Old Men 5.12
13 Seam As It Ever Was Variation
14 Faith Flake 5.11a
15 El Cracko Diablo 5.10a
16 El Cracko Diablo Direct 5.11+
17 Coup d'Etat 5.11+

REFLECTOR POST #2
18 School Room #1
19 Doctor Strange Flake 5.10
20 Fist Full of Potash 5.10a
21 Fist Full of Potash Direct 5.10
22 Above a Fist Full 5.11
23 Last Tango in Potash 5.11b
24 Last Tango in Potash 5.12
25 Pinhead 5.10b
26 Potash Sanction 5.11a
27 Short but Cute 5.10, A4
28 Below Zero A3+
29 Astro Lad – Astro Champ 5.11a, A2+
30 Another Roadside Distraction 5.10b
31 Project
32 Mother Trucker 5.11c
33 Knapping with the Alien 5.11c/d
34 Half Pipe 5.10+/5.11-
35 Welcome to Anexia 5.12

REFLECTOR POST #3
36 Movie Project
37 Bad Moki Roof 5.9
38 Eyes of Falina 5.9R
39 Eyes of Falina Direct 5.10, AO
40 Flakes of Wrath 5.9+
41 Flakes of Wrath Direct 5.11c/d
42 Mississippi High Step 5.12-
43 Zig Zag 5.10a

REFLECTOR POST #4
44 Frogs of a Feather 5.10c
45 Shoot Up or Shut Up 5.11a
46 Shoot Up or Shut Up Corner 5.12a
47 Wake of the Flood 5.10c
48 Flash Flood 5.11a
49 High Over Datura 5.11+
50 Visible Panty Line 5.10a
51 Pounding the Frog Direct 5.11
52 Pounding the Frog 5.10bR
53 Smell of Dead Euro-Peons 5.11
54 Bolts to Bumpy Land 5.11a/b
55 Ring Pin Boulder 5.9+
56 Jug Roof 5.10a
57 Tune In, Turn On, Drop Out summit pitch 5.11a, A0
58 Chimney Sweep 5.10a
59 Jingus Launch 5.12 R/X
60 Mystery Route 5.11d
61 Summit Chimney 5.9
62 Wild–Eyed Dear 5.12a

REFLECTOR POST #5
63 Twitin Shinkies 5.11b
64 Blowin' Chunks 5.11b/c
65 Chunder Bunny 5.12-
66 Sand and Steel 5.11b
67 Bolted Route 5.11a
68 Right Side In 5.9
69 30 Seconds Over Potash 5.8
70 Lucy in the Sky with Potash 5.10a
71 Pedigree Poodles 5.9+
72 Manicured Lawns 5.9+
73 Dunn-Copeland Route 5.5
74 Nervous in Suburbia 5.10a
75 Under the Boardwalk 5.12b/c
76 Something Nasty 5.12b
77 I Love Loosey 5.11c
78 Baby Blue 5.11a
79 Desp-Aréte 5.12b
80 Beyer Offwidth 5.9+

REFLECTOR POST #6
81 Slab 5.8
82 Hot Ash 5.10+ R/X
83 Eat the Rich 5.10c
84 Knight Moves 5.11
85 Three Sheeps to the Wind 5.11
86 Tired of Talus 5.12
87 Static Cling 5.11a/b
88 Potash Bong Hit 5.10
89 Skeletonic 5.11+
90 Top Forty 5.8
91 Lacto Mangulation 5.10b
92 School Room #2
93 Grama and the Green Suede Shoes 5.7

REFLECTOR POST #7
94 She-La the Peeler 5.9
95 She-La the Peeler Direct 5.10a
96 Slab Route 5.7 R
97 Puppy Love 5.9 R
98 Steel Your Face 5.10a
99 Flakes of Bongo 5.10
100 Chriscross 5.11a R
101 Just Another Pretty Face 5.10a R
102 Just Another Pretty Face Variation
103 Unfinished 5.12
104 Don Smurfo 5.10 R
105 Big Sky Mud Flaps 5.10d
106 Impasse 5.12+
107 Walk on the Wide Side 5.10a
108 Armageddon 5.12a/b
109 Jacob's Ladder 5.10+
110 Shadowfax 5.11-

REFLECTOR POST #8
111 White Way 5.11 R
112 White Way Variation 5.6
113 Unknown
114 Honer's Odyssey 5.11 b/c

NOTE: Routes #111 through #114 are not shown on photos.

*WALL STREET INDEX: Routes listed by Name**

* Route Number in parentheses

(meters) between routes and/or points from designated parking signs or Reflector Posts along the cliff side of the roadway, beginning from the "Park In Designated Areas Only" sign near Mile Post 11 at the beginning of Wall Street.

If one wishes to find *Bad Moki Roof* for instance, look up the route in the index. Bad Moki Roof is #37; turn to it and extrapolate the location either from the upriver Reflector Post or the next route upriver. For *Bad Moki Roof*, it will be #3 Reflector Post. The "Location and Access" section states that the climb is reached 30 feet (6m) left of the description for #36 (*Movie Project*)–which is 31 feet (9m) left of #3 Reflector Post, thus *Bad Moki Roof* is 61 feet (19m) left of #3 Reflector Post.

NOTE: A Reflector Post painted red indicates the point where the lane changes from a passing to no passing zone (or visa versa). Black Reflector Posts indicate a culvert running beneath the roadway. White-tipped Reflector Posts are generic, positioned along the road to aid night-time navigation.

It may be helpful in noting distances between some climbs to remember that 500 feet (152m) is equal to approximately 0.1 mile (0.16km).

Climbing Rack

The rack for Wall Street is (2) set of Friends; (1) set of TCUs; (1) set of wired stoppers; quickdraws; (1 or 2) ropes, depending on length of climb. Many routes may require triple sets of Friends.

The Best 10 of Wall Street

Rated on quality of rock, most classic line, climbability at its grade, safe protection: (1) *30 Seconds Over Potash*, 5.8 crack (dihedral); (2) *Nervous in Suburbia*, 5.10a face; (3) *Knapping with the Alien*, 5.11c/d face; (4) *Steel Your Face*, 5.10a slab/face; (5) *Just Another Pretty Face*, 5.10a face/slab; (6) *Flakes of Wrath*, 5.9+ crack and *Flakes of Wrath Direct*, 5.11c/d crack/face; (7) *Baby Blue*, 5.11a crack (dihedral); (8) *Static Cling*, 5.11a/b crack (dihedral); (9) *Wild-Eyed Dear*, 5.12a face; (10) *Astro Lad*, 5.11a crack.

Best Cracks:

Mother Trucker 5.11c, *Sibernetics* 5.8+, *El Cracko Diablo* 5.10a, *Eat the Rich* 5.10c, *Something Nasty* 5.12b.

Best Faces:

Bolts to Bumpy Land 5.11a/b, *Big Sky Mudflaps* 5.10d, *Twitin' Shinkies* 5.11b, *Shoot Up or Shut Up* 5.11a, *Blowin' Chunks* 5.11b/c, *Last Tango in Potash* 5.11b.

Classics (but too inaccessible to most for its grade):

Mississippi High Step 5.12–, *Desp-aréte* 5.12b, *Gonad the Barbarian* 5.11b, *Armageddon* 5.12a/b.

1 ANOTHER PUSSY BOLT ROUTE I, 5.12, 1 pitch, 60 feet (18m), ★★★

First Ascent: Jim Beyer, solo, January 1990.

Location and Access: To reach *Another Pussy Bolt Route*, drive 0.3 mile (0.4km) downriver from the Jaycee Campground. The climb is above the sign: "Park in Designated Areas Only, next 1 mile." The nearest legal parking is at the Jaycee Campground. Hike to the route which is on the crackless face right of a 120-foot-high (37m) two-tower structure leaning against the upper wall (this is the same formation which *Let's Go to Pluto* climbs on the lower right). *Another Pussy Bolt Route* begins right of the parking sign, up a friction slab on an arête. Veer up and left to double rappel anchors where light-colored rock meets dark varnished rock above (approximately 10 feet [3m] above and 10 feet [3m] right of *Let's Go to Pluto* rappel anchors). Approach the friction slab from the right, then traverse up and left to the arête. Nine anchors are in view from the base of the climb.

Paraphernalia: Nine quickdraws.

Descent: Rappel the route from anchors (visible from below and directly above the parking sign) on light-colored rock below a black rock band.

2 FACE OFF I, 5.11a, 1 pitch, 50 feet (21m), ★★★

First Ascent: Jim Beyer, solo, 1990.

Location and Access: *Face Off* climbs to *Let's Go to Pluto* rappel anchors. Begin left of a juniper tree where there is a petroglyph goat at the base of the wall. Climb between two petroglyph sheep facing each other 15 feet (4.5m) up the wall. The route was established with no fixed anchors placed. The climb has now been degraded by the placement (by an unknown culprit) of six bolts. The ancient hieroglyphs were left by Anasazi indians who were in the area 1300 to 700 years b.p. (before present time).

Paraphernalia: Six quickdraws.

Descent: Rappel the route.

SIGN: "PARK IN DESIGNATED AREAS ONLY, NEXT 1 MILE" AND MILE POST 11

3 LET'S GO TO PLUTO I, 5.10, 1 pitch, 50 feet (21m)

First Ascent: Jim Beyer, solo, January 1990.

Location and Access: *Let's Go to Pluto* is 30 feet (9m) left of a sign reading "Park in Designated Areas Only, next 1 mile," or 60 feet (18m) left of *Face Off*. This is a point below and right of the edge of a two tower formation leaning against the upper wall. Begin with fingers up a left-facing dihedral and continue up a wide crack passing an overhang (the crux) on its right side before reaching rappel anchors visible from below. The only fixed gear on the route is a chock below the overhang.

Paraphernalia: A selection up to 3" size; RPs at the crux; (1) quickdraw.

Descent: Rappel the route.

NOTE: There are three petroglyph panels between *Let's Go to Pluto* and *Gonad the Barbarian*.

Wall Street

Photo: Bill Godschalx

Reflector Post #1
6 Scratch and Sniff
7 Seibernetics
8 Seibernetics Direct
9 Unemployment Line
10 Unemployment Line Variation
11 Seam As It Ever Was
12 Rude Old Men
13 Seam As It Ever Was Variation
14 Faith Flake
15 El Cracko Diablo
16 El Cracko Diablo Direct
17 Coup d'Etat

4 GONAD THE BARBARIAN I, 5.11b, 2 pitches, 120 feet (37m), ★★★★

First Ascent: Kyle Copeland, Sue Kemp, Andy Pitas, Wendy Pitas, February 1990.

Location and Access: *Gonad the Barbarian* is 65 feet (20m) left of *Let's Go to Pluto.*

Pitch 1: Climb an obvious 4th class ramp (traversing right to left) several yards right of the rappel anchors, 100 feet (30m) downriver from the parking sign.

Pitch 2: Face climb past two bolts to a handcrack, 80 feet (24m). The bolts have two drilled pitons a few inches above them. Continue past two more bolts, then climb up a right-facing dihedral to the top of the pillar. The crux is a chimney at the top of the route. Rappel slings are visible from below.

Paraphernalia: One set of Friends; TCUs.

Descent: One double-rope rappel down the route.

Wall Street

Photo: Bill Godschalx

1 Another Pussy Bolt Route
2 Face Off
3 Let's Go to Pluto
4 Gonad the Barbarian
5 Kokopelli Seam

5 KOKOPELLI SEAM I, 5.10, 1 pitch, 40 feet (12m)

First Ascent: Doug Sinor, Jenni Sinor, February 1994.

Location and Access: *Kokopelli Seam* is 70 feet (21m) left of Pitch 1 of *Gonad the Barbarian*. The route may be climbed as a variation to Pitch 1 of *Gonad the Barbarian*. Climb a seam past two drilled pitons on the face, ending on the ramp near the middle of Pitch 1 of *Gonad*. The route may be top-roped from the 4th class Pitch 1 of *Gonad*.

Paraphernalia: One #1 Friend for the bottom of the route (below the first bolt); (2) quickdraws.

Descent: Rappel the route or downclimb the 4th class ramp of Pitch 1 of *Gonad*.

#1 REFLECTOR POST (WHITE)

6 SCRATCH AND SNIFF I, 5.11, 1 pitch, 80 feet (24m), ★★★★★

First Ascent: Kyle Copeland, solo, 1991.

Location and Access: This hard slab route is 40 feet (12m) left of #1 Reflector Post. Begin up a seam and climb a 5.11 slab 8 feet (2.4m) right of *Seibernetics*. Climb past two drilled pitons, then angle far right to a bolt. Continue far left and pass another bolt. The crux is above the top desert varnish. A rappel chain is visible from below.

Paraphernalia: One #1 Friend for the bottom of the route (below the first bolt); (4) quickdraws.

Descent: Rappel the route.

NOTE: The route is one of Jimmy Dunn's "right hand only" climbs.

7 SEIBERNETICS I, 5.8+, 1 pitch, 80 feet (24m), ★★★★★

First Ascent: Unknown.

Location and Access: *Seibernetics* is 25 feet (7.6m) left of *Scratch and Sniff*, 65 feet (19.8m) left of #1 Reflector Post. Climb up and left to a right-facing dihedral past two drilled baby angles, then straight up to a rappel chain below a right-sloping ceiling. The crux is at the second piton.

Paraphernalia: One set of Friends #1 through #3.5; TCUs helpful; small wires; (2) quickdraws.

Descent: One rope rappel down the route.

8 SEIBERNETICS DIRECT (Top-rope) I, 5.10–, 1 pitch, 80 feet (24m)

First Ascent: Unknown.

Location and Access: Top-rope the face right of and below *Seibernetics* anchors, 10 feet (3m) left of *Scratch and Sniff*. Begin directly below the start of a small right-facing, right-curving crack system.

Paraphernalia: Top-rope.

Descent: Rappel from *Seibernetics* anchors.

9 UNEMPLOYMENT LINE (aka Bush Line) I, 5.10+, 2 pitches, 120 feet (37m)

First Ascent: Linus Platt, Kyle Copeland, 1991.

Location and Access: *Unemployment Line* is 74 feet (23m) left of #1 Reflector Post, right of a deep chimney with a large hackberry tree at its lower end.

Pitch 1: Begin 15 feet (5m) left of *Seibernetics* and climb up a right-trending, right-facing dihedral. Visible directly above is a drilled baby angle on the left bulge of the upper dihedral. The crux of Pitch 1 is below the piton. A few feet beyond the anchor is a ledge with bushes atop the pillar formed by the dihedral. On the ledge behind a desert holly bush are rappel anchors visible from below, 80 feet (24m).

Pitch 2: From the left side of the ledge climb up angling right past three drilled pitons to rappel slings in view from below, 5.10+, 40 feet (12m).

Paraphernalia: One set of Friends; (1) quickdraw.

Descent: Rappel the route.

10 UNEMPLOYMENT LINE VARIATION (Direct Start) Rating unknown

First Ascent: Unknown

Location and Access: This variation is an easier beginning to *Unemployment Line*. Begin as for *Seibernetics* and climb up and left, traversing after a few feet to the *Unemployment Line* crack system.

11 SEAM AS IT EVER WAS I, 5.11b/c, 1 pitch, 85 feet (26m), ★★★★

First Ascent: Dan Mannix, Alison Sheets, 24 November 1987.

Location and Access: *Seam As It Ever Was* is 45 feet (14m) left of *Unemployment Line*, 10 feet (3m) left of a deep chimney with a prominent hackberry tree. The wall the route climbs is only 4 feet (1m) from the edge of the road. Begin with a few difficult moves up a 10-foot-high (3m) left-facing dihedral, then ascend a fingertips crack to anchors visible from below. Kevin Chase: "A crack to flare to bulge." The crux is a thin crack through the bulge 15 feet (4.5m) off the ground. There is a single bolt above the bulge on the left wall.

Paraphernalia: TCUs with several #0; small wires; quickdraws.

Descent: Rappel 85 feet (26m) down the route.

12 RUDE OLD MEN I, 5.12, 1 pitch, 60 feet (18m), ★★★★

First Ascent: Charlie Fowler, Kyle Copeland, May 1989.

Location and Access: *Rude Old Men* is 18 feet (5.4m) left of *Seam As It Ever Was*. Face climb to a bolt, then right toward *Seam As It Ever Was* and a second bolt, then third and fourth bolts, one drilled piton. Finally move left following two more bolts to anchors below a prominent bedding seam.

Paraphernalia: Seven quickdraws.

Descent: Rappel anchors visible from below.

13 SEAM AS IT EVER WAS VARIATION Rating unknown

First Ascent: Unknown.

Location and Access: Begin up *Rude Old Men* and at the third bolt traverse right to *Seam As It Ever Was*.

Paraphernalia: Same as *Seam As It Ever Was*.

Descent: Rappel *Seam As It Ever Was*.

14 FAITH FLAKE I, 5.11a, 1 pitch, 60 feet (18m), ★★

First Ascent: Jake "The Snake" Tradiak, April 1990.

Location and Access: *Faith Flake* is 30 feet (9m) left of *Rude Old Men* and is recognized by a sling around the "Faith Flake" behind a small hackberry tree. Climb broken rock past "Faith Flake," then past one bolt and two drilled pitons. Protect with a #3 Friend at the start, then unclip to reduce rope drag. (There is a bolt hole just below rappel anchors). Kevin Chase: "Climb the corner, clip the A4 sling that is tied around the A2+ flake, then clip drilled pins to anchors." The crux is in leaving a "no hands" rest above the flake and thin moves through a bulge.

Paraphernalia: One #3 Friend at the start; (1) #0.75 TCU for protection high up; (3) quickdraws.

Descent: One 60-foot (18m) rappel from bolts visible from below.

CAUTION: The "Faith Flake" makes the route potentially dangerous.

Wall Street

Photo: Bill Godschalx

Reflector Post #2
18 School Room #1
19 Doctor Strange Flake
20 Fist Full of Potash
21 Fist Full of Potash Direct
22 Above a Fist Full
23 Last Tango in Potash
24 Last Tango in Potash (Top-rope)
25 Pinhead
26 Potash Sanction
27 Short but Cute

15 EL CRACKO DIABLO I, 5.10a, 1 pitch, 55 feet (17m), ★★★★

First Ascent: Charlie Fowler, Nancy Prichard, Sue Wint, April 1989.

Location and Access: *El Cracko Diablo* is 13 feet (4m) left of *El Cracko Diablo Direct.* Climb a fingercrack which ends in a handcrack over a bulge, then continue to obvious rappel anchors. The crux is approximately 5 feet (1.5m) below the rappel slings.

Paraphernalia: One set of Friends #1 through #3; (1) set of TCUs with (1) #0.5 TCU for high up.

Descent: One 55-foot (17m) rappel from a 2-bolt anchor at the top of the route.

NOTE: The route is one of Jimmy Dunn's "right hand only/left hand only" climbs.

16 EL CRACKO DIABLO DIRECT I, 5.11+, 1 pitch, 55 feet (17m), ★★★★

First Ascent: Spanish climbers, Fall '96.

Location and Access: Four bolts have been placed by an unknown party on this previously top-rope route. Climb the face 13 feet (3.9m) right of *El Cracko Diablo* (left of *Faith Flake*). The crux is 12 feet (3.6m) above ground.

Wall Street Photo: Bill Godschalx

Reflector Post #2 18 School Room #1

Paraphernalia: Four quickdraws.

Descent: One 55-foot (17m) rappel from a 2-bolt anchor.

17 COUP D'ETAT I, 5.11+, 1 pitch, 50 feet (15m)

First Ascent: Linus Platt, Kyle Copeland, Spring 1991.

Location and Access: *Coup d'Etat* is a prominent small right-facing dihedral splitting a black varnished wall 15 feet (4.5m) left of *El Cracko Diablo*. Climb past one drilled piton and one bolt on the right wall to rappel slings visible above a bulge. The crux is off the ground. Lisa Hathaway: "The route is desperately hard!"

Paraphernalia: Small Friends; small TCUs; small nuts; (2) quickdraws.

Descent: Rappel the route from a single bolt.

#2 REFLECTOR POST (RED)

18 SCHOOL ROOM #1 (Top-rope Area)

This area of Wall Street contains climbing problems up to 50 feet (15m) in length and in the 5.4 to 5.10 range of difficulty. *School Room* begins at the #2 Reflector Post approximately 225 feet (69m) left of *Coup d'Etat*.

First Ascent: Unknown.

Location and Access: *School Room #1* is between the routes *Coup d'Etat* and *Doctor Strange Flake*. There are five sets of top-rope anchors in place. A 4th class approach

Wall Street

Photo: Bill Godschalx

27 Short but Cute
28 Below Zero
29 Astro Lad-Astro Champ
30 Another Roadside Distraction
31 Project
32 Mother Trucker
33 Knapping with the Alien
34 Half Pipe
35 Welcome to Anexia

to top-rope anchors begins behind a large hackberry tree (the largest tree along the School Room area) approximately 76 feet (23m) right of *Doctor Strange Flake* or 155 feet (47m) left of #2 Reflector Post.

Paraphernalia: Top-rope.

Descent: Rappel or downclimb to the large hackberry tree.

NOTE: Top-rope bolts in the *School Room* area are not always rappel anchors. Downclimbing is recommended.

19 DOCTOR STRANGE FLAKE I, 5.10, 1 pitch, 40 feet (12m)

First Ascent: *Kyle Copeland, Sue Kemp*, 2 December 1987.

Location and Access: *Doctor Strange Flake* is 72 feet (22m) left of the hackberry tree at the 4th class approach to *School Room* anchors, the route ascends a light colored rock face. Three bolts are in place, although at the time of this writing ⅜" hangers and nuts are needed. Rappel anchors are not visible from below.

Paraphernalia: Possibly (3) ⅜" hangers; (3) quickdraws.

Descent: Rappel the route or downclimb the 4th class *School Room* approach.

Wall Street

Photo: Bill Godschalx

18 School Room #1
19 Doctor Strange Flake
20 Fist Full of Potash
21 Fist Full of Potash Direct
22 Above a Fist Full
23 Last Tango in Potash
24 Last Tango in Potash (Top-rope)
25 Pinhead
26 Potash Sanction

20 FIST FULL OF POTASH I, 5.10a, 1 pitch, 40 feet (12m), ★★★

First Ascent: Charlie Fowler, Geoff Tabin, Tom Dickey, 2 December 1987.

Location and Access: *Fistfull of Potash* is 17 feet (5m) left of *Doctor Strange Flake*. The face route climbs to a wide slot up and left. There is one bolt, then two drilled pitons on the route. Rappel slings are visible on the downriver (south) facing wall. The crux is slab moves to a fingercrack.

Paraphernalia: Friends #0.75, #1; TCUs #0.75, #1, #1.5; (3) quickdraws.

Descent: Rappel 40 feet (12m) down the route.

21 FIST FULL OF POTASH DIRECT (Top-rope) I, 5.10, 1 pitch, 40 feet (12m)

First Ascent: Kyle Copeland, solo, 1989.

Location and Access: Top-rope the face 6 feet (1.8m) left, and below *Fist Full of Potash* anchors, joining *Fist Full of Potash* below the bulge.

Paraphernalia: Top-rope.

Descent: Rappel the route.

22 ABOVE A FIST FULL I, 5.11, 3 pitches

First Ascents: Pitch 1: Peter Verchick, Jeff Slider, Dave (from Alaska), 1995. Pitch 2: Bob Novellino. Pitch 3: Peter Verchick, Lou.

Location and Access: *Above a Fist Full* is on the wall above *Fistfull of Potash.* Approach from *School Room #1.*

Pitch 1: Begin at the left edge of *School Room* and climb past five bolts, 5.11, 75 feet (23m).

Pitch 2: Climb a 5.8 chimney, 40 feet (12m).

Pitch 3: Climb to rappel slings visible from a point a few yards upriver.

Paraphernalia: Standard desert rack; (5) quickdraws.

Descent: Rappel the route.

23 LAST TANGO IN POTASH I, 5.11b, 1 pitch, 60 feet (18m), ★★★★★

First Ascent: Kyle Copeland, *Alison Sheets*, 30 November 1987.

Location and Access: This popular route is 39 feet (12m) left of *Fist Full of Potash.* Follow anchors up a seam through a slab of desert varnish. Three drilled pitons, then two bolts are in place. Rappel slings are visible from below on the left wall.

Paraphernalia: TCUs (1) #0.4, #0.5, #0.25; small wires; (5) quickdraws.

Descent: Rappel the route.

24 LAST TANGO IN POTASH (Top-rope) I, 5.12, 1 pitch, 60 feet (18m)

First Ascent: Kyle Copeland, solo, 1989.

Location and Access: The top-rope is 25 feet (7.6m) right of *Last Tango in Potash* and climbs up a broken left-facing dihedral. Traverse left and join *Last Tango in Potash* rappel anchors.

Paraphernalia: Top-rope.

Descent: Rappel *Last Tango in Potash.*

25 PINHEAD (aka Mystery Route) I, 5.10b, 2 pitches, 80 feet (34m)

First Ascent: Unknown. First Free Ascent: Charlie Fowler, Franci Stagi, March 1991.

Location and Access: *Pinhead* is 16 feet (4.8m) left of *Last Tango in Potash.* Climb a broken multi-crack system to triple anchors atop Pitch 1. Continue up, then high on the climb make an obvious left traverse past two bolts side by side. Rappel slings at the 50-foot (15m) and approximately 80-foot (24m) levels.

Paraphernalia: One set of Friends; long runners; (2) quickdraws.

Descent: Rappel the route.

26 POTASH SANCTION I, 5.11a, 1 pitch, 65 feet (20m), ★

First Ascent: Charlie Fowler, solo, 12 February 1988.

Location and Access: *Potash Sanction* is 32 feet (10m) left of *Pinhead* and climbs a shallow left-facing dihedral. Lieback 5.9 and continue past a drilled baby angle (on left wall), then pass a small roof on its right side, 5.11a. Continue to rappel anchors. The route climbs an old aid line put up by an unknown party.

Paraphernalia: One set of Friends; (1) #5 Camalot; (4) small Tri-cams; (1) set of TCUs; wires; (1) quickdraw.

Descent: One 65-foot (20m) rappel down the route.

27 SHORT BUT CUTE I, 5.10, A4, 1 pitch, 65 feet (20m)

First Ascent: Kyle Copeland, solo, November 1988.

Location and Access: *Short but Cute* is 22 feet (7m) left of *Potash Sanction*. One bolt and rappel slings are visible from below on the left wall.

NOTE: *Short but Cute* is not recommended because of crack degradation resulting from piton placements, thus paraphernalia and descent information are not given. Please be responsible! Kevin Chase: "Two stupid aid lines. Not recommended as the visual impact is shitty. If you desire to climb these routes, then here is some advice: There are plenty of cracks to nail on the desert, get off the road and find one."

28 BELOW ZERO (aka Less than Zero) I, A3+, 1 pitch, 70 feet (21m)

First Ascent: Kyle Copeland, Charlie Fowler, February 1989.

Location and Access: *Below Zero* is 23 feet (7m) left of *Short but Cute*.

NOTE: *Below Zero* ascends a thin aid crack and is not recommended because of rock destruction from piton placements, thus paraphernalia and descent information are not given. Please be responsible!

29 ASTRO LAD-ASTRO CHAMP I, 5.11a A2+, 3 pitches, 200 feet (60m), ★★★★★

First Ascent: Pitch 1-Astro Lad: Jim Beyer, Pat McInerney, October 1989. Pitches 2-3-Astro Champ: Darrel Watson, Paul O'Brien, April 1997.

Location and Access: Pitch 1 of *Astro Lad* steps out on the face (left) to a bolt, then back (right) into the corner. Jim Beyer. "Like the changing corners pitch on *Astro Man* (Washington Column, Yosemite)."

Pitch 1 (Astro Lad): Climb thin cracks in the first right-facing dihedral 42 feet (13m) left of *Below Zero*. There is a bolt on the left wall two-thirds of the way up, and rappel slings visible from below. The cruxes are after the bolt and overhanging thin crack moves on a north (right-facing) wall, 5.11a, 55 feet (17m).

Pitch 2 (Astro Champ): Climb with aid through a broken roof to a drilled ring angle visible on the left wall from below (much thin nailing), A2+.

Pitch 3: Continue with aid up a dihedral to just past a small roof. Rappel anchors are visible on the right wall from below, A2+.

Paraphernalia: Friends up to #3; small TCUs; (1) set of nuts; many thin pitons, Lost Arrows, Beaks and Peckers; (2) 200 foot (60m) ropes; (1) quickdraw.

Descent: Rappel the route from double-anchors.

30 ANOTHER ROADSIDE DISTRACTION I, 5.10b, 1 pitch, 45 feet (14m), ★★

First Ascent: Jim Beyer, Pat McInerney, October 1989.

Location and Access: *Another Roadside Distraction* ascends the right-facing dihedral 21 feet (6m) left of *Astro Lad*. Begin up 5.7 rock 5 feet (1.5m) left, then step back right before a fingercrack, 5.10b. Continue to a stance below rappel anchors on the left wall. There is no fixed gear on the route. Bob Novellino: "The crux is loose bottom and pumpy top."

Paraphernalia: Friends (3) #0.75, #2, #4; nuts.

Descent: Rappel the route from triple anchors.

Wall Street

Photo: Bill Godschalx

REFLECTOR POST #3
36 Movie Project
37 Bad Moki Roof
38 Eyes of Falina
39 Eyes of Falina Direct
40 Flakes of Wrath
41 Flakes of Wrath Direct
42 Mississippi High Step

31 PROJECT (aka Unfinished Line) I, 1 pitch, 25 feet (8m)

First Ascent: Peter Verchick, solo.

Location and Access: *Project* is 34 feet (10m) left of *Another Roadside Distraction* on a left-facing dihedral. A fixed piton is low on the route on the left wall and a rappel piton is visible on the right wall.

NOTE: The climb is an unfinished project and not recommended, thus no further information is given.

32 MOTHER TRUCKER I, 5.11c, 1 pitch, 50 feet (15m), ★★★★★

First Ascent: Jim Beyer, Pat McInerney, October 1989. First on-sight: Linus Platt, Spring 1990.

Location and Access: *Mother Trucker* is 26 feet (8m) left of *Project* and is climbed with stemming and face moves up a thin crack system in a left-trending dihedral. There is no fixed gear in place. The cruxes are at the top below a ceiling and the lunge for slings (or the grade of the climb is harder than 5.11c).

Wall Street

Photo: Bill Godschalx

26 Potash Sanction
27 Short but Cute
28 Below Zero
29 Astro Lad –Astro Champ
30 Another Roadside Distraction
31 Project
32 Mother Trucker
33 Knapping with the Alien
34 Half Pipe
35 Welcome to Anexia

Paraphernalia: Thin protection; nuts.
Descent: Rappel the route.

33 KNAPPING WITH THE ALIEN I, 5.11c/d, 1 pitch, 45 feet (14m), ★★★★★

First Ascent: Kyle Copeland, Linus Platt, Spring 1991.

Location and Access: *Knapping with the Alien* is 26 feet (7.9m) left of *Mother Trucker*. The climb is rated 5.11b for a tall climber, 5.11c/d if short. Ascend a face past five drilled baby angles. The route is easily identified by a 1-foot-deep (0.3m) shelf 5.5 feet (1.6m) off the ground. Between the third and fifth pitons one may climb up and left or up and right. Begin up the shelf, then traverse (from a baby angle) up and past a second baby angle. Continue up and left past three more pitons to rappel chain visible from below. The crux is getting to and past the fourth anchor.

Paraphernalia: Optional #1 Friend at the start; thin to handsize protection; (5) quickdraws.

Descent: A rappel chain is visible from below.

34 HALF PIPE I, 5.10+/5.11–, 1 pitch, 55 feet (17m), ★★★

First Ascent: Jim Beyer, solo, January 1991.

Location and Access: *Half Pipe* is 72 feet (22m) left of *Knapping with the Alien* and 75 feet (23m) right of *Bad Moki Roof*. Begin up the left side of a left-facing dihedral. One bolt, then one piton are fixed on the left wall high on the route. Rappel anchors are visible on the right side of the dihedral.

Paraphernalia: Thin to hand-size protection; a few Friends to #3; TCUs; many small wires; (2) quickdraws.

Descent: Rappel anchors are visible.

35 WELCOME TO ANEXIA I, 5.12, 1 pitch, 40 feet (12m), ★★★

First Ascent: Jake "The Snake" Tradiak. First Free Ascent: Kyle Copeland.

Location and Access: *Welcome to Anexia* is 2 feet (0.6km) left of *Half Pipe*, 22 feet (6.7m) right of #3 Reflector Post (which is positioned at the right side of *Bad Moki Roof*). Climb past four bolts, then one drilled angle to a rappel chain visible from below on a south (downriver) facing wall. Begin on a left-sloping 5-foot-long (1.5m) ramp at the start of *Half Pipe*. Ascend up and left to a high angle shoulder, then to rappel anchors. The route is a face climb with the crux down low.

Paraphernalia: (5) quickdraws.

Descent: Rappel the route.

#3 REFLECTOR POST (BLACK AND WHITE)

36 MOVIE PROJECT

First Ascent: Hollywood.

Location and Access: There is a rappel anchor under the lip (on the right side) of *Bad Moki Roof*, 31 feet (9.4m) left of #3 Reflector Post.

37 BAD MOKI ROOF I, 5.9, 1 pitch, 45 feet (14m), ★★

First Ascent: Kyle Copeland, solo, April 1988.

Location and Access: *Bad Moki Roof* is 30 feet (9m) left of *Movie Project* (#36) or 61 feet (19m) left of #3 Reflector Post, and is an obvious, dominant feature along Wall Street. Climb the crack system in a right-facing dihedral with a small roof 20 feet (6m) off the ground. Begin up a fingercrack with an undercling to negotiate the roof, then up to rappel slings visible from below. The crux is pulling the sandy roof.

Paraphernalia: Small pieces with large protection for the roof.

Descent: Rappel the route or downclimb the gully to the right.

38 EYES OF FALINA I, 5.9 R, 1 pitch, 90 feet (27m)

First Ascent: Kyle Copeland, solo, March 1988.

Location and Access: *Eyes of Falina* is 3 feet (0.9m) left of *Bad Moki Roof*. Climb up and left to a bolt on the wall below an overhang, then a piton left of the overhang. Continue to rappel anchors on a loose face.

Paraphernalia: One set of Friends; wires.; (2) quickdraws.

Descent: One double-rope rappel down the route.

39 EYES OF FALINA DIRECT I, 5.10, A0, 1 pitch, 90 feet (27m)

First Ascent: Jim Beyer, solo.

Location and Access: Begin 18 feet (5.4m) left of *Eyes of Falina*. There were three bolts in place, but the route now has only two with the graffito of an empty hole from a chopped bolt. Begin behind a large rabbit brush left of a 12-foot-high (3.5m) circular broken area (created by blasting rock during road construction). Pass a small overhang on its right and continue to rappel anchors.

CAUTION: Beware of poison ivy at the base of the climb.

Paraphernalia: Unknown

Descent: Rappel the route.

40 FLAKES OF WRATH I, 5.9+, 1 pitch, 60 feet (18m), ★★★★★

First Ascent: Alison Sheets belayed by Paul Firestone, 29 January 1988.

Location and Access: *Flakes of Wrath* is 3 feet (1m) left of *Eyes of Falina Direct*. Begin up a left angling handcrack. Continue with a lieback to a thin undercling around the left side of a large flake/ceiling, 5.9. The crux is low down at the finger pockets 8 feet (2.4m) above the first overhang. There is no fixed gear on the climb.

CAUTION: Beware of poison ivy at the base of the climb.

Paraphernalia: One each #1.5 through #3.5 Friends with extra #2, #2.5; TCUs (1) #4, #0.1; medium stoppers for the crux.

Descent: Rappel the route.

41 FLAKES OF WRATH DIRECT I, 5.11c/d, 1 pitch, 60 feet (18m), ★★★★★

First Ascent: Brent Bartholomeu, Summer 1995.

Location and Access: Begin up the face with a lieback 8 feet (2.4m) left of *Flakes of Wrath*, then climb fingercracks to a hard face move using the *Flakes of Wrath* anchors. The crux is pulling the bulge. The route was previously a top-rope line which was led by the late Brent Bartholomeu in the summer of '95 prior to his death in a climbing accident the following winter.

CAUTION: Beware of poison ivy at the base of the wall.

Paraphernalia: Standard Wall Street rack.

Descent: Rappel the route.

42 MISSISSIPPI HIGH STEP I, 5.12–, 1 pitch, 40 feet (12m), ★★★★

First Ascent: Linus Platt, Kyle Copeland, March 1990.

Location and Access: *Mississippi High Step* is 28 feet (9m) left of *Flakes of Wrath*. Begin with a hard start where light-colored rock on the left meets desert varnished rock on the right–a point 6 feet (1.8m) in from the roadway. Climb a left trending broken flake/crack system. Continue past bolts to a rappel chain right of a small ceiling and visible from below. There are five anchors fixed on the route; one bolt 15 feet (4.5m) up, then a drilled piton, a bolt, another bolt, and finally a drilled baby angle. There is a difficult crux off the ground (at the first bolt). A second crux is between the third and fourth bolts.

CAUTION: Beware of poison ivy at the base of the wall.

Paraphernalia: Five quickdraws.

Descent: Rappel the route.

NOTE: Left of Mississippi High Step there is approximately 120 feet (37m) of light-colored smooth wall with no routes, then a broken seam to wide crack system (unclimbed). Left of this is another 100 feet (30m) of dark varnished rock. At this point the wall begins to cut back from the road and climbing lines begin to appear, beginning with Zig Zag.

43 ZIG ZAG I, 5.10a, 1 pitch, 75 feet (23m), ★★★

First Ascent: Jim Beyer, solo, February 1991.

Location and Access: The route zig-zags up the face 27 feet (8m) right of #4 Reflector Post. Begin behind small willow bushes and climb past one bolt 12 feet up (3.6m), then continue, angling left to a second bolt. Veer up and right past a shelf, then another bolt, and climb up past a fourth bolt. Angle left up a small ramp passing a fifth bolt. Surmount a bulge to reach rappel anchors. Kevin Chase in his precursor guide to Wall Street: "Unclipping bolts after you pass helps with rope drag problems." Jim Beyer: "Clip third bolt and downclimb, unclip second bolt, then second climbs straight up corner, 5.8/5.9."

Paraphernalia: One #1 Friend; (1) #0.75 cam; (5) quickdraws.

Descent: Rappel the route.

#4 REFLECTOR POST (WHITE)

44 FROGS OF A FEATHER I, 5.10c, 1 pitch, 80 feet (24m), ★★

First Ascent: Kyle Copeland, Paul Seibert, July 1989.

Location and Access: *Frogs of a Feather* is 7 feet (2m) left of #4 Reflector Post, immediately left of two blasting holes 4 feet (1.2m) above ground, and 27 feet (7m) left of *Zig Zag*. Begin at the same start as *Shoot Up or Shut Up* (sharing anchors). Ascend by lieback and jams to a stance right of the second bolt on *Shoot Up or Shut Up*. Climb a fingercrack up light-colored rock, then traverse high with the crux after the traverse. Join *Shoot Up or Shut Up* or continue a couple of feet left and ascend to rappel anchors. A bolt protects the hard move (crux) near the top of the climb.

Paraphernalia: Friends up to #3 with many #1; TCUs; (1) quickdraw.

Descent: Rappel anchors are shared with *Shoot Up or Shut Up*.

NOTE: If *Frogs of a Feather* is climbed, one may top-rope *Shoot Up or Shut Up*, or visa-versa.

45 SHOOT UP OR SHUT UP I, 5.11a, 1 pitch, 80 feet (24m), ★★★★★

First Ascent: Kyle Copeland, Charlie Fowler, Marc Hirt, Tim Hudgel, February 1989.

Location and Access: Climb right of a left-facing dihedral 100 feet (30m) right of the first designated parking area. Begin at the same start as *Frogs of a Feather*. Ascend past three bolts, one piton, then two bolts up an arête formed by the dihedral. Continue to anchors shared with *Frogs of a Feather*. The climb's crux is reached past the third bolt where a fixed piton is in place.

Paraphernalia: One #3 Friend; small wires; (6) quickdraws.

Descent: Rappel anchors are shared with *Frogs of a Feather*.

46 SHOOT UP OR SHUT UP CORNER (Top-rope) I, 5.12a, 1 pitch, 80 feet (24m)

First Ascent: Kyle Copeland, solo, 1989.

Location and Access: Top-rope the corner 10 feet left (3m) of *Shoot Up or Shut Up*, climbing an arête of a left-facing dihedral. The crux is the first 15 feet (4.5m).

Paraphernalia: Top-rope.

Descent: Rappel the route.

47 WAKE OF THE FLOOD I, 5.10c, 1 pitch, 60 feet (18m), ★★★

First Ascent: Kyle Copeland, Ron Olevsky, August 1989.

Location and Access: *Wake of the Flood* is 36 feet (11m) left of #4 Reflector Post. Begins behind willow trees 17 feet (5m) left of *Shoot Up or Shut Up Corner*. Climb past two fixed pitons (first on right wall, second on left wall) up an intermittent widening crack and seam. Pass a double overhang (the crux) and continue to a belay/rappel station visible from below. Kyle Copeland: "The route was put up after the flooding of Wall Street." Lisa Hathaway: "The moves are delicate."

Paraphernalia: One set of Friends; (1) set of TCUs; wires; (2) quickdraws.

Descent: Rappel the route.

NOTE: Rappel anchors are shared with *Flash Flood*, thus the routes may be top-roped from each other.

48 FLASH FLOOD I, 5.11a, 1 pitch, 60 feet (18m), ★★★

First Ascent: Kyle Copeland, Dave Dawson, July 1989.

Location and Access: *Flash Flood* climbs a steep face 7 feet (2m) left of *Wake of the Flood*. Begin behind small willow trees and ascend a seam/crack system. There is one bolt and one piton fixed on the route and visible from below. Kyle Copeland: "The first ascent party found the true meaning of a flash flood when caught in the midst of a sudden heavy rainstorm."

Paraphernalia: Friends (1) #1, #2, #2.5, #3; TCU (1) #2, #3; #5 Stopper; (2) quickdraws.

Descent: Rappel anchors are shared with *Wake of the Flood*.

49 HIGH OVER DATURA (aka High on Datura) I, 5.11+, 1 pitch, 60 feet (18m), ★★★★

First Ascent: Charlie Fowler, Kyle Copeland, 1989.

Location and Access: *High Over Datura* is a face climb 5 feet (1.5m) left of *Flash Flood* and right of *Visible Panty Line*. Begin behind small willow trees and right of a small datura bush. There are three pitons and two bolts fixed on the steep pitted route. Climb light-colored rock to rappel anchors on dark rock. The crux is low on the route.

Paraphernalia: Five quickdraws.

Descent: Rappel the route.

50 VISIBLE PANTY LINE I, 5.10a, 1 pitch, 70 feet (21m), ★★★

First Ascent: Kyle Copeland, Layton Kor, December 1988.

Location and Access: *Visible Panty Line* ascends past a bolt up four thin cracks 8 feet (2m) left of *High Over Datura*. Begin up a shallow chimney/crack system. Climb light-colored rock with patches of desert varnish low on the route. There is a drilled angle piton high on the climb. Rappel slings are visible on a left-facing wall.

Paraphernalia: Small Friends; TCUs; wires; (2) quickdraws.

Descent: Rappel the route.

Wall Street

Photo: Bill Godschalx

55 Ring Pin Boulder
56 Jug Roof
57 Tune In, Turn On, Drop Out, summit pitch
58 Chimney Sweep
59 Jingus Launch
60 Mystery Route
61 Summit Chimney
62 Wild-Eyed Dear

REFLECTOR POST #5
63 Twitin' Shinkies

NOTE: Routes 51, 52, 53, and 54 are at the first designated parking area, across from the parking sign downriver from the beginning of Wall Street.

51 POUNDING THE FROG DIRECT I, 5.11, 1 pitch, 70 feet (21m)

First Ascent: Kyle Copeland, Marabel Loveridge, 1990.

Location and Access: Ascend the face 5 feet (1.5m) left of *Visible Panty Line*, climbing past three fixed pitons to *Visible Panty Line* anchors.

Paraphernalia: Two quickdraws.

Descent: Rappel from *Visible Panty Line* anchors.

Wall Street

Photo: Bill Godschalx

43 Zig Zag
REFLECTOR POST #4
44 Frogs of a Feather
45 Shoot Up or Shut Up
46 Shoot Up or Shut Up Corner
47 Wake of the Flood
48 Flash Flood
49 High Over Datura
50 Visible Panty Line
51 Pounding the Frog Direct
52 Pounding the Frog
53 Smell of Dead Euro-Peons
54 Bolts to Bumpy Land

52 POUNDING THE FROG I, 5.10b R, 1 pitch, 40 feet (12m), ★★

First Ascent: Kyle Copeland, Paul Seibert, July 1989.

Location and Access: *Pounding the Frog* is 11 feet (3.3m) left of *Pounding the Frog Direct* and shares anchors with *smell of Dead Europeans*. Climb a face past one bolt then one piton to a rappel chain visible from below just inside a gully. Lisa Hathaway: "There are spooky moves to the first clip."

Paraphernalia: Two quickdraws.

Descent: Rappel the route.

53 SMELL OF DEAD EURO-PEONS (Top-rope) I, 5.11, 1 pitch, 40 feet (12m)

First Ascent: Kyle Copeland, solo, 1989.

Location and Access: This top-rope problem is 12 feet (4m) left of *Pounding the Frog*. Begin up a right-facing flake above three boulders in the back right of the asphalt parking area. Climb a right-facing crack/flake system straight up to *Pounding the Frog* anchors.

Paraphernalia: Top-rope.

Descent: Rappel *Pounding the Frog*.

54 BOLTS TO BUMPY LAND (aka Sedan Delivery) I, 5.11a/b, 1 pitch, 110 feet (36m), ★★★★★

First Ascent: Jake "The Snake" Tradiak, July 1989.

Location and Access: *Bolts to Bumpy Land* is an excellent face climb at the back right side of the gully at the first parking area. It may be identified by three small boulders on the ground in front of the route. Begin 3 feet (1m) left of *Smell of Dead Euro-Peons*. Face climb past fourteen left-trending bolts. Kyle Copeland: "New bolts have sprouted a variation to the left." The cruxes are a hard mantel at the first bolt, thin face moves at the third and fourth bolts, and a side cling traverse to a bumpy face at the seventh bolt.

Paraphernalia: Two ropes; (14) quickdraws.

Descent: Double-rope rappel the route.

55 RING PIN BOULDER I, 5.9+, 1 pitch, 20 feet (6m)

First Ascent: Unknown.

Location and Access: *Ring Pin Boulder* is on the left (downriver) side of the designated parking area, 55 feet (17m) left of *Bolts to Bumpy Land*. Climb a right-angling crack to a ring piton (removed at the time of this writing) on the left side of a gully. The crux is off the ground at 5.9+.

Paraphernalia: None required.

Descent: Rappel the route or downclimb.

56 JUG ROOF I, 5.10a, 1 pitch, 90 feet (27m), ★★★★

First Ascent: Jim Beyer, solo, November 1989.

Location and Access: *Jug Roof* is 100 feet (30m) left of *Ring Pin Boulder* and climbs a face and a 4-inch (10cm) crack to a large right-facing corner, over a roof, then up and left to anchors shared with *Tune In*, *Chimney Sweep*, and *Jingus Launch*. Jim Beyer: "*Jug Roof* is a good route, and given its grade, 5.10a, should be popular, but is not because it has never been recorded correctly."

Paraphernalia: Friends to #4; wires.

Descent: Rappel the route from shared anchors not visible from below.

NOTE: The following three routes, Tune In, Chimney Sweep, and Jingus Launch share the same start and may be top-roped from their shared rappel anchors.

57 TUNE IN, TURN ON, DROP OUT, SUMMIT PITCH III, 5.11a, A0, 4 pitches, 370 feet (113m)

First Ascent: Jim Beyer, solo, November 1989.

Location and Access: Begin 23 feet (7m) left of *Jug Roof*.

Pitch 1: *Tune In* ★★★ Climb right past two hard-to-see black bolts. The crux of is near the top of the pitch, 5.10b/c, 90 feet (27m). Protect with Friends to #1.5; TCUs.

Pitch 2: *Turn On* ★★★★ Climb a 5.10, then 5.11a sustained crack system past seven bolts to a double anchor belay station, 130 feet (40m). Paraphernalia: Seven quickdraws.

Pitch 3: *Drop Out* Traverse left, then stem up a right-facing system (single point of aid). Continue past an easy-undercling overhang, then 5.10d to a belay, 5.10d, A0.

Pitch 4: *Summit Pitch* Climb 5.10 offwidth ending up a 5.6 chimney, 150 feet (46m) from the top of Turn On to the top of Summit Pitch. Forty feet (12m) higher the top of Summit Chimney is reached. Paraphernalia for Pitches 3 and 4: Two sets of Friends; (1) 5" piece; TCUs; wires; quickdraws.

Descent: Top anchor is a single bolt on an arête. Rappel 40 feet (12m) to the top of Summit Pitch, then 150 feet (46m) to the top of Drop Out (slings are visible from the top of Shoot Up). Rappel to the top of Tune In. Rappel from anchors shared with *Jug Roof*, *Tune In*, *Chimney Sweep*, and *Jingus Launch* (not visible from below).

58 CHIMNEY SWEEP I, 5.10a, 1 pitch, 80 feet (24m)

First Ascent: Jim Beyer, Leslie McCormic, Pat McInerney, October 1989.

Location and Access: Begin 19 feet (5.7m) left of *Jug Roof*. Ascend a loose-appearing chimney with the crux near the start of the route and with no fixed gear in place.

Paraphernalia: Friends to #3; wires.

Descent: Rappel the route from anchors shared with *Jug Roof*, *Tune In*, and *Jingus Launch*.

59 JINGUS LAUNCH I, 5.12 R/X, 1 pitch, 80 feet (24m), ★★

First Ascent: Jim Beyer, Pat McInerney, October 1989.

Location and Access: *Jingus Launch* is 19 feet (5.7m) left of *Jug Roof*. Climb up and left, following bolts and fixed anchors to the belay/rappel station. There is a runout above the second bolt, although it is possible to place a 1" TCU. There are six anchors fixed on the route, but the upper ones are hard to see from below the climb.

Paraphernalia: TCUs to 1"; wires; (6) quickdraws.

Descent: Rappel the route from anchors shared with *Jug Roof*, *Tune In*, and *Chimney Sweep*.

60 MYSTERY ROUTE I, 5.11d, 1 pitch, 80 feet (24m)

First Ascent: Unknown.

Location and Access: *Mystery Route* climbs the first right-facing dihedral 36 feet (11m) left of *Jingus Launch* and ends at a large block. There is no fixed gear on the route and rappel anchors are out of sight.

Paraphernalia: Unknown.

Descent: Rappel the route.

61 SUMMIT CHIMNEY III, 5.9, 4 pitches, 410 feet (125m)

First Ascent: Jim Beyer, solo, March 1991.

Location and Access: *Summit Chimney* is two crack systems, or 31 feet (9.4m) left of *Mystery Route* and climbs to the top of the rimrock.

Pitch 1: The crux, 5.9 offwidth.

Pitch 2: Climb a 5.9 handcrack.

Pitch 3: Continue up a 5.8 offwidth chimney.

Pitch 4: Finish up a 5.7 chimney.

Paraphernalia: Up to 5" protection; cams and nuts.

Descent: Third class down and right to a rib right of a chimney/gully. Rappel from a single bolt 40 feet (12m) to the top of Drop Out. Continue down the route with double 150 foot (46m) ropes.

62 WILD-EYED DEAR (aka Black Horse, Dark Horse) I, 5.12a, 1 pitch, 65 feet (20m), ★★★★★

First Ascent: Jim Beyer, solo, April 1991.

Location and Access: *Wild-Eyed Dear* is a face climb 7 feet (2m) right of #5 Reflector Post and 3 feet (1m) left of *Summit Chimney*. Climb past seven bolts with black painted hangers, up and left around a bulge. The crux is at the bottom and finishes at the seventh anchor. Lisa Hathaway: "A super classic Potash face route." Jim Beyer: "Red point 5.11d, flash on-sight 5.12a."

Paraphernalia: Seven quickdraws.

Descent: Rappel the route.

#5 REFLECTOR POST (WHITE)

63 TWITIN' SHINKIES I, 5.11b, 1 pitch, 50 feet (15m), ★★★★

First Ascent: Kyle Copeland, solo, July 1989. First free solo: Linus Platt, 1992.

Location and Access: *Twitin' Shinkies* is rated 5.11a for tall people, 5.11b for short. The route is 24 feet (7m) left of *Wild-Eyed Dear*, 17 feet (5m) left of #5 Reflector Post. Begin up the steep face left of a left-facing dihedral. Climb past three drilled pitons (2 on left wall, 1 on right wall) to a belay/rappel station. The crux is getting to the fingercrack at the bulge at the second piton.

Paraphernalia: Friends (2) #2; (1) #5 RP; (3) quickdraws.

Descent: Rappel the route.

64 BLOWIN' CHUNKS (aka Sharp Arête) I, 5.11b/c, 1 pitch, 60 feet (18m), ★★★★

First Ascent: Kyle Copeland, John McMullen, November 1989.

Location and Access: *Blowin' Chunks* is 31 feet (9.4m) left of *Twitin Shinkies*, at the right edge of an obvious curving overhang 60 feet (18m) above the roadway. Thin face climb up the arête of a left-facing dihedral to a rappel chain where the left-facing dihedral becomes right-facing. Four fixed anchors are in place: one piton (right wall), bolt, piton, bolt (left wall). Rappel anchors are visible from the river side of the highway only. The crux is between the second and third bolts.

Paraphernalia: Camalots (4) #0.75; many ⅛"–⅜" wires; small Aliens; (4) quickdraws.

Descent: Rappel the route.

65 CHUNDER BUNNY (Top-rope) I, 5.12–, 1 pitch, 60 feet (18m)

First Ascent: Kyle Copeland, 1989.

Location and Access: *Chunder Bunny* ascends the face left of *Blowin' Chunks*.

Paraphernalia: Top-rope from *Blowin' Chunks* anchors.

Descent: Rappel *Blowin' Chunks*.

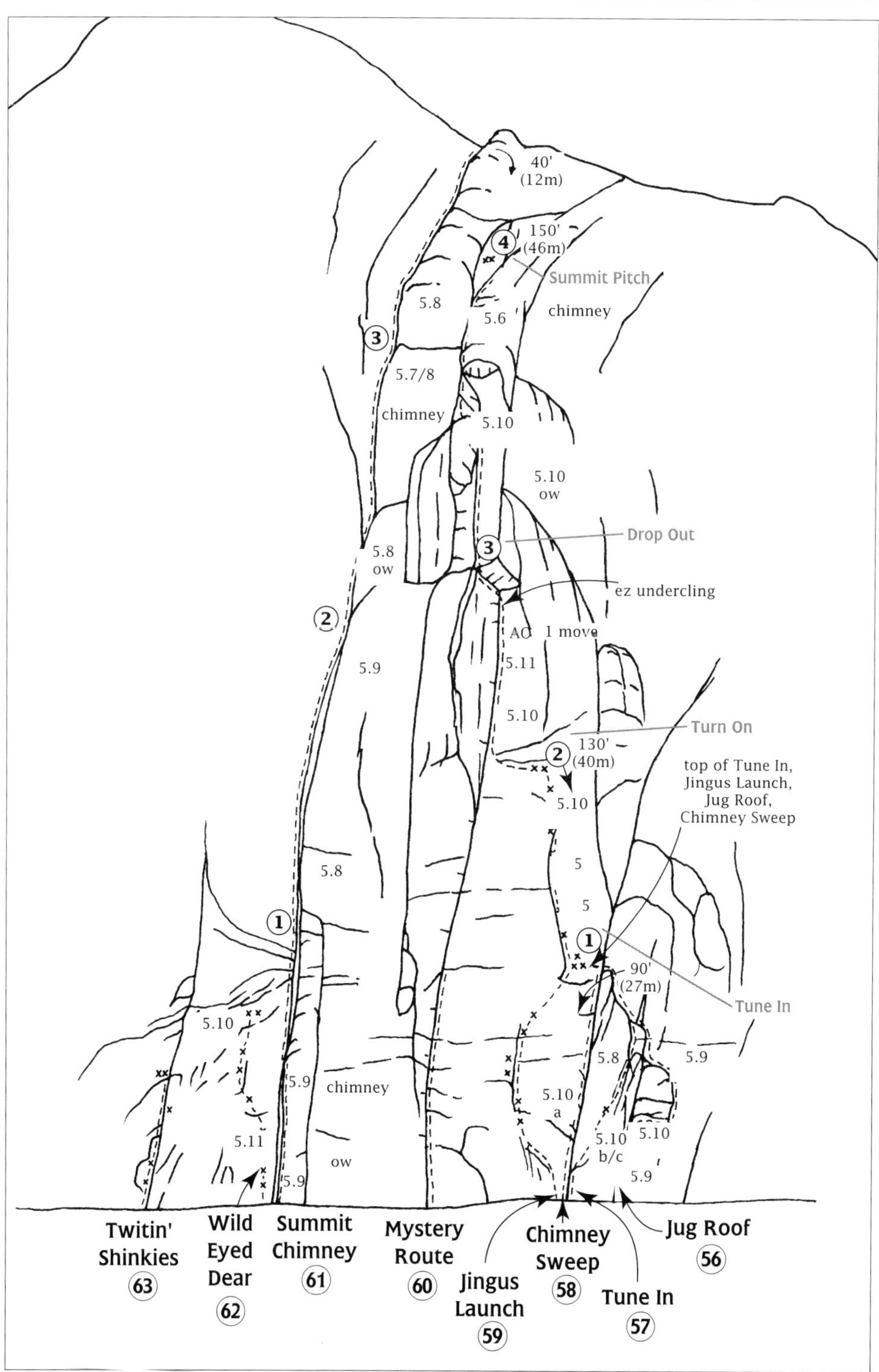
40'
(12m)
150'
(46m)
4
Summit Pitch
5.8
5.6
chimney
3
5.7/8
chimney
5.10
5.10
ow
Drop Out
3
5.8
ow
ez undercling
2
AO 1 move
5.9
5.11
5.10
Turn On
130'
(40m)
2
5.10
top of Tune In,
Jingus Launch,
Jug Roof,
Chimney Sweep
5.8
5
5
1
1
90'
(27m)
Tune In
5.10
5.8
5.9
5.9
chimney
5.10
a
5.11
5.10
b/c
5.10
ow
5.9
5.9
Twitin' Shinkies
63
Wild Eyed Dear
62
Summit Chimney
61
Mystery Route
60
Jingus Launch
59
Chimney Sweep
58
Tune In
57
Jug Roof
56

Wall Street

Photo: Bill Godschalx

75 Under the Boardwalk
76 Something Nasty
77 I Love Loosey
78 Baby Blue
79 Desp-Aréte
80 Beyer Offwidth

REFLECTOR POST #6
81 Slab
82 Hot Ash

NOTE: Sand and Steel, Bolted Route, Right Side In, and 30 Seconds Over Potash share a rappel bench and thus may be top-roped from one another.

66 SAND AND STEEL I, 5.11b, 1 pitch, 60 feet (18m)

First Ascent: Tony Calderone, Michael Taylor, 21 March 1994.

Location and Access: *Sand and Steel* is between *Blowin' Chunks* and *Bolted Route*, 27 feet (8m) left of *Chunder Bunny* and climbs a face for 20 feet (6m), then continues up a right-facing corner to rappel anchors visible from below. Traverse left to a ledge. The crux is an overhang at the top of the route.

Paraphernalia: Small cams; (1) quickdraw.

Descent: Rappel the route.

Wall Street

Photo: Bill Godschalx

64 Blowin' Chunks
65 Chunder Bunny
66 Sand and Steel
67 Bolted Route
68 Right Side In
69 30 Seconds Over Potash
70 Lucy in the Sky with Potash
71 Pedigree Poodles
72 Manicured Lawns
73 Dunn-Copeland Route
74 Nervous in Suburbia

67 BOLTED ROUTE I, 5.11a, 1 pitch, 60 feet (18m), ★★

First Ascent: Unknown

Location and Access: *Bolted Route* is one crack left (32 feet, 10m) of *Sand and Steel* from which it may be top-roped. The crux is under a small roof. There are five fixed pitons on the right wall.

Paraphernalia: Five quickdraws.

Descent: Rappel *Sand and Steel.*

68 RIGHT SIDE IN I, 5.9, 1 pitch, 60 feet (18m)

First Ascent: Jim Beyer, solo, October 1989.

Location and Access: *Right Side In* is one crack (19 feet, 5.7m) left of *Bolted Route*. Begin 5.9 up a 5-inch (13cm) crack, then 5.9 offwidth ending with 5.9 hands at double-anchors. There are no fixed anchors on the route.

Paraphernalia: Friends and TCUs to #4, with #5 optional.

Descent: Rappel the route or traverse left to *30 Seconds Over Potash*, or right to *Bolted Route* rappel anchors.

69 30 SECONDS OVER POTASH I, 5.8, 1 pitch, 50 feet (15m), ★★★★★

First Ascent: Kyle Copeland, solo, November 1988.

Location and Access: This popular route is 24 feet (7.3m), or one crack system left of *Right Side In*. Climb a large left-facing dihedral. There is no fixed gear on the climb. The cruxes are off the ground and 30 feet (9m) up the route. Kyle Copeland: "Note the bomb above the route, can it last 5 minutes or 5 million years?"

Paraphernalia: Friends to #3.5; TCUs; wires.

Descent: Rappel the route from a rappel chain.

70 LUCY IN THE SKY WITH POTASH I, 5.10a, 1 pitch, 60 feet (18m), ★★★★

First Ascent: Linus Platt, Charlie Fowler, 1989.

Location and Access: *Lucy in the Sky with Potash* climbs a left-facing dihedral which is the next line (18 feet, 5.4m) left of *30 Seconds over Potash*. Beware of a loose flake at top of the climb. There is no fixed gear in place. The crux is where the crack thins to a seam.

Paraphernalia: Small selection of Friends to #3; TCUs to #2; small wires.

Descent: Rappel the route from anchors on the left wall.

71 PEDIGREE POODLES I, 5.9+, 1 pitch, 20 feet (6m)

First Ascent: Cameron Burns, Rab Cummings, Steve Porcella, March 1990.

Location and Access: *Pedigree Poodles* is right of *Manicured Lawns* and climbs the right side of a leaning flake with an anchor at its top. Begin at *Lucy in the Sky with Potash*.

Paraphernalia: None required.

Descent: Rappel from a fixed anchor (not visible from below) or lower off.

72 MANICURED LAWNS I, 5.9+, 1 pitch, 20 feet (6m)

First Ascent: Cameron Burns, Rab Cummings, Steve Porcella, March 1990.

Location and Access: *Manicured Lawns* climbs the face of the leaning flake between *Pedigree Poodles* and the *Dunn–Copeland Route*.

Paraphernalia: None required.

Descent: Rappel from a fixed anchor (not visible from below) or lower off.

73 DUNN–COPELAND ROUTE I, 5.5, 1 pitch, 20 feet (6m)

First Ascent: Jimmy Dunn, Kyle Copeland, 1989.

Location and Access: Ascend the left edge of the leaning flake (left of *Manicured Lawns*).

Paraphernalia: None required.

Descent: Rappel from a fixed anchor (not visible from below) or lower off.

74 NERVOUS IN SUBURBIA I, 5.10a, 1 pitch, 55 feet (17m), ★★★★★

First Ascent: Kyle Copeland, Joy Kor, November 1988.

Location and Access: *Nervous in Suburbia* is 30 feet (9m) left of *Lucy in the Sky with Potash*. Face climb up heavily chalked rock past one piton, three bolts, then one piton to a belay/rappel station. The first crux is getting to the first bolt. A second crux is moving beyond the first bolt.

Paraphernalia: Five quickdraws.

Descent: Rappel the route.

75 UNDER THE BOARDWALK I, 5.12b/c, 1 pitch, 60 feet (18m), ★★★

First Ascent: Charlie Fowler, Kyle Copeland, 1989.

Location and Access: *Under the Boardwalk* is 40 feet (12m) left of *Nervous in Suburbia*. Begin up a right-facing dihedral left of a tamarisk bush 17 feet (5m) from the right side of a deep gully. Face climb past four bolts (angling left), then ascend an arête past one piton and three bolts to a belay/rappel station visible from below.

Paraphernalia: Eight quickdraws.

Descent: Rappel the route.

76 SOMETHING NASTY I, 5.12b, 1 pitch, 60 feet (18m), ★★★★★

First Ascent: Kyle Copeland, solo, December 1988.

Location and Access: *Something Nasty* is on the left side of a large gully with a large oak tree, on the steep wall behind and left of a culvert which carries water under the Potash Road to the river. Climb a thin fingercrack (with hard start) which becomes right-trending. There is no fixed gear in place. The crux is at the bottom of the route. Kyle Copeland: "Don't forget your edging shoe on the left and a smear shoe on the right."

Paraphernalia: Three #1 Friends (for the top of the climb), (3) #3, #4; TCUs; small wires.

Descent: Rappel the route from anchors visible from below.

77 I LOVE LOOSEY (aka I Love Lucy) I, 5.11c, 1 pitch, 45 feet (13.7m), ★★★★★

First Ascent: Charlie Fowler, Kyle Copeland, December 1988.

Location and Access: *I Love Loosey* is 18 feet (5m) left of *Something Nasty*. Begin on the left corner of a prominent gully. Climb a rounded arête with four bolts in place (third bolt at time of writing is missing). The first bolt is difficult to clip unless a stick-clip is used.

Paraphernalia: Stick-clip; (4) quickdraws.

Descent: A rappel chain is visible right of an overhang.

78 BABY BLUE I, 5.11a, 1 pitch, 40 feet (12m), ★★★★★

First Ascent: Charlie Fowler, Kyle Copeland, January 1989.

Location and Access: *Baby Blue* is a short but excellent route 18 feet (5m) left of *I Love Loosey*. Climb a fingercrack in a left-facing dihedral to triple rappel anchors. No fixed gear is in place. The crux is the last 9 feet (4m). Kevin Chase: "The route is the best looking thin crack on Wall Street." Lisa Hathaway: "Classic moves with great pro and killer rests."

Paraphernalia: Friends to #2.5; TCUs (2) #0.4, #0.5; wires.

Descent: Rappel the route.

Wall Street

Photo: Bill Godschalx

92 School Room #2
93 Grama and the Green Suede Shoes
91 Lacto Mangulation
REFLECTOR POST #7

79 DESP-ARETE I, 5.12b, 1 pitch, 50 feet (15m), ★★★★★

First Ascent: Kyle Copeland, Linus Platt, Spring 1991.

Location and Access: *Desp-arête* is 52 feet (16m) or two crack systems left of *Baby Blue*, 17 feet (5m) right of #6 Reflector Post. Begin on the right wall of a gully and climb an arête protected by five drilled baby angles. Dave Medara: "Style or denial (hard)."

Paraphernalia: Five quickdraws; staying power.

Descent: Rappel the route.

CAUTION: Beware of poison ivy at the base of the wall.

80 BEYER OFFWIDTH I, 5.9+, 1 pitch, 80 feet (24m)

First Ascent: Jim Beyer, solo, 1989.

Location and Access: *Beyer Offwidth* begins 3 feet (0.9m) left of *Desp-arête*. Climb a wide crack system around the left corner from *Desp-arête* to double-anchors on a south-facing wall. Begin up a loose chimney ending at a wide flaring crack.

Wall Street Photo: Bill Godschalx

83 Eat the Rich
84 Knight Moves
85 Three Sheeps to the Wind
86 Tired of Talus
87 Static Cling
88 Potash Bong Hit
89 Skeletonic
90 Top Forty

Paraphernalia: Wide crack protection up to 5".

Descent: Rappel the route.

CAUTION: Beware of poison ivy at the base of the wall.

#6 REFLECTOR POST (WHITE-BLACK)

81 SLAB I, 5.8, 1 pitch, 60 feet (18m), ★★

First Ascent: Jake "The Snake" Tradiak, Ray Huntsinger, 1989.

Location and Access: *Slab* climbs a light-colored fin with a wide crack system on the left side of a gully 28 feet (9m) left of #6 Reflector Post. Begin behind willows and a large tamarisk tree. Stay to the middle of the slab and climb past five fixed anchors (one bolt, piton, three bolts) to rappel anchors visible from below. Lisa Hathaway: "Thin daunting-looking moves that are totally do-able."

Paraphernalia: Five quickdraws.

Descent: Rappel the route.

82 HOT ASH (aka Death Flake) I, 5.10+ R/X, 1 pitch, 80 feet (24m)

First Ascent: Jimmy Dunn, Betsy McKittrich, Summer 1991.

Location and Access: *Hot Ash* ascends the face 18 feet (5m) left of *Slab*. Climb up a corner with a large thin leaning flake. Climb past two drilled pitons to an anchor on the right wall, or begin a few feet right and climb up and left past the drilled pitons.

Paraphernalia: Friends; (2) quickdraws.

Descent: Rappel the route.

83 EAT THE RICH I, 5.10c, 1 pitch, 40 feet (12m), ★★★★

First Ascent: Kyle Copeland, Ron Olevsky, May 1989.

Location and Access: *Eat the Rich* is 36 feet (11m) left of *Hot Ash*. Ascend a shallow right-facing dihedral with a fingercrack. Begin direct or 3 feet (1m) right up an easier ramp (for 8 feet, 2.4m), then cross left. Continue using both the left and right crack systems to a rappel chain visible from below. The crux is at the top of the pitch.

Paraphernalia: Friends #2, #2.5; TCUs; stoppers.

Descent: Rappel the route.

84 KNIGHT MOVES I, 5.11, 1 pitch, 40 feet (12m)

First Ascent: Kyle Copeland, Ron Olevsky, May 1989.

Location and Access: *Knight Moves* is 20 feet (6m) or one crack left of *Eat the Rich* and climbs a left-facing dihedral. Pass an overhang on its right and continue to rappel anchors (right wall) visible from below. There is one drilled piton on the right wall at the overhang.

Paraphernalia: One set of Friends; TCUs; (1) quickdraw.

Descent: Rappel the route from a difficult-to-see fixed hex inside a crack.

85 THREE SHEEPS TO THE WIND I, 5.11, 2 pitches, pitch 1 85 feet (30m)

First Ascent: Kyle Copeland, Dave Dawson, May 1989.

Location and Access: *Three Sheeps to the Wind* is 29 feet (9m) or one crack left of *Knight Moves*. Begin up a right-facing dihedral. Pitch 1 climbs 85 feet (26m). Information is unknown about Pitch 2.

NOTE: Because the climb starts above petroglyphs please respect BLM rules and your own ecologic consciousness–do not climb this route.

86 TIRED OF TALUS II, 5.12, 3 pitches, pitch 1 85 feet (30m), ★★★★

First Ascent: Pitch 1 Bret Ruckman, Gary Olsen, 5.11b, May 1988. Pitch 2, 3 Jim Beyer, Pat McInerney, 5.12, 1991.

Location and Access: *Tired of Talus* is 12 feet (3.6m) left of and shares rappel anchors with *Three Sheeps to the Wind*. Begin at the right edge of the second designated parking area.

Pitch 1: Climb a left-facing corner by liebacking past a wide bottom section, then continue up thin cracks to rappel anchors, 5.11b, 85 feet (30m)

Pitch 2: Begin left up light-colored rock, then continue up and with moderate 5th class to a rappel station where dark rock meets lighter colored rock on the right wall of a right-facing dihedral. Anchors are visible from the river side of the highway only.

Pitch 3: Climb a 5.12 lieback up a right-facing corner to double-anchors visible on the right wall.

Photo: Gary Olsen

Bret Ruckman on first ascent of *Tired of Talus*

Paraphernalia: Friends (4) #0.75, #2.5, (1) #4; Camalot #4; many medium wires; Blue Lowe Balls recommended for dicey protection at the roof (crux).

Descent: Rappel the route.

87 STATIC CLING I, 5.11a/b, 1 pitch, 70 feet (21m), ★★★★★

First Ascent: Jim Beyer, Pat McInerney, February 1990. First free solo: Linus Platt, 1991.

Location and Access: *Static Cling* is 27 feet (8m) left of *Tired of Talus*. The route ascends a left-facing dihedral with a thin crack system. The first crux is pulling up to under the roof. The second crux is the roof. No fixed anchors are on the route. Rappel slings are visible on the right wall.

Paraphernalia: Friends to #3; a selection of (9) nuts.

Descent: Rappel the route from anchors shared with *Potash Bong Hit*.

88 POTASH BONG HIT (Top-rope) I, 5.10, 1 pitch, 70 feet (21m)

First Ascent: Jim Beyer, solo, February 1990.

Location and Access: *Potash Bong Hit* climbs a face and crack system 8 feet (2m) left of *Static Cling*.

NOTE: There is a loose flake level with the ceiling on *Static Cling*.

Paraphernalia: Top-rope.

Descent: Rappel *Static Cling*.

89 SKELETONIC I, 5.11+, 1 pitch, 70 feet (21m), ★★★★

First Ascent: Eric Decaria, Peter Verchick, Dave Medara.

Location and Access: *Skeletonic* climbs the first dihedral (right-facing) left of *Static Cling*. Begin right of a Russian olive tree. Ascend a thin crack system up a right-facing dihedral (with bullet hole graffiti on the right wall) past three bolts on the right wall. Continue to the top of a pillar and rappel anchors visible from below.

Paraphernalia: Friends to #2; TCUs; medium wires; (3) quickdraws.

Descent: Rappel the route.

90 TOP FORTY I, 5.8, 2 pitches, 70 feet (21m)

First Ascent: Jeff Slider, Jorma Hayes, 1 October 1995

Location and Access: *Top Forty* is 32 feet (9.7m) or the first crack left of *Skeletonic*. Climb a left-facing dihedral up light-colored rock past two pitons to anchors on the left wall. Pitch 2 angles up and right to anchors shared with *Skeletonic*.

Paraphernalia: Camalot (1) #1; TCUs (1) #0.5, #0.75; (2) quickdraws.

Descent: Rappel the route.

91 LACTO MANGULATION I, 5.10b, 1 pitch, 50 feet (15m)

First Ascent: Jorma Hayes, 1 April 1995.

Location and Access: *Lacto Mangulation* is 26 feet (8m) from the first crack left of *Top Forty*. Climb past one piton, two bolts, then one piton up a right-facing dihedral to rappel slings visible from below.

Paraphernalia: Friends (2) #4 Friend; (3) quickdraws.

Descent: Rappel the route.

92 SCHOOL ROOM #2 (Top-rope Area)

There are numerous top-rope problems in the School Room #2 area left of *Lacto Mangulation*. To reach, fourth class approach from the dirt gully opposite #7 Reflector Post, 100 feet (30m) left of *Grama and the Green Suede Shoes*.

93 GRAMA AND THE GREEN SUEDE SHOES I, 5.7, 40 feet (12m)

First Ascent: Unknown climbers, 1995.

Location and Access: *Grama and the Green Suede Shoes* climbs a deep crack system 57 feet (17m) left of *Lacto Mangulation*, directly across from a sign on the river side of the road reading "Parking."

Paraphernalia: Large cams.

Descent: Downclimb to the left of the route.

SIGN: "PARKING" WITH ARROW, #7 REFLECTOR POST (WHITE)

94 SHE-LA THE PEELER I, 5.9, 1 pitch, 60 feet (18m)

First Ascent: Warren Egbert, Mattias Holiday, Cindy Furman, May 1992.

Location and Access: *She-La the Peeler* climbs the right side of a slab at the left end of Schoolroom #2, 15 feet (4.5m) left of a young cottonwood tree. Begin 150 feet (46m) left of #7 Reflector Post up a "step" just above ground, then traverse right and up to double-rappel anchors, 5.8. There are two fixed bolts on the route. The crux is through the calcite (white) rock band, 5.9.

Paraphernalia: Two quickdraws.

Descent: Walk-off right or rappel the route.

95 SHE-LA THE PEELER DIRECT (Top-rope) 5.10a, 1 pitch, 60 feet (18m)

First Ascent: Warren Egbert, Mattias Holiday, Cindy Furman, May 1992.

Location and Access: Climb vertically to rappel anchors from the right side of the original route.

Paraphernalia: Top-rope.

Descent: Rappel the route.

96 SLAB ROUTE I, 5.7 R, 1 pitch, 90 feet (27m)

First Ascent: Unknown.

Location and Access: *Slab Route* climbs a low-angle runout 30 feet (9m) left of *She-la the Peeler*. Two bolts are in place. Begin 5 feet (1.5m) right of a large hackberry tree. The crux is at the first bolt.

Paraphernalia: Two quickdraws.

Descent: Rappel the route 90 feet (27m) or downclimb loose rock 4th class to the right (upriver) side of the climb.

97 PUPPY LOVE I, 5.9 R, 1 pitch, 60 feet (18m), ★★

First Ascent: Mike Baker, Leslie Henderson, 1994.

Location and Access: *Puppy Love* is 121 feet (37m) left of *Slab Route*, 12 feet (3.6m) right of *Steel Your Face*. Begin left of and behind a hackberry tree. Climb past three drilled pitons (right of a seam) and one drilled piton below rappel anchors on the wall left of the seam.

Paraphernalia: Friends (1) #2.5; TCUs to protect the runouts; (4) quickdraws.

Descent: Rappel the route.

Wall Street

Photo: Bill Godschalx

97 Puppy Love
98 Steel Your Face
99 Flakes of Bongo
100 Chriscross
101 Just Another Pretty Face
102 Just Another Pretty Face Variation
103 Unfinished
104 Don Smurfo
105 Big Sky Mud Flaps
106 Impasse
107 Walk on the Wide Side
108 Armageddon
109 Jacob's Ladder
110 Shadowfax

REFLECTOR POST #8

98 STEEL YOUR FACE I, 5.10a, 1 pitch, 80 feet (24m), ★★★★★

First Ascent: Kyle Copeland, Charlie Fowler, November 1988.

Location and Access: *Steel Your Face* is a face climb 12 feet (3.6m) left of *Puppy Love*. Begin 15 feet (5m) right of a prominent left-facing dihedral. Pass one piton, two bolts, one piton and finally two bolts before angling left to a bolt and up to a chain rappel anchor. The crux is thin moves past the fourth bolt.

Paraphernalia: Seven quickdraws.

Descent: Rappel the route from anchors shared with *Flakes of Bongo*.

NOTE: The route is one of Jimmy Dunn's "right hand/left hand only" climbs.

Wall Street Photo: Bill Godschalx

94 She-La the Peeler 95 She-La the Peeler Direct 96 Slab Route

99 FLAKES OF BONGO (Top-rope) I, 5.10, 80 feet (24m)

First Ascent: Kyle Copeland, Dave Dawson, May 1989.

Location and Access: Climb an arête 15 feet (5m) left of *Steel Your Face* and just in from the outside of the left-facing dihedral climbed by *Chriscross*. The route traverses right to join *Steel Your Face*.

Paraphernalia: Top-rope.

Descent: Rappel the route from shared anchors with *Steel Your Face*.

100 CHRISCROSS I, 5.11a R, 1 pitch, 70 feet (21m)

First Ascent: Chris Pendleton, Gary Olsen, March 1984.

Location and Access: *Chriscross* begins up a left-facing dihedral, then continues onto the face. The crux is at the third of six fixed anchors leading to the rappel station. Kyle Copeland: "Subsequent ascents have cleaned off key holds at the crux, and a bolt of dubious quality has been added."

Paraphernalia: Friends (1) #2, #3.5; small wire; (6) quickdraws.

Descent: Rappel the route .

Note: One may top-rope *Chriscross* (5.11a) after climbing *Flakes of Bongo*, or visa versa.

101 JUST ANOTHER PRETTY FACE I, 5.10a R, 1 pitch, 70 feet (21m), ★★★★★

First Ascent: Kyle Copeland, solo, November 1988.

Location and Access: Begin 5 feet (1.5m) left of *Chriscross* behind cocklebur bushes (dogs beware). Face climb past three bolts with a 5.8 runout to the first bolt, then one piton and two bolts. The route climbs to a rappel chain visible from below. The crux is between the third and fourth bolt. Please do not add additional bolts to this route.

Paraphernalia: Six quickdraws.

Descent: Rappel the route from shared anchors with *Don Smurfo*.

NOTE: *Just Another Pretty Face* may be top-roped after climbing *Don Smurfo*, or visa versa. The route is one of Jimmy Dunn's right hand only/left hand only climbs.

102 JUST ANOTHER PRETTY FACE VARIATION Rating unknown

First Ascent: Unknown.

Location and Access: The variation climbs the first 15 feet (4.5m) of *Chriscross*, avoiding the runout to the first bolt. Traverse left to the first bolt of *Just Another Pretty Face*, then back-clean the crack (a must).

103 UNFINISHED (Top-rope) I, 5.12, 1 pitch, 50 feet (15m)

First Ascent: Kyle Copeland, Charlie Fowler, Marc Hirt, November 1988.

Location and Access: *Unfinished* is 11 feet (3m) left of *Just Another Pretty Face*. Face climb between *Just Another Pretty Face* and *Don Smurfo*.

Paraphernalia: Top-rope.

Descent: Rappel the route.

104 DON SMURFO I, 5.10 R, 1 pitch, 70 feet (21m)

First Ascent: Kyle Copeland and party from Nebraska, May 1989.

Location and Access: *Don Smurfo* is 13 feet (4m) left of *Unfinished* and climbs a discontinuous right-facing dihedral. There is a runout above the first piton, then traverse right and join *Just Another Pretty Face* at a drilled piton.

Paraphernalia: Three quickdraw.

Descent: Rappel anchors are shared with *Just Another Pretty Face*.

105 BIG SKY MUD FLAPS I, 5.10d, 1 pitch, 110 feet (34m), ★★★★★

First Ascent: Kyle Copeland, Charlie Fowler, Marc Hirt, November 1988.

Location and Access: *Big Sky Mud Flaps* is 15 feet (5m) left of *Don Smurfo*. Ascend a thin seam passing a bulge and nine fixed anchors (starting with one bolt, one piton, three bolts to a small overhang, then pass one bolt above and right of the overhang). Climb up and left past two more bolts and one piton. Continue up and right to a headwall above a bedding seam, then to the varnished rock above. Rappel anchors are on dark rock above a light-colored face. There are cruxes at the second and third bolts (past a small roof).

Paraphernalia: Nine quickdraws.

Descent: Rappel the route with double-ropes.

NOTE: The route is one of Jimmy Dunn's "right hand only" climb.

106 IMPASSE I, 5.12+, 1 pitch, 90 feet (27m)

First Ascent: Kyle Copeland, Dave Dawson, top-rope, February 1989. First Lead: Jim Beyer, Pat McInerney, to fourth bolt, October 1989.

Location and Access: *Impasse* climbs the first crack left of *Big Sky Mud Flaps.* Ascend a discontinuous crack system past two pitons (left wall), then face climb sharply right past two pitons (right wall) to the eighth anchor (bolt) of *Big Sky Mud Flaps.*

Paraphernalia: One set of Friends; (6) quickdraws.

Descent: Rappel the route.

107 WALK ON THE WIDE SIDE I, 5.10a, 1 pitch, 90 feet (27m), ★★★

First Ascent: Peter Gallagher, Kyle Copeland, Charlie Fowler, December 1987.

Location and Access: *Walk on the Wide Side* climbs the first (wide) crack left of *Impasse* to rappel slings visible below a prominent bedding seam where the lower light-colored wall meets the upper dark rock. The crux is wide pro.

Paraphernalia: Protection for 2–6" crack; (1) quickdraw.

Descent: Rappel the route.

108 ARMAGEDDON I, 5.12a/b, 1 pitch, 50 feet (15m), ★★★★

First Ascent: Linus Platt, Charlie Fowler, 1992

Location and Access: *Armageddon* is 22 feet (7m) left of *Big Sky Mud Flaps*. Face climb past three bolts and two pitons to the rappel station visible from below. Lisa Hathaway: "Lots of technique, great but desperate!"

Paraphernalia: Five quickdraws.

Descent: Rappel the route.

109 JACOB'S LADDER I, 5.10+, 1 pitch, 40 feet (12m), ★★★

First Ascent: Jake "The Snake" Tradiak, July 1989.

Location and Access: *Jacob's Ladder* is 25 feet (8m) left of *Walk on the Wild Side*, directly across from a Reflector Post (red) on the river side of the highway. Face climb right of a crack system where two large rabbit brushes are growing. Continue up and right past four bolts to rappel anchors visible from below. The cruxes are past the first and fourth bolts.

Paraphernalia: Protection for 2–6" crack; (4) quickdraws.

Descent: Rappel the route.

110 SHADOWFAX I, 5.11–, 1 pitch, 50 feet (15m), ★★★

First Ascent: Kyle Copeland, Bego Gerhart, July 1989.

Location and Access: *Shadowfax* is 15 feet (5m) left of *Jacob's Ladder*. Begin right of a deep chimney/drainage, left of two large rabbit brushes growing 15 feet (4.5m) up the wall. Climb a face past five pitons with the cruxes at the first and fourth bolts. The first 5.11 section can be avoided by starting to the left with 5.6.

Paraphernalia: Five quickdraws.

Descent: Rappel the route.

#8 REFLECTOR POST (BLACK)

NOTE: The remaining Wall Street climbs (#111-114) are not shown on photos.

111 WHITE WAY I, 5.11 R, 1 pitch, 100 feet (30m), ★

First Ascent: Peter Gallagher, Kyle Copeland, Layton Kor, with Sue Kemp working on the lower wall, November 1988.

Location and Access: *White Way* is 49 feet (15m) left of #8 Reflector Post, in front of a healthy cottonwood tree. Face climb a hogback past one piton, then four anchors with a 60-foot (18m) runout at the top of the route (with one bolt in the middle). Begin up the first white rock (calcium deposit) downriver from *Shadowfax* and right of the petroglyph panel (directly below the route's obvious rappel anchors).

Paraphernalia: Six quickdraws.

Descent: Rappel the route.

112 WHITE WAY VARIATION I, 5.6, 1 pitch, 90 feet (27m)

First Ascent: Unknown.

Location and Access: The variation avoids the 5.11 climbing by beginning to the left of the original start.

Paraphernalia: Quickdraws.

Descent: Rappel the route.

113 UNKNOWN Rating unknown, I, 1 pitch, 60 feet (18m)

First Ascent: Unknown.

Location and Access: *Unknown* is one crack right of *Honer's Odyssey*, two cracks left of *White Way*. Begin up a splitter crack, then climb broken rock to a shelf, 60 feet (18m).

114 HONER'S ODYSSEY II, 5.11b/c, 2 pitches, 150 feet (46m), ★★★★★

First Ascent: Kyle Copeland, Dave Dawson, June 1989

Location and Access: *Honer's Odyssey* is one crack left of *Unknown*, above a petroglyph panel. To avoid the petroglyphs and climb the route legally, approach from a gully to the right, then step across a chimney to clip a piton for a tension traverse to the belay for Pitch 2.

Descent: Rappel the route.

Williams Bottom

Williams Bottom (identified on the Moab West map) is roughly the region downriver from the "Indian Writings" signs (south of Wall Street) to the dinosaur tracks at the Poison Spider Mesa trailhead.

POLKA DOTS AND MOONBEAMS I, 5.10, 1 pitch, 70 feet (21m)

First Ascent: Bill Robins, Erin Riffel, 17 February 1991.

Location and Access: *Polka Dots and Moonbeams* is climbs a right-facing crack up dark rock to the top of a pillar leaning against the rimrock. Rappel slings are visible on the wall behind and above the pillar.

Paraphernalia: Hand-size protection.

Descent: Rappel the route.

PROJECT I, 5.10, 1 pitch, 35 feet (11m)

First Ascent: Kyle Copeland, solo, 1989.

Location and Access: *Polka Dots and Moonbeams* is 90 feet (27m) upriver from a yellow diamond-shaped sign with a curved arrow (on the river side of the road) indicating an upcoming curve for north-bound (upriver) traffic. This is also a point downriver (past a black Reflector Post) from the second Indian Writing sign. At the base of the route "RHS 1953" is inscribed in the rock, a curious date since the Potash Road was not built until 1960.

Project downriver from the first Reflector Post south of the second Indian Writing sign. The route climbs the second hogback right of a prominent gully. Begin behind hackberry trees, and right of a large juniper tree. Climb the left side of a curving slab to a fixed piton. Move up and left to a second anchor.

Paraphernalia: Two quickdraws.

Descent: Rappel the route.

GUMBEES EDGE I, 5.11 A0, 2 pitches

First Ascent: Jim Beyer, solo, February 1990

Location and Access: *Gumbees Edge* is right of an unimproved campground and 20 feet (6m) right of a petroglyph panel low on the wall. The location is mid-way between signs on the river side of the Potash Road reading: "Park in Designated Areas Only, next 1 mile" and "North 279 Scenic Byway."

Pitch 1: Begin up a left-facing dihedral one crack left of the right prow of the wall. Pass two chopped bolts, then one bolt (right wall) to rappel anchors on the left wall visible from below.

Pitch 2: Continue up a corner system to the top and rappel anchors not visible from below.

Paraphernalia: Protection up to 3"; (1) quickdraw.

Descent: Rappel the route.

PROJECT I, 5.12, A1+, 1 pitch, 28 feet (9m)

First Ascent: Jorma Hayes, Joeff Sluyter, Chad Davis, November 1995.

Location and Access: Approach to the right of the first turn into the unimproved campground upriver from the Dinosaur Tracks. *Project* climbs an overhanging alcove behind a tall hackberry tree. The high point is a ring angle piton visible from the ground.

Paraphernalia: Quickdraw.

Descent: Lower off the piton.

DODGING BULLETS I, 5.10, 1 pitch

First Ascent: Mike Baker, Roger Rumsey, 14 October 1991.

Location and Access: *Dodging Bullets* is 8 feet (2m) or one crack right of *Black Friday*. Climb a corner crack system past loose rock. Rappel anchors are visible from below at a prominent bedding seam below a smooth wall marred with bullet holes.

Paraphernalia: Medium to small cams.

Descent: Rappel the route from two drilled angle pitons.

BLACK FRIDAY I, 5,9+, 1 pitch, ★★

First Ascent: Mike Baker, Leslie Henderson, 14 October 1991.

Location and Access: *Black Friday* is in a large deep chimney 8 feet left (2m) of *Dodging Bullets*. Ascend a chimney, then a left-facing dihedral to rappel anchors visible below a small round cave.

Paraphernalia: Wide protection.

Descent: Rappel the route.

LOOK MA NO HANDS I, 5.10, 1 pitch, ★★★

First Ascent: Mike Baker, Leslie Henderson, 26 April 1991.

Location and Access: *Look Ma No Hands* is 8 feet (2m) or one crack left of *Black Friday*. Climb face nubbins and edges past three drilled angles to a ledge, then traverse right to rappel anchors visible from below. The crux is a mantle-shelf.

Paraphernalia: Tech-Friend (1) #10; nut (1) #10; (3) quickdraws.

Descent: Rappel the route.

CAMPGROUND CRACK I, 5.9, 1 pitch

First Ascent: Indians and cowboys from the fourth-class back side.

Location and Access: *Campground Crack* ascends the crack system of a left-facing dihedral on the south side of a large boulder in the unimproved campground upriver from the Dinosaur Tracks. The route may be top-roped by scrambling atop the boulder from the back side. The boulder has also been climbed right (5.9) and left (5.10) of *Campground Crack*.

Paraphernalia: A selection of Friends.

Descent: Downclimb the back side.

NOTE: There are petroglyphs low on the wall right of the dihedral.

ENIGMA CAMPGROUND ROUTE I, 5.10c, 2 pitches, 150 feet (46m)

First Ascent: Enigmatic ascent team.

Location and Access: The route is 50 yards (46m) left of *Campground Crack*, or 150 feet (46m) left of the dirt turn to the Campground Boulder. A short trail climbs the scree to the beginning of the route.

Pitch 1: Begin behind a willow tree on up-sloping rock. Climb past a bolt to a ledge, then past a second bolt to a rappel chain on a steep wall.

Pitch 2: Continue up a crack system in a right-facing dihedral, past five bolts, to a rappel station near the lip of the wall.

Paraphernalia: Friends #2 through #4; a selection of Tri-cams; (8) quickdraws.

Descent: Double-rope rappel down the route.

Poison Spider Mesa Trail Area

War and *Shrubhead Ranger* are on the wall above the parking area of Poison Spider Mesa Trail, which begins at the Dinosaur Tracks sign. *Taste of Venom* is 0.5 mile (0.8km) up the trail from the Potash Road.

WAR (On Drugs) I, 5.10c, 2 pitches, 150 feet (46m)

First Ascent: Kyle Copeland, Sonja Paspal, Ron Olevsky, November 1989.

Location and Access: *War* climbs a short prow-shaped buttress with a crack splitting it in half. Begin up the central crack system visible from the Potash Road.

Paraphernalia: One set of Friends.

Descent: Downclimb a chimney to the north.

SHRUBHEAD RANGER I, 5.9, 1 pitch, ★★

First Ascent: Sonja Paspal, Kyle Copeland, Ron Olevsky, November 1989.

Location and Access: *Shrubhead Ranger* is left of *War* on a south-facing wall with a steep handcrack.

Paraphernalia: One set of Friends.

Descent: Downclimb a chimney to the north.

TASTE OF VENOM I, 5.11, 1 pitch, 85 feet (26m), ★★★★★

First Ascent: Kyle Copeland, Holly Gorden, November 1988.

Location and Access: To reach *Taste of Venom* hike a short trail above the first switchback on the Poison Spider Mesa Trail. Begin up an obvious crack above the trail. Pass a double overhang to its right. There is one drilled piton fixed below the upper (right) bomb bay overhang, 5.10 offwidth. Rappel slings are visible 8 feet (2.4m) below the top of the wall.

Paraphernalia: Two sets of Friends racked in order; (1) quickdraw.

Descent: Rappel the route.

NOTE: There is the negative and positive footprint of a dinosaur a few yards right of *Taste of Venom*. To locate, walk the base of the wall, watching for a large boulder split in two. The track is inside the split.

Middle Earth

Middle Earth is the section of wall along Potash Road downriver from the Dinosaur Tracks to Culvert Canyon. *Spur of the Moment*, although on the east side of the river, is included because it is approached from the Middle Earth area and the route is isolated from other climbs established across the Colorado River.

WHERE EGOS DARE I, 5.10c, 1 pitch, 75 feet (23m), ★★★★★

First Ascent: Kyle Copeland, Andy Pitas, Wendy Pitas, November 1989.

Location and Access: *Where Egos Dare* is right of the fourth Reflector Post downriver (cliff side) from Mile Post 7. Approach with 3rd class scrambling left of the route. Begin up a left-slanting 3" to 4" crack (7.6–10cm), passing a loose block on a right-facing dihedral 120 feet (37m) right of a large, deep chimney, then curve right. The route climbs a 3-inch crack (7.6cm) narrowing to 2.5-inches (6.3cm) and finally 2-inches (5cm). Pass two small stances before reaching double rappel anchors visible from below.

Paraphernalia: Friends (1) #1, (3) #2, #2.5, (2) #3, (1) #3.5, #4; TCUs (1) #0.75.

Descent: Rappel the route.

SPUR OF THE MOMENT—LOVE-RIDGE IV, 5.11 R, A2+, 4 pitches, 415 feet (126m)

First Ascent: Kyle Copeland, Linus Platt, Marc Hirt, 11 February 1992.

Location and Access: *Love-Ridge* climbs a crack system on a tower semi-attached to the rimrock, directly across the Colorado River from Gold Bar Canyon. Approach by boat or a long hike from the Amasa Back Trail. Climb a fracture line on the left side of the Spur Tower obvious from the Corona Arch trailhead parking area.

Pitch 1: Begin from the left ascending third-class to a 3-inch crack (7.6cm), then up a 5.9 R crack (.75"–1.9cm) past a ledge and a fixed anchor (A0) Continue up a 1" to 2" crack (2.5–5cm) at 5.10 to a good belay ledge with double-anchors, 100 feet (30m).

Pitch 2: Climb 5.10, then 5.11 (or A1) to a belay ledge with double-anchors, 85 feet (26m).

Pitch 3: Climb 5.9 up a classic 2–3-inch crack (5–7.6cm) finishing with 5.10 at a good belay ledge with double-anchors, 80 feet (24m).

Pitch 4: Move right and ascend (5.11) a 2–3-inch crack (5–7.6cm), passing a ledge on the right, then (5.10) up a 1-inch crack (2.5cm) with aid to triple rappel anchors on the summit, 150 feet (46m).

Paraphernalia: Two sets of Friends with (3) sets of hand-sizes; (2) knifeblades; Micro Nuts and medium nuts; long runners; (1) quickdraw.

Descent: Rappel 150 feet (46m) to the top of Pitch 3. Continue 80 feet (24m) to the top of Pitch 2 (or 165 feet–50m to the top of Pitch 1). Rappel 85 feet (26m) to the top of Pitch 1, then 100 feet (30m) to the third-class ground at the beginning of the climb.

NOTE: The route is dedicated to Marabel Loverage who died in an avalanche (winter of 1992) in the LaSal Mountains above Moab.

Potash Road South

Potash Road South is the area downriver from Culvert Canyon to Long Canyon, the greatest concentration of routes are between Day and Long Canyons. Climbs from *Unknown Route One* to *Green Coloradan* are on the dark varnished buttress of vertically fractured Wingate, in view 0.3 mile (0.4km) directly ahead when viewed downriver from the entrance to Day Canyon.

UNKNOWN ROUTE ONE

Unknown Route One is 0.4 mile downriver (0.6km) from Day Canyon. There are double-anchors on a left-facing, dark-varnished wall approximately five crack systems right of *Uno Mo-Mo*. The route climbs a left-facing dihedral up thin fingers to offwidth to hands. Further information is unknown.

UNO MO-MO I, 5.10, 1 pitch, 50 feet (15m)

First Ascent: Ron Olevsky, solo, October 1989.

Location and Access: *Uno Mo-Mo* is .35 mile downriver from Day Canyon or five crack systems left of *Unknown Route One*. One crack right of *Dos Mo-Mos* climb a right-facing dihedral up a thin crack to rappel slings visible from below on the right wall.

Paraphernalia: Friends (1) #0.5, #0.75 to #4.

Descent: Rappel the route.

DOS MO-MOS I, 5.10, 1 pitch, 100 feet (30m), ★★

First Ascent: Kyle Copeland, Ron Olevsky, October 1987.

Location and Access: *Dos Mo-Mos* begins right of a lone juniper tree. Climb a wide crack (in light-colored rock) up a large overhanging right-facing dihedral to a ledge with rappel slings visible on the right wall.

Paraphernalia: Friends (1) #0.5, #0.75 through #5.

Descent: Rappel the route.

UNKNOWN ROUTE TWO

Unknown Route Two is one crack right of *Skin Walker*. Climb to double rappel anchors on the right wall. Further information is unknown.

SKIN WALKER I, 5.11c, 1 pitch, 140 feet (43m), ★★★★★

First Ascent: Jay Smith, Jo Smith, April 1992.

Location and Access: *Skin Walker* is 1.5 miles downriver (2.4km) from Long Canyon. Begin right of a loose looking stacked-rock pedestal. Ascend the fragile rock of the pedestal on its left, past two anchors (5.10), then up a thin handcrack (5.11c). Continue up a "super-pod" to double rappel anchors below the center of three overhangs, 5.10 hands. Linus Platt: "Superb."

Paraphernalia: Friends (1) #1, (2) #1.5, (5) #2, (4) #2.5, (2-3) #3; (2) quickdraws; runners.

Descent: Rappel the route from double anchors.

Photo: Eric Bjørnstad

Potash Road South: *Dos Mo-Mos, Uno Mo-Mo*

SAY YOUR PRAYERS (Top-rope) I, 5.13, 1 pitch, 140 feet (43m), ★★

First Ascent: Jay Smith, almost!

Location and Access: *Say Your Prayers* climbs top-rope beginning further up the pedestal (left) from the start of *Skin Walker*.

Paraphernalia: Top-rope.

Descent: Rappel from *Skin Walker* anchors.

HARD DIRT I, 5.12, A1, 1 pitch, 150 feet (46m)

First Ascent: Jay Smith, Kyle Copeland, May 1992.

Location and Access: *Hard Dirt* is 400 yards (366m) left of *Skin Walker*. A few free moves lead to three points of aid. Climb past a small lip beyond two fixed anchors low on the wall. Continue past a pod, then up a left-facing corner, 5.10+. The upper part of the route climbs 5.12 up a left-facing dihedral, left under a roof, then continues 5.12 up a right-facing system to double rappel anchors on the left wall.

Paraphernalia: Friends (2) #1, (7-8) #1.5, (1) #2; TCUs (3) #0.4, (1) #0.75, #1.5, #1.75; (5) quickdraws.

Descent: Rappel the route.

GREEN COLORADAN I, 5.11b, 2 pitches, 150 feet (46m), ★★★★

First Ascent: Bret Ruckman, Gary Olsen, May 1988.

Location and Access: *Green Coloradan* is 1.5 miles (2.4km) north (right) of Long Canyon, or approximately four cracks left of *Skin Walker* and above a (broken in two) pillar at the base of the Wingate wall.

Pitch 1: Climb a left-facing "V" formation with liebacking to a ledge, 5.11–, protect with #4, then #2.5 Friend.

Pitch 2: Continue to rappel anchors below where the crack widens to a chimney, 5.11b, protect with #2 Friend.

Paraphernalia: Friends, many #2, #2.5 (1) #4.

Descent: Rappel the route.

UNKNOWN ROUTE THREE I, 1 pitch

Unknown slings are visible on the right wall atop the first right-facing dihedral 150 feet (46m) right of *Offwidths are Beautiful*. Further information is unknown.

OFFWIDTHS ARE BEAUTIFUL (aka Frenchie's Nightmare) I, 5.10a, 2 pitches, 190 feet (58m), ★★★★★

First Ascent: Craig Luebben, George Hurley, Sari Schmetterer, Katy Cassidy, Earl Wiggins, May 1988.

Location and Access: *Offwidths are Beautiful* is 1 mile upriver (1.6km) from Jug Handle Arch, or 600 feet downriver (183m) from Mile Post 3. The route climbs a wide crack on the right side of an obvious pillar leaning against the Wingate wall. Begin up a 5-inch crack (13cm) at 5.10 which widens to 7-inches (18cm). The top of the route has a 5.8 runout up a chimney before reaching double rappel anchors. The climb is offwidth at its crux, and was done as one 190 foot (58m) pitch on the first ascent, but will probably be climbed in two pitches on future ascents.

Paraphernalia: Pitch 1: Friends #1 through #3.5; small Tri-cams. Pitch 2: Friends (1) #3.5; Big Bros. (2) #1, #2, (3) #3.

Descent: Rappel the route from two fixed anchors, downclimbing the last 15 feet (4.5m) of Pitch 1. Rappel slings are visible upriver from the climb.

Photo: Eric Bjørnstad

Potash Road South: *Offwidths are Beautiful*

RAILROAD WRITING ROUTE Rating unknown, I, 1 pitch

First Ascent: Unknown.

Potash Road South: *Offwidths are Beautiful, Unknown Route Three*

Location and Access: *Railroad Writing Route* is 0.9 mile downriver (1.4km) from Day Canyon. It is identified by white lettering at the base of the wall (notations made by a railroad crew). Rappel slings are visible from below (upriver from the climb), but difficult to see without binoculars.

Paraphernalia: Unknown.

Descent: Rappel the route.

ALCOVE ROUTE I, 5.8, 1 pitch, 30 feet (9m)

First Ascent: Unknown.

Location and Access: *Alcove Route* is behind a large hackberry tree and sandstone block at the right side of a large alcove approximately 130 feet right (40m) of *Taco Bender*. Begin behind the block which is approached through the right side of the tree, then climb small hands to rappel anchors.

Paraphernalia: Friends (1) #1.5, #2.

Descent: Rappel the route.

TACO BENDER I, 5.9, 1 pitch, 50 feet (15m)

First Ascent: Charlie Fowler, Sue Wint, November 1986.

Location and Access: *Taco Bender* is 0.6 mile upriver (0.9km) from Long Canyon, or 1.3 miles downriver (2km) from Day Canyon. The rock is marked with faded white lettering part of the way up (a notation made by a railroad crew). Begin approximately 10 feet (3m) from the railroad tracks at an overhang and climb 5.9 hands up a right-facing dihedral to a fixed piton rappel anchor visible from below.

Paraphernalia: Friends #2.5 through #3.5.

Descent: Rappel the route.

UNBENT TACO I, 5.8, 1 pitch, 40 feet (12m)

First Ascent: Chad Wiggle, Ron Wiggle, 19 December 1988.

Location and Access: *Unbent Taco* ascends the first fracture system left of *Taco Bender*, 20 feet (6m). Climb a hands-to-wide crack system.

Paraphernalia: Friends #1.5 through #4.

Descent: Traverse right (5.1) and walk off/downclimb the backside (5.4) belaying from slings around a bush.

Descent: Rappel the route.

BUGS ON THE JUG I, 5.8, 1 pitch, 85 feet (26m)

First Ascent: Robert Bauer, Elliot Brown, Jerry Erb, Chris Williams, April 1994.

Location and Access: *Bugs on the Jug* is right of *Jug Handle Arch*. Begin between *Jug Handle Arch* and the crack system obvious below rappel slings. Climb 30 feet (9m)) up a left-facing corner to a long bench. Traverse right and climb up, then right to a left-facing crack system. Pass an offwidth section and continue with hands to rappel anchors visible from below.

Paraphernalia: Medium Friends and TCUs; Camalot (1) #4.

Descent: Rappel to the bench at the start of the climb, then scramble off to the right.

JUG HANDLE ARCH—HANDLE WITH CARE II, 5.8, 3 pitches, 300 feet (91m)

First Ascent: Alen Bartlette, Eric Johnson, March 1989. Pitch 1 and 2 were first climbed by John Bouchard belayed by Titoune Bouchard, 1985.

Location and Access: *Jug Handle Arch* is on the northeast corner of Long Canyon, 15 miles (24km) down the Potash Road from U.S. Highway 191. It is indicated with a sign before the turn into Long Canyon, downriver from Mile Post 2.

Pitch 1: Climb 5.8 past a loose area to a belay stance, 5.8, 50 feet (15m).

Photo: Eric Bjørnstad

Potash Road South: ***Jug Handle Arch***

Pitch 2: Continue past death blocks to a hanging belay, 100 feet (30m).

Pitch 3: Begin with a right traverse. Protect the end of the traverse with a #2.5 Friend. Move up using large TCUs for protection. There is a 60-foot (18m) runout of 5.4. Continue, protecting with #3 and #4 Friends, up easy but loose ground, then 4th class angling right. It is possible to continue to the rim at about 5.7/5.8 climbing.

Paraphernalia: One set of Friends with (2) #2.5 through #3.5; (1) set of TCUs; stoppers.

Descent: Move 4th class diagonally right, then walk 250 feet (76m) upriver and descend the last (second possible) water groove with two double-rope rappels.

Offwidth City

This is the wall (facing Potash Road) beyond the turn up Long Canyon (to the left). Bear left on an old mining road immediately left after the turn up Long Canyon. Usually it is possible to approach with 2-wheel-drive to the base of the Wingate wall, but conditions vary storm to storm and 4-wheel-drive may be required or a short hike from the mouth of Long Canyon.

MAYOR II, 5.11+, 4 pitches, 300 feet (91m)

First Ascent: Kennan Harvey, Topher Donahue, 1994. First Free Ascent: Topher Donahue, Craig Luebben, 7 November 1995.

Location and Access: *Mayor* is one crack left of *Done-Loubin'* (see Potash Road Side Canyons chapter) and climbs a large left-facing dihedral to the rimrock.

Paraphernalia: Friends #1 through #4 with double #1.5; Camalots #1 through #5; Big Bros. (2) #1, (3) #2, (6) #3.

Descent: Rappel from the summit to the top of a pillar. Rappel (double-rope) from the pillar to the base of the climb.

OFF I, 5.12b, 1 pitch, 160 feet (49m)

First Ascent: Craig Luebben, Topher Donahue, 14 November 1994.

Location and Access: *Off* climbs the first crack left of *Mayor* and ascends an offwidth system (up through fingers) to rappel anchors visible from below. It may also be identified as the first crack right of a prominent window visible from below the wall.

Paraphernalia: Friends (1) #1, (3) #1.5, (3-4) #2, (2-3) #2.5, (1) #4; Camalots (2) #4; Big Bros. (3) #1, (1) #2, (2) #3; Hex (1) #9.

Descent: Rappel the route from double anchors.

BIRTH CANAL I, 5.10, 2 pitches, 140 feet (42m)

First Ascent: Pitch 1: Doug Snively, Jimmy Dunn, November 1994. Pitch 2: Craig Luebben, Silvia DeVito, Topher Donahue, Kennan Harvey, October 1995.

Location and Access: *Birth Canal* is 150 feet (46m) left of *Off*.

Pitch 1: Begin up a chimney and climb left past a hole in the rock.

Pitch 2: Climb an offwidth and chimney. There are three bolts in place.

Paraphernalia: Big Bros. (2) #3, #4 and (1) #5, or protection for 12-17" crack; (3) quickdraws.

Descent: Rappel the route.

APOLOGY I, 1 pitch, 60 feet (18m)

First Ascent: Jimmy Dunn, Lisa Hathaway, May 1995.

Offwidth City: (left to right) ***Incredible Pooh, Pillar Route, Black n'Stacks, Apology, Birth Canal, Off, Mayor*** Photo: Eric Bjørnstad

Location and Access: *Apology* is two cracks left of *Birth Canal* and climbs a "V" formation. Rappel slings are visible on the left wall.

Paraphernalia: Camalots (1) set to #4.

Descent: Rappel the route.

BLACK N' STACKS I, 5.10+, 2 pitches, 160 feet (49m)

First Ascent: Pitch 1: Jimmy Dunn, Craig Luebben, Doug Snively, Lisa Hathaway, Topher Donahue, 80 feet (24m), November 1994. Pitch 2: Topher Donahue, Peter Dukette, 80 feet (24m), Spring 1995.

Location and Access: *Black N' Stacks* is one crack left of *Apology*.

Pitch 1: Climb fingers, then hands to a belay, 5.10+.

Pitch 2: Continue up a wide system with hands, then offwidth.

Paraphernalia: Camalots: Pitch 1 (4) #4, Pitch 2 (1) #4; Big Bro (3) #3.

Descent: Rappel the route.

PILLAR ROUTE I, 5.10+, 3 pitches, 220 feet (67m)

First Ascent: Pitch 1: Kyle Copeland. Pitches 2, 3: Craig Luebben, Kennan Harvey, Spring 1995.

Location and Access: *Pillar Route* is left of *Black 'n' Stacks* and climbs past an obvious pillar leaning against the Wingate wall. Three sets of rappel slings are visible from below.

Pitch 1: Climb 5.10+ fingers to a shelf and double anchors part of the way up the pillar.

Pitch 2: Continue to the top of the pillar.

Pitch 3: Move right to wide climbing and ascend hands to a thin splitter crack, then to rappel anchors visible from below.

Paraphernalia: Two sets of Friends.

Descent: Rappel the route.

INCREDIBLE POOH I, 5.11a, 1 pitch, 70 feet (21m)

First Ascent: Eric Decaria, Kevin Chase, 12 December 1995.

Location and Access: *Incredible Pooh* is left of *Pillar Route*. Climb a left-facing dihedral to rappel slings visible on the left wall.

Paraphernalia: Friends (1) #0.5, #0.75, (2) #1 through #3; small wires.

Descent: Rappel the route.

MAIN STREET I, 5.11c, 1 pitch, 80 feet (24m)

First Ascent: Jay Smith, Jo Smith, 24 April 1992.

Location and Access: *Main Street* is two cracks left of *Incredible Pooh*. Hike the upper mining road or trail until blocked by large boulders, then scramble diagonally up and left. Climb up a right-facing finger corner up light-colored rock to double rappel anchors (visible from below) on the left wall.

Paraphernalia: Friends (2) #0.4, (1) #0.5, (4) #0.75, (3) #1, (1) #2.5, #3.

Descent: Rappel the route from double rappel hangers.

SIDE STREET I, 5.10+, 1 pitch, 80 feet (24m)

First Ascent: Jay Smith, Jo Smith, 24 April 1992.

Location and Access: *Side Street* is one crack left of *Main Street*. Climb a left-facing corner (5.10+) with thin hands to double rappel hangers.

Paraphernalia: Friends (2) #1.5, #2, (4) #2.5, (1) #3.

Descent: Rappel the route from double rappel hangers.

HAND SANDWITCH I, 5.10d, 1 pitch

First Ascent: Rush Bowers, Kent Wheeler, October 1987.

Location and Access: *Hand Sandwitch* is 0.25 mile (0.4km) past Long Canyon. Climb a right-facing chimney, then make a face traverse left to a handcrack and continue offwidth to rappel anchors. No further information is known about this route's location.

Paraphernalia: Friends (2) #3 through #4; Camalot (1) #4; Tri-cam (1) #7.

Descent: Rappel the route.

Weak Bosons, Strong Muons, Energy Decay, Hand Sandwitch

Weak Bosons is 0.5 mile (0.8km) south of the turn into Long Canyon. Park on the river side of the roadway where there is a yellow caution sign with a serpentine arrow at the downriver end of the pull out. Approach *Strong Muons*, *Energy Decay* and *Hand Sandwitch* from the same parking area.

Photo: Bret Ruckman

Gary Olsen on *Weak Bosons*

WEAK BOSONS I, 5.11+, 1 pitch, 135 feet (41m), ★★★★★

First Ascent: Bret Ruckman, Gary Olsen, May 1988.

Location and Access: Climb a right-facing corner protected with #2 Friends, 5.11. Move left on a ledge, then up to a second ledge and a rappel station. Rappel slings are visible from the Potash Road with binoculars.

Paraphernalia: Friends (2) #0.75, #1.5, (10) #2, (2) #2.5, (1) #4.

Descent: One double-rope rappel.

STRONG MUONS I, 5.12, 1 pitch, 135 feet (41m), ★★★★★

First Ascent: Bret Ruckman, Gary Olsen, May 1988.

Location and Access: *Strong Muons* is 30 feet (9m) left of *Weak Bosons*. The route was originally climbed top-rope from *Weak Boson*'s anchors. It was first climbed on lead by an unknown party. Begin up the first crack left of Weak Bosons and climb a small roof, then up a 3-inch (7.6cm) off-set corner to a pod and rappel slings visible from below.

Paraphernalia: Friends (2) #0.5, (1) #1.

Descent: Rappel *Weak Bosons* with double-ropes.

ENERGY DECAY I, 5.10+, 1 pitch, 75 feet (23m)

First Ascent: Bret Ruckman, Gary Olsen, May 1988.

Location and Access: *Energy Decay* climbs a handcrack in a left-facing corner 100 yards (91m) left of *Strong Muons*. Approach from the right up a break in the Chinle cliffs. Climb a prow to rappel slings visible below two side by side overhangs.

Paraphernalia: Friends (3) #2, (1) #2.5, (3) #3, (2) #3.5, (1) #4.

Descent: Rappel the route.

Dingleberry Rock, Chimney Rock

Dingleberry Rock is on the right side of the Potash Road as it winds past the Potash Ash settling ponds below Chimney Rock. Chimney Rock is a prominent tower obvious as one continues down the Potash Road past the mine toward the White Rim Road and Island-in-the-Sky District of Canyonlands National Park. The spire may be approached (with route finding) from the mesa top from the north region of Dead Horse Point State Park. To reach from the bottom drive 7.1 miles downriver (11.4km) from Long Canyon. The road becomes 2-wheel drive dirt beyond the BLM river put-in.

DINGLEBERRY ROCK I, A1, 1 pitch

First Ascent: Cameron Burns, Michael Schillaci, May 1989.

Location and Access: Dingleberry Rock is a large boulder beside the Potash Road below Chimney Rock. A register was left on top of the climb by the first ascent party.

Paraphernalia: A selection of pitons.

Descent: Rappel the route.

CHIMNEY ROCK–MIDNIGHT EXPRESS IV, 5.10, A3–, 6 pitches, 330 feet (101m)

First Ascent: Daryl Miller, Bruce Bundy, Kyle Copeland, 29 March 1989.

Location and Access: The first ascent party approached from the mesa top where they rappel to the notch between the rimrock and the tower from three ropes tied together and left fixed for a return prusik. The rappel point is left (west) of the

Brett Ruckman on *Weak Bosons*

buttress of rimrock opposite Chimney Rock. Approach from below is longer but may be more feasible.

Pitch 1: From the notch 4th class up the left side of a small pillar at the beginning of the tower.

Pitch 2: From the top of the pillar climb a crack system to a belay ledge, 5.6.

Pitch 3: Climb up a bulge to double rappel anchors atop a small pillar near the left side of the tower, 5.10.

Pitch 4: Begin with a roped jump from the pillar (right) to the main rock of the tower, then 4th class diagonally up and right and finally straight up a right-facing corner to a belay ledge.

Pitch 5: Climb A1 up a 1.5-inch (3.8cm) crack (passing a fixed anchor), and continue up overhanging rock with some free moves in pods. Pass two more fixed anchors and continue A3 (with hooks) to a belay ledge.

Pitch 6: Climb to a ledge with double rappel anchors, then move left and make one 5.6 move before 4th class rock leads to the summit.

Paraphernalia: Two sets of Friends with a #5 or #6 useful; Tri-cam (1) #7; TCUs (1) set; medium stoppers; Leeper Hook; quickdraws.

Descent: Downclimb to the ledge above the ledge of Pitch 5. Rappel 150 feet (46m) to the top of Pitch 3. Downclimb and rope-jump to the top of the pillar at the top of Pitch 2. Rappel 165 feet (50m) to the beginning of Pitch 1, then 4th class to the notch and prusik to the mesa top.

The region last explored [the Colorado Plateau] is, of course, altogether valueless. It can be approached only from the south, and after entering it there is nothing to do but to leave. Ours has been the first, and will doubtless be the last, party of whites to visit this profitless locality . . . . Excepting when the melting snows send their annual torrents through the avenues to the Colorado, conveying with them sound and motion, these dismal abysses, and the arid table-lands that enclose them, are left, as they have been for ages, in unbroken solitude and silence.

Lieutenant Joseph C. Ives, *Report upon the Colorado River of the West*, 1861

Although the Southwest is littered with ruins, one of its greatest charms is its emptiness. There is a profound sense of peace in the great reaches of open country and the silence and solitude of its canyons. The sky and the weather are so important a part of the Southwest that it is easy to understand how the people who have lived there have been governed by the march of the seasons and the cycles of sun and moon and stars.

Harold Gladwin, *Southwestern Archaeology*, 1957

Photo: Judy Ruckman

Long Canyon, *Program Director*

POTASH ROAD SIDE CANYONS

Despite these inroads upon the desert, its greater body remains untouched. To it millions of us make pilgrimages. We glimpse its brief display of spring flowers, find a breathing space free from urban smog, and, when confused and fragmented at heart, seek escape from our conscious mind.

In silence and solitude we find a spiritual oasis amidst the clamor of the world's voices and the tyranny of our unceasing conscious thoughts. How strangely familiar is this unfamiliar domain which mysteriously mirrors our unconscious. It calls forth instant response from that hidden font within us, eternal as the desert itself.

Frank Waters, *Eternal Desert*

Potash Road Side Canyons are shown on the Moab West map, and in downriver order are Culvert Canyon, Day Canyon, and Long Canyon. Long Canyon's dirt road requires 4-wheel drive above Maverick Buttress if approaching from Potash Road, or the road may be descended with a 2-wheel drive vehicle from the Island-in-the-Sky Mesa off State Highway 313. Culvert and Day Canyons not only have great climbs but are beautiful hikes.

Culvert Canyon

Culvert Canyon is the first canyon downriver 0.4 mile (0.16km) from the Corona Arch Trailhead or 10.1 miles (16.2km) from the junction of U.S. 191 and the Potash Road. The canyon is identified by the only culvert in view from Potash Road, under the railroad tracks, which can be walked through to access a canyon. Climbs on the east (right) wall are approached by hiking a trail which diagonals up and right over the railroad tracks before entering the culvert. Once over the tracks, hike past boulders with petroglyphs on the way to the Wingate buttress above. Climbs on the west wall are reached by hiking through the culvert, then 3rd class to the base of the wall on the left. Traverse along prominent benches upcanyon to the location of the routes.

Culvert Canyon East

Climbs in Culvert Canyon East are listed right to left.

LK AND KC I, 5.10, 4 pitches, 300 feet (91m)

First Ascent: Layton Kor, Kyle Copeland, 30 November 1991.

Location and Access: *LK and KC* ascends a block tower obvious on the right at the entrance to Culvert Canyon.

Pitch 1: Begin 5.9 and climb past a fixed anchor to a one-bolt belay station. One may also start to the right with 5.10 fist.

Pitch 2: Continue up a 4-inch (10cm) right-facing crack, passing a small overhang (5.9+ stem) on its right, then to a second belay ledge off a shelf below the tower above.

Pitch 3: Continue 4th class around the formation to the right (back) to a belay below the upper landform.

Pitch 4: Third-class diagonally up and left, then straight up at 5.4 to double-rappel anchors at the summit.

Paraphernalia: One set of Friends with double #2.5, #3, #3.5; stoppers; (1) quickdraw.

Descent: One 150-foot (46m) rappel to the top of Pitch 2, then scramble and walk down the bench around to the right.

ROUND HEAD RUCKUS I, 5.9, 2 pitches, 125 feet (38m)

First Ascent: Bob Novellino, Tom Gilje, 1994.

Location and Access: *Round Head Ruckus* is at the first corner left of *LK and KC* at the right side of Culvert Canyon. The route climbs to the top of the Wingate, passing rappel slings visible at the top of Pitch 1.

Pitch 1: Climb 75 feet (23m) to rappel/belay slings visible from below.

Pitch 2: Continue to the top, 5.9, 50 feet (15m).

Paraphernalia: Friends (2) #2, #2.5, #3, #3.5, #4.

Descent: Rappel the route.

NOTE: There are petroglyphs on the summit block to the right of the climb.

POWER COSMIC I, 5.11c, 1 pitch, 60 feet (18m), ★★★

First Ascent: Bob Novellino, Tom Gilje, 1994.

Location and Access: *Power Cosmic* is a face climb right of *Corner*. Climb past five bolts to rappel slings visible from below.

Paraphernalia: Five quickdraws.

Descent: Rappel the route.

CORNER I, 5.10, 1 pitch, 60 feet (18m), ★

First Ascent: Tom Gilje, Bob Novellino, 1994.

Location and Access: Corner climbs broken rock up the next crack system left of *Power Cosmic*. Begin at the same start as *El Nacho*, and climb a left-facing dihedral, then continue with face climbing to rappel slings are not visible from below the climb.

Paraphernalia: Friends (3) #0.75, (1) #1, #1.5; Hex (1) #7.

Descent: Rappel the route.

EL NACHO I, 5.9, 1 pitch, 100 feet (30m), ★★

First Ascent: Todd Marder, Millie Birdwell, 1992.

Location and Access: *El Nacho* shares a start with *Corner*, then climbs up and left up a left-facing dihedral to a notch giving a view of both sides of the wall. The crux is at the beginning of the route. Rappel slings are not visible from below the climb.

Paraphernalia: Friends (1) #1, #1.5, (3) #2.5, (2) #3.

Descent: Rappel the route.

FINGER FOOD I, 5.9, 1 pitch, 75 feet (23m)

First Ascent: Todd Marder, Millie Birdwell, 1992.

Location and Access: *Finger Food* climbs a left-facing dihedral between *El Nacho* and *Kor Route*.

Paraphernalia: One set of Friends; Camalot (1) #4.

Descent: Rappel the route.

KOR ROUTE I, 5.9, 2 pitches, 150 feet (46m)

First Ascent: Unknown.

Location and Access: *Kor Route* is left of *Finger Food*, and climbs to an offwidth crack system. The route's name refers to an old piton found on the route with "L.K." stamped on it.

Paraphernalia: A selection of Friends; hexes (2) #1.5 through #4.

Descent: Rappel the route.

PEAS IN A POD I, 5.10c/d, 2 pitches, 190 feet (58m)

First Ascent: Bob Novellino, Tom Gilje, 1994.

Location and Access: *Peas in a Pod* climbs to the top of the rimrock the first crack left of the corner as one walks from the south-facing to the west-facing wall of Culvert Canyon.

Pitch 1: Climb to a belay in a pod (rappel slings are not visible from below), 90 feet (27m).

Pitch 2: Continue to the top of the rimrock, 100 feet (30m).

Paraphernalia: Friends (1) #0.75, #1, #1.5, #2, (3) #2.5, (3) #3, (3) #3.5, (2) #4.

Descent: Rappel the route.

SECOND HAND SMUTE I, 5.11c/d, 2 pitches, 120 feet (37m), ★★★

First Ascent: Bob Novellino, Tom Gilje, Eric Decaria, 1994.

Location and Access: *Second Hand Smute* climbs the first major crack system left of *Peas in a Pod*.

Pitch 1: Climb a left-facing dihedral to an obvious (loose looking) chockstone with rappel slings visible from below, 70 feet (21m). There is one bolt fixed below the chockstone.

Pitch 2: Continue 50 feet (15m) to a rappel station. The pitch is not recommended due to poor quality rock.

Paraphernalia: Standard desert rack; TCUs; (1) quickdraw.

Descent: Rappel the route.

FART KNOCKER I, 5.11+, 1 pitch, 100 feet (30m), ★★

First Ascent: Tom Gilje, Bob Novellino, 1994.

Location and Access: *Fart Knocker* is a "powdery classic" left of *Second Hand Smute*. The route may also be identified by its position 200 feet (61m) right of a bench (high on the left) with a thin horizontal arch at its outside edge. Begin up light-colored rock above a large split-in-two boulder on the talus slope. Climb a handcrack that thins halfway up and ends at a left-facing dihedral. Rappel slings are visible from below.

Paraphernalia: Standard desert rack with extra #2.5 and #4s.

Descent: Rappel the route.

Photo: Eric Bjørnstad

Gold Bar Tower

Culvert Canyon West

Climbs at Culvert Canyon West begin from a bench at the same level as the climbs on the east (right) side of the canyon and can be viewed with binoculars from the east bench. Routes are listed left to right.

VICIOUS DIGIT I, 5.11a, 1 pitch, 40 feet (12m)

First Ascent: Alex Hogel, Bob Novellino.

Location and Access: *Vicious Digit* is across from *Fart Knocker*, and is an incomplete project.

Paraphernalia: Standard desert rack.

Descent: Rappel the route.

BOB'S OFFWIDTH I, 5.10a/b, 1 pitch, 85 feet (26m)

First Ascent: Bob Novellino, Peter Verchick, Eric Decaria, 1994.

Location and Access: *Bob's Offwidth* begins up a face, then continues up a splitter crack left of *The Sluice*.

Paraphernalia: Standard desert rack with extra #4.

Descent: Rappel the route.

THE SLUICE I, 5.9+, 1 pitch, 75 feet (23m)

First Ascent: Bob Novellino, Peter Verchick, Eric Decaria, 1994.

Location and Access: *The Sluice* climbs offwidth and a chimney up sharp rock 10 feet (3m) right of *Bob's Offwidth*.

Paraphernalia: Standard desert rack.

Descent: Rappel the route.

NOSE CORNER I, 5.10c/d, 1 pitch, 75 feet (23m)

First Ascent: Peter Verchick, Eric Decaria, 1994.

Location and Access: *Nose Corner* climbs a prominent right-facing corner 25 feet (7.6m) right of *The Sluice*.

Paraphernalia: Friends (3) #1, #1.5, (2) #2, (1) #2.5, (3) #3.5.

Descent: Rappel the route.

5.10 CORNER I, 5.10, 1 pitch, 65 feet (20m)

First Ascent: Bob Novellino, Peter Verchick, Spring 1995.

Location and Access: *5.10 Corner* is right of *Nose Corner*.

Paraphernalia: Standard desert rack; TCUs several #0.75.

Descent: Rappel the route.

NOTE: There are several other routes, not documented, upcanyon.

Gold Bar Tower

Gold Bar Tower is approximately 1 mile (1.6km) up Gold Bar Canyon (next canyon downriver from Culvert Canyon) but is best approached by hiking Culvert Canyon. When the canyon splits into three, ascend the left fork. The tower is obvious ahead and to the left.

FORT KNOX I, 5.10, 1 pitch, 120 feet (37m)

First Ascent: George Hurley, Katy Cassidy, Earl Wiggins, March 1988.

Location and Access: The route climbs the east face of the landform.

Paraphernalia: One set of Friends; a few large tubes.

Descent: One double-rope rappel down the route.

Day Canyon

Day Canyon is 1.2 miles (1.9km) downriver from Culvert Canyon, or 1.4 miles upriver (2.2km) from Long Canyon. There is a pedestrian gate (cows don't fit) at the downriver side of the canyon entrance. Although a sign reads "Property of RRCO No Trespassing," the canyon is BLM land and access is legal to the public. Hike into the canyon, keeping to its left side to avoid difficult bushwhacking. Routes are listed as one hikes from the Potash Road.

KISS OF THE SPIDER WOMEN I, 5.12, 1 pitch, 150 feet (46m), ★★★★★

First Ascent: Jimmy Dunn, Craig Luebben, Lisa Hathaway, Betsi McKittrick, May 1994.

Location and Access: *Kiss of the Spider Women* is on the left side of Day Canyon, left of the gully left of *Working Class Hero*. The location is beyond the tamarisk brush where an old 4-wheel-drive mining road is reached and large potholes appear in the stream's bedrock. The first crux is a crack that thins to an awkward 1-1.5 inches (2.5–3.8cm). A second crux is pulling the undercling at the roof, then moving to good hands.

Paraphernalia: Friends (4) #1, (3) #1.5, (3) #2.5, (2) #3, #3.5, #4; Camalot (1) #5; TCUs (2) #0.75, #0.5.

Descent: Rappel the route.

WORKING CLASS HERO I, 5.9+, 1 pitch, 70 feet (21m), ★★★

First Ascent: Kyle Copeland, Eric Johnson, August 1989.

Location and Access: *Working Class Hero* is right of the prominent gully right of *Kiss of the Spider Women*, on the left (south) side of the canyon before reaching Bootleg Tower. Climb a thin fingercrack splitting white rock. The color is a result of the relatively recent exfoliation of a thin slab from the green lichen-covered wall. Rappel slings are visible from below.

Paraphernalia: Friends (3) #0.75, #1, (2) #1.5, (1) #2, #2.5.

Descent: Rappel the route.

Photo: Eric Bjørnstad

Day Canyon: ***Kiss of the Spider Woman***

BEE LINE I, 5.10c, 1 pitch, 75 feet (23m)

First Ascent: Katy Cassidy, Earl Wiggins, March 1988.

Location and Access: *Bee Line* is upcanyon from *Working Class Hero*, on the right (opposite) wall. Begin at a large dihedral that faces west (upcanyon). Ascend a 5.9+ face for 15 feet (4.5m) to get to the beginning of a straight-in crack. Thin jamming leads up a steep wall for 30 feet (9m) until it is possible to switch to the left crack and continue to a hanging belay on the left wall. An overhang is passed on its left side. Rappel slings are visible from below the climb.

Paraphernalia: Friends (2) sets #1 through #3.5, (1) #4; a few wired stoppers.

Descent: Double-rope rappel the route from two fixed anchors.

BEE LINE (Top-rope), I, 5.11+, 1 pitch, 75 feet (23m)

First Ascent: Unknown.

Location and Access: The variation climbs left of the original route.

Paraphernalia: Top-rope.

Descent: Same as *Bee Line*.

Raptor Tower, Bootleg Tower

Raptor and Bootleg Towers are 0.75 mile (1.2km) up Day Canyon from the Potash Road. Raptor Tower is the larger spire on the left, Bootleg the smaller tower on the right. *Bootleg*

Photo: Eric Bjørnstad

Day Canyon: *Working Class Hero*

was named by the first ascent team for a moonshine still reported to have once operated in the canyon.

RAPTOR TOWER:

ENIGMATIC ROUTE I, 1 pitch, 100 feet (30m)

First Ascent: Unknown

Location and Access: Rappel slings are visible below a ceiling in a dihedral at the left side of the tower when viewed from the mining road.

Paraphernalia: Unknown

Descent: Rappel the route.

PROHIBITION CRACK I, 5.11+, 3 pitches, 300 feet (91m)

First Ascent: Keith Reynolds, Alan Stevenson, March 1995.

Location and Access: The tower is adjacent (left) to Bootleg Tower. Begin on the right (Bootleg) side of the tower.

Pitch 1: Climb a wide squeeze crack at 5.10+ offwidth to a belay ledge with an anchor visible from below, 100 feet (30m).

Pitch 2: Continue up a chimney (offwidth/squeeze) past 1 bolt and 1 drilled piton. Exit the main crack system and traverse left, then climb up to a large ledge (no anchors in place). Belay from natural gear.

Pitch 3: Climb straight above the ledge, passing 2 bolts, then traverse up and left to obvious holes, 5.10+/5.11–. Continue up and left mantling to the top as soon as possible. Belay from a single directional bolt.

Paraphernalia: Two sets of Friends; Big Bro (1) #3, #4; Lowe Balls; (5) quickdraws.

Descent: Move right from the top of Pitch 3, then rappel the west face from double bolts, 165 feet (50m) to the notch between the tower and the Wingate wall behind.

BOOTLEG TOWER:

MOONSHINE I, 5.10+, 1 pitch, 175 feet (53m) long side, 70 feet (21m) backside

First Ascent: Eric Bjørnstad, Ron Wiggle, Terry McKenna, 5.7, A2, 30 May 1974. First Free Ascent: Charlie Fowler, Dan McGee, Doug Barry (led by all), September 1989.

Location and Access: *Moonshine* climbs the tower's short (up-hill) side. Begin up a 5.7 body stem at a chimney, then climb an arête passing four bolts before following an obvious crack system to a ledge below the summit on the northwest corner of the tower.

Paraphernalia: Gear in ascending order: medium stopper; Friends #3.5, #2.5, #2.5 (or smaller), above ledge (1) #4 Friend; (4) quickdraws.

Descent: One double-rope rappel down the route.

MOONSHINE SUMMIT VARIATIONS I, 5.7, 5.9, 5.11+

First Ascent: Charlie Fowler, Dan McGee, Doug Barry, 1989.

Location and Access: From the ledge below the summit one may move left and reach the top with 5.9 or move right around a corner (loose rock) and climb at 5.7. The direct finish between the two is 5.11+.

BUZZ LUST I, 5.12, 1 pitch, 100 feet (30m), ★★★★

First Ascent: Kevin Chase, Jimmy Symans, 27 April 1995.

Location and Access: *Buzz Lust* climbs a steep arête past nine bolts on the west (back) side of the tower, right of *Moonshine.*

Paraphernalia: Nine quickdraws.

Descent: Rappel the route.

Photo: Eric Bjørnstad

Day Canyon, left to right: *Raptor Tower, Bootleg Tower, Androids Waffle Hot Line, Christine's Way Buff Saab, Brush-Painted Datsun*

Androids Waffle Hot Line, Christine's Way Buff Saab, Brush-Painted Datsun

The following routes climb the Wingate buttress behind Bootleg Tower

ANDROIDS WAFFLE HOT LINE I, 5.10+, 2 pitches, 190 feet (58m) 190 feet (58m), ★★★★★

First Ascent: Kyle Copeland, Eric Johnson (supported by Warren Harding), September 1989.

Location and Access: *Androids Waffle Hot Line* climbs the Wingate wall behind and right of Bootleg Tower. Ascend a prominent dihedral left of *Brush-Painted Datsun*.

Pitch 1: Climb a 4-inch crack (10cm) to a hanging belay from bolts, 5.10+, 100 feet (30m).

Pitch 2: Begin up a 4-inch (10cm) then 3-inch crack (7.6cm), then continue up a handcrack past a small pod on the right wall. Move left to belay on a ledge from bolts, 5.10, 90 feet (27m). The crux is above the pod. Rappel slings are visible from below.

Paraphernalia: Friends (1) #1, (2) #1.5, #2, #2.5, #3, (3) #3.5, (4) #4.

Descent: Rappel from fixed anchors 100 feet (30m) to the top of Pitch 1, then from fixed anchors 90 feet (27m) to the ground.

CHRISTINE'S WAY BUFF SAAB I, 5.9+, 1 pitch, 80 feet (24m), ★★

First Ascent: Kyle Copeland, Eric Johnson, August 1989

Location and Access: *Christine's Way Buff Saab* climbs a 5.9+ handcrack in a large left-facing dihedral right of *Androids Waffle Hot Line*. Rappel slings are visible from below.

Paraphernalia: Friends (1) #1, #1.5, #2, (2) #2.5, (4) #3.

Descent: One double-rope rappel.

BRUSH-PAINTED DATSUN I, 5.10, 1 pitch, 100 feet (30m), ★★★★★

First Ascent: Kyle Copeland, Eric Johnson, September 1989.

Location and Access: Begin right of *Christine's Way Buff Saab* up a 6-inch crack (15cm) angling right. Pass a flake on its right and continue up a 3-inch crack (7.6cm). A perfect handcrack takes one to double rappel anchors visible from below.

Paraphernalia: Friends (2) #2, (3) #2.5, (4) #3, #5.

Descent: One double-rope rappel down the route.

Acromaniac, Aerobicide, Handyman Splits, Unknown Route, Pillar of Bubdom, Bi-Hedral

These routes are up canyon from Bootleg Tower.

ACROMANIAC I, 5.10, A0, 2 pitches, 235 feet (72m), ★★★★★

First Ascent: Kyle Copeland, Ron Olevsky, September 1989.

Location and Access: *Acromaniac* is across the canyon from Bootleg Tower. Climb a splitter crack angling left up a blank wall with concave stress lines in the rock.

Pitch 1: Begin with aid, then climb fingers to a hanging belay, 160 feet (49m). The pitch ascends from a 0.25 to 2-inch crack (0.6–5cm).

Pitch 2: Climb perfect hands to a sloping belay stance below a headwall, 75 feet (32m). The pitch climbs from a 2.5 to 4-inch crack (6.3-10cm).

Paraphernalia: Many Friends; TCUs; Ball Nuts.

Descent: Two rappels down the route.

Photo: Eric Bjørnstad

Day Canyon: *Acromaniac*

Photo: Eric Bjørnstad

Day Canyon: *Aerobicide*

AEROBICIDE I, 5.11c, 2 pitches, 160 feet (49m), ★★★★★

First Ascent: Kyle Copeland, Carl Diedrich, Marabel Loveridge, October 1989.

Location and Access: *Aerobicide* is on the left approximately 0.5 mile upcanyon (0.8km) from Bootleg Tower. It is right of a prominent dihedral which begins on a ledge having two parallel cracks on its right. Climb two 80-foot (24m) pitches to rappel slings visible from below. The first two-thirds of the route is overhanging. Begin up the left crack (left-facing dihedral) atop a broken ledge 20 feet (6m) above the talus slope, then move to the right crack (the crux). Continue past an overhang with an offwidth flake (another crux) and continue to rappel slings above a ledge and visible from below.

Paraphernalia: Friends (2) #2, (4) #2.5, #3, (3) #3.5, (2) #4, #6.

Descent: Rappel the route.

HANDYMAN SPLITS I, 5.10, 1 pitch

First Ascent: Carl Diedrich, Kyle Copeland, October 1989.

Location and Access: *Handyman Splits* is on the right 0.25 mile upcanyon (0.4km) from *Aerobicide*. Climb a large chimney with hands up wide cracks. Rappel slings are visible from below above a ledge.

Paraphernalia: Selection of Friends.

Descent: Rappel the route.

UNKNOWN ROUTE Rating unknown

First Ascent: Unknown

Location and Access: *Unknown Route* climbs a large dihedral on the left side of the canyon, left of two towers approximately 0.5 mile upcanyon (0.8km) from Bootleg Tower. Rappel slings are visible from below.

Paraphernalia: Unknown.

Descent: Rappel the route.

Photo: Jeff Widen

Day Canyon, *Pillar of Bubdom*

PILLAR OF BUBDOM II, 5.8, A2/3, 4 pitches, 230 feet (70m)

First Ascent: Jeff Widen, Graham Frontella, John Plvan, 22 November 1994.

Location and Access: *Pillar of Bubdom* is obvious high on the left wall as one continues up Day Canyon from *Handyman Splits*. Approach from a gully left of the base of the tower. Climb two pitches ascending right to left, then scramble right to the approach ridge between the tower and the wall behind. One final lead will reach anchor bolts on the tower's summit.

Pitch 1: Scramble 5.4 up the gully and belay, 40 feet (12m).

Pitch 2: Continue up the gully to a second belay using a bush/tree for anchors at 5.8, 120 feet (37m).

Pitch 3: Move right to the tower, then climb the east face 70 feet (21m) to the summit.

Paraphernalia: Friends (1) #2.5, #3; for a belay at the base of the tower (2) #3.5, #4; (1) set of TCUs; (5) knifeblades; (4) Lost Arrows; (1) 1.5" angle; (2) large RPs; (2) Ball Nuts; (1) hook.

Descent: Rappel 70 feet (21m) to the approach ridge, then 120 feet (37m) to the top of Pitch 2 and a final rappel 40 feet (12m), then downclimb to the canyon floor.

NOTE: Pitons were cleaned with upward blows–please continue this practice so the route can go clean after a few ascents.

BI-HEDRAL I, 5.10a, 2 pitches, 165 feet (50m)

First Ascent: Kyle Copeland, Carl Diedrich, September 1989.

Location and Access: *Bi-Hedral* is across (north) from *Pillar of Bubdom* in a deep chimney with a handcrack at its back.

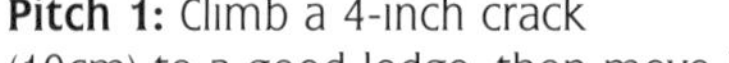

Photo: Eric Bjørnstad

Day Canyon: *Bi-Hedral*

Pitch 1: Climb a 4-inch crack (10cm) to a good ledge, then move left to belay.

Pitch 2: Climb 5.9 hands into a thin lieback into a 5.10a wide system ending up a 3-inch (7.6cm) handcrack at a ledge with rappel slings visible from below on the right wall.

Paraphernalia: One set of Friends with extra #1.5, #3.

Descent: Rappel the route.

Long Canyon

Long Canyon is the first canyon downriver from Day Canyon on Potash Road. It is approximately 4 miles (6.4km) in length and reaches east from Potash Road. The canyon contains excellent Wingate rock and has the potential for hundreds of crack climbs similar in quality to those of the *Supercrack* area of Indian Creek.

Long Canyon is easily approached by driving 15 miles south (24km) on Potash Road from U.S. 191. Turn right (west) 500 feet (305m) beyond the Jug Handle Arch viewing sign. A 2-wheel-drive vehicle will reach the approach for all climbs in the canyon (except *Sidewinder*) but to continue to the Island-in-the-Sky Mesa a 4-wheel-drive will be required a short distance beyond Maverick Buttress where a huge slab of rock fell during the winter of 1995-96. Maintenance crews have tunneled under the slab, but the road beyond is rough, steep, and narrow.

To reach Long Canyon from the top, drive 9 miles north (14.5km) of Moab and follow State Highway 313 west, then south toward Dead Horse Point. At Mile Post 6, before the road curves right, keep straight (onto a dirt road), and drive due east toward the La Sal Mountains. After 2 miles (3.2km) the dramatic fins of the Behind the Rocks area come into view. This panorama is equal to any on the Colorado Plateau and well worth the visit regardless of one's interest in Long Canyon. At the eastern edge of the Island-in-the-Sky Mesa, Pucker Pass is reached, and the road abruptly descends into Long Canyon. A 2-wheel-drive vehicle can negotiate the canyon from top to bottom, but high clearance is recommended. Climbing routes are listed upcanyon from the Potash Road. The first switchback is 2.3 miles upcanyon (3.7km), the second switchback is 2.4 miles (9.8km), the third switchback 3.1 miles (4.9km). Maverick Buttress is 3.4 miles (5.4km) from the Potash Road.

Photo: Eric Bjørnstad

Long Canyon, Jug Handle Buttress: *Generations*

Jug Handle Buttress

Jug Handle Buttress is the right (north) wall reaching from Jug Handle Arch (at the Potash Road) up Long Canyon to North Spur. Routes are listed right to left.

NOTE: Three-tenths of a mile (0.4km) up the buttress, across a dry creek bed, is a large boulder split in two with fossil fragments of an alligator-type creature that lived three hundred million years ago (twice the age of dinosaurs).

GENERATIONS (aka Porcupine Flake) I, 5.10, 1 pitch, 90 feet (27m)

First Ascent: Topher Donahue, Craig Luebben, Jimmy Dunn, Doug Snively, Doug McQueen, November 1994.

Location and Access: *Generations* climbs the left side of a leaning tower approximately 150 yards (137m) up Jug Handle Buttress from the Potash Road. Climb a squeeze chimney-to-fist to a bolt belay atop the pillar. Rappel slings are visible from below.

Paraphernalia: Friends (1) set with (3) #4; Big Bros (3) #4.

Descent: Rappel the route.

UNKNOWN RAPPEL ANCHOR Rating unknown, I, 1 pitch

First Ascent: Unknown.

Location and Access: Three crack systems right of the left end of the Jug Handle Buttress is a prominent blind arch (arch-in-the-making). An unknown anchor is above the bedding seam within the lower left side of the arch.

Paraphernalia: Unknown.

Descent: Rappel the route.

North Spur Right

North Spur Right is the right (east) side of the box canyon branching north (right) at the west end of Jug Handle Buttress approximately 0.4 mile (0.6km) up Long Canyon from the Potash Road. Routes are listed right to left as one hikes up the spur canyon.

SWEETY I, 5.11+, 1 pitch

First Ascent: Unknown.

Location and Access: On the right wall inside North Spur.

Paraphernalia: Unknown.

Descent: Rappel the route.

PEACHES I, A2, 1 pitch, 150 feet (46m)

First Ascent: Unknown.

Location and Access: *Peaches* is left of *Sweety* and climbs to a 2-bolt rappel anchor.

Paraphernalia: Unknown.

Descent: Rappel the route.

BUTT PYGMYS ON A LANDSCAPE I, 5.11, 1 pitch, 70 feet (21m)

First Ascent: Unknown

Location and Access: One crack right of *Broads Hate Pods*. Climb a widening to thin crack in a right-facing dihedral to double anchors below a prominent ceiling.

Paraphernalia: Wide to thin protection.

Descent: Rappel the route from anchors visible from the road.

BROADS HATE PODS I, 5.10, 1 pitch, 80 feet (24m)

First Ascent: Topher Donahue, Lisa Hathaway, Fall 1994.

Location and Access: *Broads Hate Pods* is one crack left of *Butt Pygmys on a Landscape*. Begin up the first crack right of the main crack system. Rappel slings are visible on the left wall above a prominent bedding seam.

Paraphernalia: One of all hand-size cams.

Descent: Rappel the route.

SHIPWRECKED I, 5.10a, 1 pitch, 85 feet (26m)

First Ascent: Kevin Chase, Eric Decaria, Cristie Wayment, 10 February 1996.

Location and Access: *Shipwrecked* is near the head of the canyon. From Long Canyon Road opposite the entrance to North Spur the route is visible right of the largest rectangular boulder (with black desert varnish) on the scree slope at the head of the canyon.

Paraphernalia: Cams 0.4 through 3.5".

Descent: Rappel the route.

TORPEDO BAY I, 5.12c, 1 pitch, 65 feet (20m), ★★★

First Ascent: Eric Decaria, Kevin Chase, Christie Wayment, 10 February 1996

Location and Access: *Torpedo Bay* climbs with fingers a splitter crack a few yards left of *Shipwrecked*. There are three cruxes above a stance (the only one) at an area where flakes of rock have broken off leaving a light-colored patch on an otherwise dark desert varnished wall.

Paraphernalia: Friends in order of ascent (1) #0.5, (2) #0.75, (3) #1, (5) #1.5; a selection of small nuts

Descent: Rappel the route.

NINA I, 5.10d, 1 pitch, 60 feet (18m), ★★★

First Ascent: Eric Decaria, Kevin Chase, Christie Wayment, 10 February 1996.

Location and Access: *Nina* is one crack left of *Torpedo Bay* and climbs a splitter crack to red painted rappel bolts.

Paraphernalia: Friend #1 through #4.

Descent: Rappel the route.

ELECTRONIC BATTLESHIP I, 5.10c, 1 pitch, 60 feet (18m), ★★★

First Ascent: Kevin Chase, Christie Wayment, Eric Decaria, 10 February 1996

Location and Access: *Electronic Battleship* ascends a splitter crack left of *Nina*.

Paraphernalia: Cams 0.4 through 4".

Descent: Rappel the route from black welded cold shuts.

North Spur Left

North Spur Left is the west side of the short box canyon. Routes are listed left to right as one hikes upcanyon.

STEWING OVER ART I, 5.12–, 1 pitch, 100 feet (30m), ★★★★

First Ascent: Stuart Ruckman, Bret Ruckman, May 1988.

Location and Access: *Stewing Over Art* appears in profile on the skyline inside North Spur Left when viewing from the Long Canyon Road. It ascends a right-facing corner, climbing past a pod to double rappel anchors. To start, either traverse right on a ledge and belay at the base of a right-facing dihedral, or climb straight up a sandy crack.

Paraphernalia: Friends (2) #0.5, (8) #0.75, (4) #1, #3.5.

Descent: Rappel the route from double-bolts.

MARCO'S ROUTE I, 5.12d, A0, 1 pitch

First Ascent: Marco Cornacchione, Bret Ruckman.

Location and Access: *Marco's Route* climbs a splitter crack to rappel chains visible below and left of a pillar on light-colored rock, 15 feet (4.6m) right of *Stewing Over Art.*

Paraphernalia: Finger-size to hand-size units with many #1.5 Friends.

Descent: Rappel the route.

RAINMAKER I, 5.9+, 1 pitch, 145 feet (44m)

First Ascent: Graham Frontella, Doug McQueen, 16 September 1995.

Location and Access: *Rainmaker* is approximately halfway up the canyon. Climb the right side of a pillar beginning with fingers, then climb a chimney up 5.8+ dirty rock to a small ledge on the left of the crack/chimney system. Continue past double-anchors, passing a semi-detached pillar on its left side. Climb hands-to-fist to armbars continuing up the right side of the landform. The crux is a little below the top at 5.9+. There are no summit anchors.

Paraphernalia: Friends (1) #4; Camalots (2) #1, (3) #2, (2) #3, (1) #4; stoppers; (2) quickdraws.

Descent: The first ascent party downclimbed the route due to lack of equipment with which to place summit anchors.

Long Canyon Right

Long Canyon Right is the north (right) side of the canyon, beginning at Deadman's Buttress (just west of North Spur) as one drives from the Potash Road. Routes are listed right to left. Some routes are referenced to a prominent hoodoo (mushroom rock) obvious on the right side of the road 1.3 miles upcanyon (2km) from the Potash Road.

Deadman's Buttress:

Deadman's Buttress is the Wingate wall on the north side of Long Canyon, beginning west of North Spur and continuing to the cottonwood trees obvious high on the scree 0.9 mile upcanyon (1.4km) from Potash Road. The first six climbs are best viewed from Long Canyon Road by a large rock on the left (south) side with faded yellow letters "TP 224" 500 feet (152m) upcanyon from the beginning of Deadman's Buttress. The last four routes are more easily seen 0.2 mile (0.3km) further up the road, or 0.8 mile (1.2km) from Potash Road. This is a location directly below a large boulder (with black varnish on top) sitting at the top edge of the Chinle cliff. Directly above the boulder (from this view) is *Program Director.* Approach Deadman's Buttress from the first break in the Chinle cliffs, near the center of the wall.

DORSEY LINE I, 5.11, 1 pitch, 100 feet (30m), ★★

First Ascent: Mike Dorsey, 1987.

Location and Access: *Dorsey Line* climbs a handcrack past offwidth pods. Begin up the first crack left of the northeast prow of Deadman's Buttress. Climb a 3-inch crack (7.6cm) leading into a chimney-size pod ("dicey to exit"). Continue with hands for 30

Long Canyon, Deadman's Buttress, left to right: *Angle Runner, Necro Dancer, Dragon's Lair, Dorsey Line*

feet (9m), then climb a gradually widening fist-to-armbars system ending at a two-piton rappel station on the left wall.

Paraphernalia: A selection of large Friends.

Descent: Rappel the route.

DRAGON'S LAIR I, 5.11, 1 pitch, 150 feet (46m), ★★

First Ascent: Craig Luebben, Greg Murphy, 15 November 1989.

Location and Access: *Dragon's Lair* is left of *Dorsey Line*, right of *Necro Dancer*. To locate, walk from *Dorsey Line* left past three arêtes, then a jagged double splitter, and finally a light-colored prow. *Dragon's Lair* is the first crack left of the prow. Climb a 4-inch crack (10cm) widening to a 7-inch (18cm) then a 10-inch crack (25cm) through two bulges. Craig Luebben: "Classic fist stacking, chicken wings, and squeeze."

Paraphernalia: Friends (1) #4; Big Bros (2) #1, (3) #2, #3, (4) #4.

Descent: Rappel the route from two fixed anchors visible from below on the left wall.

NECRO DANCER I, 5.10+, 2 pitches, 150 feet (46m)

First Ascent: Kyle Copeland, Sue Kemp, 5.10+, A2, 9 April 1987. First Free Ascent: Earl Wiggins, Katy Cassidy, Spring 1988.

Location and Access: *Necro Dancer* climbs the third crack left of *Dragon's Lair*. Begin right of a thin crack between two arêtes. The start is atop the same short pillar shared with the beginning of *Angle Runner*, 5.7.

Photo: Eric Bjørnstad

Long Canyon, Deadman's Buttress, left to right: *Unknown, Dawn of an Error, Angle Runner, Necro Dancer, Dragon's Lair*

Pitch 1: Climb 5.9 hands, then continue up a loose chimney to double piton anchors, 80 feet (24m).

Pitch 2: Climb 5.10+ hands to double anchors visible on the left wall, 70 feet (21m).

Paraphernalia: Friends (1) #1, (2) #2, (4) #2.5, #3, (2) #3.5, (1) #4; Tri-cams #1 through #7.

Descent: One 150-foot (46m) rappel down the route.

ANGLE RUNNER I, A1, 2 pitches, 155 feet (47m)

First Ascent: Kyle Copeland, Bego Gerhart, September 1989.

Location and Access: *Angle Runner* is one crack left of *Necro Dancer* and begins atop the same ledge.

Pitch 1: Climb with aid (following obvious piton scars) 115 feet (35m) up a thin crack protected with small units up to 0.75" to a hanging belay. A good pitch for practicing clean aid.

Pitch 2: Continue up less solid rock to rappel slings on the right wall, 40 feet (12m).

Paraphernalia: Friends (2) #1, #1.5, #2, (1) #2.5, #3; TCUs; a few wires; many 0.5" and ⅝" angles; 0.75"–1" pitons.

Descent: Rappel the route.

DAWN OF AN ERROR I, 5.11+, 1 pitch, 80 feet (24m), ★★★★

First Ascent: Kyle Copeland, Sue Kemp, 9 April 1987.

Location and Access: *Dawn of an Error* is three cracks left of *Angle Runner*. Climb a splitter crack to anchors on both sides of the crack.

Paraphernalia: Friends (3) #1, #1.5, (2) #2, #3, (1) #3.5.

Descent: Rappel the route from two fixed 0.5" angle pitons.

UNKNOWN Rating unknown

First Ascent: Unknown.

Location and Access: *Unknown* is three crack system left of *Dawn of an Error*. From the base of Deadman's Buttress three overhangs (low on the wall) are obvious left of *Dawn of an Error*. The route climbs the right side of the rightmost overhang, continuing through an overhang to rappel slings visible from below.

Paraphernalia: Standard desert rack.

Descent: Rappel the route.

CHALK IS CHEAP (aka Boschmania, Heronimous Bosch) I, 5.12–, 2 pitches, 175 feet (53m), ★★★★★

First Ascent: Kyle Copeland, Alison Sheets, November 1990.

Location and Access: *Chalk is Cheap* is several yards left of *Unknown*, right of the approach break in the Chinle cliff band. *Chalk is Cheap* can be identified by the seven bolts of Pitch 1, visible from below.

Pitch 1: Climb the left wall of an open book past seven bolts to a rappel chain visible from below, 5.12–, 75 feet (23m). The second bolt is right of a light-colored block sitting on a small ledge.

Pitch 2: Climb an overhanging hand-and-fist crack to a rappel station not visible from below, 5.11, 100 feet (30m).

Paraphernalia: One set of Friends with many hand-and-fist sizes; (1) set of TCUs; quickdraws.

Descent: Rappel the route.

Photo: Eric Bjørnstad

Long Canyon, Deadman's Buttress, left to right: *Chopper, Chalk is Cheap*

CHOPPER I, 5.10b/c, 2 pitches, 165 feet (50m)

First Ascent: Katy Cassidy, Earl Wiggins, Carol Petrelli, 20 March 1988.

Location and Access: *Chopper* is two cracks left of *Chalk is Cheap* and left of the break in the lower Chinle rock band. There is white aragonite on the wall left of the route. Ascend a left-facing corner. Begin on the right side and climb 5.10 to 5.10+ past a loose block/flake with two fixed anchors, then up to double rappel anchors. Kevin Chase: "The name says CHOPPER!"

Paraphernalia: Friends (1) #1, #1.5, (3) #2, #2.5, #3, (1) #3.5; (2) quickdraws.

Descent: Double-rope rappel the route.

NOTE: From the two routes which follow, cottonwood trees are in view at the left edge of Deadman's Buttress.

PROGRAM DIRECTOR I, 5.10, 2 pitches, 190 feet (58m), ★★★★★

First Ascent: Katy Cassidy, Peter Gallagher, Earl Wiggins, 24 February 1988.

Location and Access: *Program Director* is four crack systems left of *Chopper* and cannot easily be seen from the road. The route is above a large boulder at the top edge of the Chinle cliff, with a black-varnished top, and to its right a large cairn (with a stick on top). A fixed belay anchor can be seen 190 feet (58m) above the ground. Scramble up to a ledge to start the climb which can be done in one long pitch or two shorter ones. Rappel slings are visible above.

Pitch 1: A few face moves leads to the base of a straight-in crack which is followed to a belay stance, 40 feet (12m). The rock is brittle for the first few feet.

Pitch 2: Climb a straight-in handcrack in the right wall of an open book. Clean steep jamming leads 150 feet (46m) to rappel slings on the right wall.

Paraphernalia: Friends (2) #2, #2.5, (3) #3, many #3.5.

Descent: Double-rope rappel to the top of Pitch 1, then to the ground.

SHORT ROUTE Rating unknown, 1 pitch

First Ascent: Unknown.

Location and Access: *Short Route* is four crack systems left of *Program Director* and is directly above a small cairn at the edge of the Chinle cliff band. Climb a splitter crack (with flares) past an anchor to rappel slings above a prominent bedding seam.

Paraphernalia: Finger-size unites; (1) quickdraw.

Descent: Rappel the route from anchors visible from below.

Long Canyon Right, Middle Section

Long Canyon Right Middle Section is the area from the west end of Deadman's Buttress (at the cottonwood trees) to the first Long Canyon switchback.

BLOOD ON THE TRACKS I, 5.12, 1 pitch

First Ascent: Lisa Hathaway, Craig Luebben, Fall 1994.

Location and Access: *Blood on the Tracks* is right of *Gin and Tectonics*.

Paraphernalia: Standard desert rack.

Descent: Rappel the route.

GIN AND TECTONICS I, 5.11+, 3 pitches, 255 feet (78m), ★★★★★

First Ascent: Stuart Ruckman, Bret Ruckman, April 1988.

Location and Access: *Gin and Techtonics* is above the wash before the hoodoo (described in *Hot Lips p. 102*) several yards right of *Peccadillo.* At 1.2 miles (1.9km) up Long Canyon, when facing the south-facing cliff, the route is in the 10 o'clock position, and is identified as a right-facing white corner (Pitch 1) with rappel slings visible. Climb a right-facing dihedral with a prominent tower-like summit projection in the skyline. The route goes to the rim and only one wide section needs to be negotiated, a 10-foot-long (3m) squeeze chimney.

Pitch 1: Climb an overhanging corner which goes from fingers-to-hands to a 2-bolt anchor on a small ledge, 5.11, 100 feet (30m).

Pitch 2: Traverse right to a drilled angle, then climb a thin crack in a shallow corner to belay anchors below a chimney, 5.11+, 65 feet (20m).

Pitch 3: Climb a chimney, pass an overhanging handcrack, then continue up lower angled rock past jutting flakes before traversing 10 feet right (3m) to a final 10 foot long (3m) handcrack leading to rappel anchors, 90 feet (27m).

Paraphernalia: Friends (3) #1, #2, (2) #3, (1) #3.5, (1) #4; many TCUs; Big Bro #3; quickdraws.

Descent: Rappel from the top anchors 155 feet (47m) to anchors atop Pitch 1, then 100 feet (30m) to the ground.

PECCADILLO I, 5.11–, 2 pitches, 190 feet (58m), ★★★★★

First Ascent: Bret Ruckman, Gary Olsen, October 1988.

Location and Access: *Peccadillo* is several yards left of *Gin and Tectonics*. It may be identified as being approximately ten skyline projections right of The Anvil (a conspicuous protuberance in the skyline above the hoodoo described in *Hot Lips p.102*). The route climbs a splitter crack on a left wall from a chimney until the crack becomes wide. Rappel slings are visible from below.

Pitch 1: Climb 40 feet (12m) to a stance with a belay bolt, 5.9.

Pitch 2: Continue up a handcrack to a 2-bolt anchor, 5.11–, 150 feet (46m).

Paraphernalia: Two sets of Friends #2 through #3.5 with many #3.5; Camalots (1) #4. In order: Pitch 1, #3.5. Pitch 2, #3.5, #2, #3.5 (lieback flakes), #3.5 (crux at ceiling), #4 Camalot.

Descent: Two double-rope rappels down the route, 150 feet (46m) and 40 feet (12m) respectively. A short pendulum from the bottom of the first rappel is necessary to reach the single bolt anchor at the top of Pitch 1.

CHASIN' SKIRT I, 5.10, 1 pitch

First Ascent: Jeff Ofsanko, Topher Donahue, Betty sisters, 1995.

Location and Access: *Chasin' Skirt* is left of *Peccadillo*. Climb with hands up a splitter crack to blocks before traversing left and continuing up an offwidth to a thin splitter crack. Rappel anchors are in a pod.

Paraphernalia: Two sets of Friends through #5.

Descent: Double-rope rappel the route.

SHIT EATIN' GRIN I, 5.12, 2 pitches, 135 feet (41m)

First Ascent: Topher Donahue, 1995

Location and Access: *Shit Eatin' Grin* is 20 feet (6m) left of *Chasin' Skirt*, or two cracks left of a prominent sharp-cut double overhang one-third of the way up the Wingate buttress. Double rappel anchors are visible from below.

Photo: Eric Bjørnstad

Long Canyon Right, Middle Section: ***Hot Lips***

Pitch 1: Climb a hand-size crack through pods to a belay, 5.11, 75 feet (23m).

Pitch 2: Continue up a thin crack to a hand-size crack, 5.12, 60 feet (18m).

Paraphernalia: Two sets of Friends; (2) sets of TCUs.

Descent: Double-rope rappel the route.

HOT LIPS I, 5.11c, 1 pitch, 100 feet (30m)

First Ascent: Topher Donahue, Jimmy Dunn, Lisa Hathaway, December 1994.

Location and Access: *Hot Lips* is 1.5 miles upcanyon (2.4km) from the Potash Road. It may be located by driving downcanyon from the prominent hoodoo (mushroom rock) 0.1 mile (0.16km). It may also be identified by its position opposite the first band of Moenkopi Sandstone as one drives downcanyon (500 feet-152m) from the hoodoo. *Hot Lips* climbs a right-leaning splitter crack (which begins as a double splitter) with rappel slings visible from below. To approach the route go downcanyon 0.3 mile (0.4km) from the hoodoo to the first break in the Chinle cliffs. Park at a camp spot on the south. Ascend the break in the cliff break and scramble to the Wingate wall above, then traverse left (west) to the route. The crux is a bulge protected by #4 Camalots.

Paraphernalia: Friends (1) #1, (2) #1.5 through #3.5; Camalots (4) #4.

Descent: Rappel the route.

Long Canyon Right, First Switchback

Long Canyon First Switchback is 2.3 miles upcanyon (3.7km) from the Potash Road. Routes continue right to left on the right (north) wall of the canyon.

WHY DOES IT HURT WHEN I PEE I, 5.11, 1 pitch, 150 feet (46m)

First Ascent: Sonja Paspal, Dave Jones, Kyle Copeland, November 1989

Location and Access: *Why Does It Hurt When I Pee* ascends a left-facing dihedral at the far right end of the buttress viewed from the first switchback. Climb a 4-5-inch crack system (10-12.7cm) in a corner to rappel anchors visible from below. The crux is at the top of the route. Kyle Copeland: "Sustained."

Paraphernalia: Friends (1) #3.5 with many #5.

Descent: Double-rope rappel the route.

NO MORE TEARS I, 5.11–, 1 pitch, 140 feet (43m), ★★★★★

First Ascent: Bret Ruckman, Judy Ruckman, 5 May 1988.

Location and Access: *No More Tears* is approximately 200 yards (183m) left of *Peccadillo*, above the first switchback. A perfect left-facing corner is climbed with liebacks and jams, with the crux low on the route. Rappel slings are visible from below.

Paraphernalia: Friends (2-3) sets. In ascending order #1.5, #4, #2.5, #2.5, #2, #2.5.

Descent: Rappel the route.

Reptilian Wall

Reptillian Wall is the Wingate buttress north (right) of the road, across from Maverick Buttress. Approach from the second switchback 0.7 mile upcanyon (1.2km) from the first switchback), or 2.4 miles (9.8km) up Long Canyon from the Potash Road. Park at the second switchback and scramble up the obvious drainage above. Routes are listed left to right.

Photo: Eric Bjørnstad

Long Canyon Right, Reptilian Wall: ***Seventh Serpent***

SEVENTH SERPENT I, 5.11+, 1 pitch, 110 feet (34m), ★★★

First Ascent: Kyle Copeland, Dave Dawson, April 1990.

Location and Access: *Seventh Serpent* is several yards left of the top of the approach drainage to Reptilian Wall. Begin up an awkward 7-inch crack (18cm) at 5.10+ climbing, then continue up a right-angling 2.5-inch crack (6cm) which then angles left up a 2-inch-wide (5cm) ramp. Climb a 2.5-inch (6cm), then 1.5-inch system (3.8cm), and finish at hard 5.11+ at rappel anchors on the left wall of the crack system.

Paraphernalia: Friends (7) #2, (2) #3.

Descent: Rappel the route.

WEEKEND WITH A SNAKE EATER I, 5.10+, 1 pitch, 100 feet (30m)

First Ascent: Lisa Hathaway, Tony Calderone, 17 February 1996

Location and Access: *Weekend with a Snake Eater* climbs the fifth crack right of a large chimney/drainage system (in light-colored rock). This is a location directly above the parking area at the second switchback. Begin behind a large square block (right side) and ascend a "V" formation. There are three fixed pitons on the curving crack above. The route may also be identified by a prominent curving overhang.

Paraphernalia: Friends (1) #1, #1.5; Camalots (2) #0.4, (1) #0.5, #0.75; TCUs (3) #0, (3) #1, (2) #1.5; (3) quickdraws.

Descent: Rappel the route.

MYSTERY ROUTE Rating unknown

First Ascent: Unknown.

Location and Access: *Mystery Route* is approximately eight crack systems left of *Lizard Lust*. Rappel slings are visible from below.

Paraphernalia: A selection of Friends.

Descent: Rappel the route.

Photo: Eric Bjørnstad

Long Canyon Right, Reptilian Wall: *Weekend with a Snake Eater*

Long Canyon Right, Reptilian Wall, left to right: *Mystery Route, Lizard Lust, Stealth Belly, Anaconda*

LIZARD LUST I, 5.10d, 1 pitch, 80 feet (24m), ★★★

First Ascent: Dave Dawson, Linus Platt, April 1990.

Location and Access: *Lizard Lust* is the first crack left of *Stealth Belly*. Climb past a ceiling up a left-facing thin handcrack to rappel anchors visible from below on the right wall. The crux is sustained thin hands up a crack that tends to be lined with calcite dust and can be slippery.

Paraphernalia: Small to medium Friends with many #2s.

Descent: Rappel the route.

STEALTH BELLY I, 5.10a, 1 pitch, 45 feet (14m)

First Ascent: Warren Egbert, Cindy Furman, October 1996.

Location and Access: *Stealth Belly* is one crack right of *Lizard Lust*. Begin right of a pillar and climb a left-facing dihedral to its top. A rappel bolt is visible from below.

Paraphernalia: Friends (1) #1.5; Camalots (1) #2, #3.

Descent: Rappel the route.

ANACONDA I, 5.11b, 2 pitches, 150 feet (46m), ★★★★

First Ascent: Linus Platt, Dave Dawson, April 1990.

Location and Access: *Anaconda* is two cracks right of *Stealth Belly*. Climb a left-facing dihedral beginning with 5.10 thin-hands, then up a 5.9+ chimney with a bolt protecting a squeeze to a belay. Continue 5.11b thin-hands to double rappel anchors visible on the left wall.

Paraphernalia: One set of Friends with extra #1.5, #2, #2.5.

Descent: Rappel the route.

Photo: Eric Bjørnstad

Long Canyon Right, Reptilian Wall, from left to right: *Lizard Lust, Stealth Belly, Anaconda, Don Iguana, No Name, Snake Charmer, Wiggle, Hidden Door, Splitter Crack*

DON IGUANA I, 5.10c, 1 pitch, 90 feet (27m), ★★★

First Ascent: Linus Platt, Dave Dawson, April 1990

Location and Access: Ascend a hand-size splitter crack in a right-facing dihedral two cracks right of *Anaconda*. Hand-and-fist moves mark the crux. Double rappel anchors are visible on the right wall below a ceiling.

Paraphernalia: One set of Friends with extras #2.5.

Descent: Rappel the route.

NO NAME Rating unknown, I, 1 pitch

First Ascent: Topher Donahue, 16 February 1996

Location and Access: *No Name* is four cracks right of *Don Iguana*. Climb a smooth wall up a right-facing dihedral. There is one bolt low on the route.

Paraphernalia: Friends; (1) quickdraw.

Descent: Rappel the route.

SNAKE CHARMER I, 5.12, 1 pitch, 140 feet (43m), ★★★★★

First Ascent: Topher Donahue, Patience Gribble, 17 February 1996.

Location and Access: *Snake Charmer* is between *No Name* and *Wiggle*. Left of the route is a black waterstreak on a dihedral. When the route is viewed from Maverick Buttress, it is above three large light-colored talus boulders positioned in a line. Climb a smooth dark-colored wall up a "V" slot, past a fixed anchor, to a rappel station with slings visible from below. Topher Donahue: "The crux is where you find it."

Paraphernalia: Friends; (1) quickdraw.

Descent: Rappel the route.

WIGGLE I, 5.10, 1 pitches, 70 feet (21m)

First Ascent: Topher Donahue, Patience Gribble, 17 February 1996.

Location and Access: *Wiggle* is one crack right of *Snake Charmer*, or 30 feet (9m) left of *Hidden Door*, which is identified by a window high on the route. Climb thin cracks in a slot to double rappel anchors with slings visible from below.

Paraphernalia: Two sets of Friends with (5) #1; TCUs (2) sets; (1) Big Bros #4.

Descent: Rappel the route.

HIDDEN DOOR I, 5.11–, 2 pitches, 140 feet (43m), ★★★★★

First Ascent: Topher Donahue, Patience Gribble, 16 February 1996.

Location and Access: *Hidden Door* is 30 feet (9m) right of *Wiggle*.

Pitch 1: Begin up the crack system right of an obvious window high on the route. Climb 5.9 to 5.10 offwidth and belay in a chimney.

Pitch 2: Climb through the window, left over a ceiling, and up a 5.10– splitter crack on a pillar to double rappel/belay anchors above a ledge. The crux (5.11–) is up perfect hands (with nothing for the feet) at the roof reached after climbing through the window. Topher Donahue: "The window is one of the most amazing passages I have ever climbed on the desert."

Paraphernalia: Two sets of Friends with extra #2.5, #3, #3.5, #4; TCUs; (1) Big Bro #1, #3.

Descent: Double-rope rappel from the top of the pillar.

SPLITTER CRACK Rating unknown, I, 1 pitch

First Ascent: Unknown

Location and Access: *Splitter Crack* is right of a tall juniper tree, left of the right prow of Reptilian Wall. Climb a large left-facing dihedral, two large dihedrals right of *Hidden Door*. Continue through a small roof a third of the way up to a rappel anchor visible from below.

Paraphernalia: Unknown.

Descent: Rappel the route.

Sidewinder

Sidewinder is on the north side of Long Canyon 0.7 mile upcanyon (1.1km) from Maverick Buttress, or 0.1 mile upcanyon (0.16km) from the fallen boulder the road tunnels behind. This is a location where the canyon narrows to cut through the Wingate formation. The route climbs a wide crack system up a left-facing dihedral to a ledge.

SIDEWINDER I, 5.11, 1 pitch, 160 feet (49m), ★★★★

First Ascent: Craig Luebben, Thor Keiser, April 1990.

Location and Access: To approach *Sidewinder*, scramble down the dirt-bank from the road, then traverse right on a narrow ledge. Begin the climb at a prominent corner where there is a fixed belay piton at the base of the route.

Paraphernalia: Friends #2.5 through #4; Big Bro (2) #1, (4) #2, (2-3) #3, (4) #4.

Descent: Walk-off to the left.

Long Canyon Left

Climbs are listed left to right as one progresses up Long Canyon from the Potash Road.

Photo: Eric Bjørnstad

Long Canyon: *Sidewinder*

DONE-LOUBIN' (aka Open Up Wide) III, 5.11, 5 pitches, 400 feet (122m)

First Ascent: Craig Luebben, Sari Schmetterer, Pitch 1, April 1988. Craig Luebben, Jimmy Dunn, Pitches 2-5, 8 November 1994.

Location and Access: *Done-Loubin'* climbs (to the rimrock) the right side of a large pillar leaning against the prow at the southwest corner of Long Canyon, one crack right of *Mayor.* Approach from parking immediately after turning into Long Canyon off Potash Road, or take an obvious left branch (old mining road) uphill to the base of the cliff (4-wheel-drive may be necessary).

Pitch 1: Begin 5.10, then 5.11 up the right side of the pillar and belay in slings from double-anchors behind (inside) the pillar, 130 feet (40m).

Pitch 2: Climbs through a tight squeeze at 5.10 to a fixed anchor and belay from a ledge behind (inside) the pillar.

Pitch 3: Climbs 5.9 hands, then fingers at 5.10a to a belay atop the pillar.

Pitch 4: Continue with hands past a loose block, then offwidth to a belay ledge, 5.10d.

Pitch 5: Fourth class to the summit.

Paraphernalia: One set of Friends with (2-3) #3.5, (1-2) #4; Camalot (1) #4; Big Bro (1) #4, (3) #2, (4) #3, #4; (1) set of stoppers; quickdraws.

Descent: Downclimb to the top of Pitch 4, then lower from a drilled angle piton to the top of Pitch 3. Rappel 150 feet (46m) to double-rappel anchors on the left side of the pillar, and finally rappel 160 feet (49m) to the ground.

DOUBLE CRACKS I, 5.11, 1 pitch, 85 feet (26m)

First Ascent: Jimmy Dunn, Betsi McKittrick, Alf, December 1994.

Location and Access: Right of *Done-Loubin'*. Begin up a handcrack switching to the left crack before reaching rappel anchors visible from the base of the climb.

Paraphernalia: Friends #2, #2.5, #3. #3.5, #4; including units for 6" and 7" cracks.

Descent: Rappel the route with double-ropes.

NO NAME II, 5.11a, 3 pitches, 300 feet (91m)

First Ascent: Jimmy Dunn, Craig Luebben, Bob Novellino, November 1994.

Location and Access: *No Name* is right of *Double Cracks*.

Paraphernalia: Two sets of Friends; TCUs; Stoppers; Big Bro (1) #1, #2, (2) #3, #4; hexes (1)#7 through #9.

Descent: Rappel the route.

LEANING TOWER Rating unknown, I, 1 pitch

First Ascent: Unknown.

Location and Access: *Leaning Tower* climbs the left side of a large chunky tower leaning against the Wingate wall behind. Approach by traversing the wall right of *No Name*. Begin inside the tower on the right side. Climb a dihedral where dark-colored rock forms the left face of a dihedral with light rock forming the right wall. Rappel slings are visible from the road with binoculars.

Paraphernalia: Unknown.

Descent: Rappel the route.

UNKNOWN ROUTE Rating unknown, I, 1 pitch, 70 feet (21m)

First Ascent: Unknown.

Location and Access: *Unknown Route* is three crack systems right of *Leaning Tower*. Begin up a splitter crack, then continue up a right-facing dihedral of dark rock on the left, light rock on the right. Rappel slings are visible from below. The route is directly above a 4-foot high (1.2m) branching dead snag a few feet down the talus slope, and directly opposite *North Spur*.

Paraphernalia: Standard desert rack.

Descent: Rappel the route.

UNDOCUMENTED ROUTE Rating unknown, 1 pitch, 60 feet (18m)

First Ascent: Unknown.

Location and Access: *Undocumented Route* is right of *Unknown Route* and right of a green juniper on the talus slope below the wall. There is a deep broken chimney left and right of the route. Rappel anchors are above a bedding seam on the wall right of the crack system. "DAVID 5/2/92" is scratched below the route in large 2-foot-high (0.l6m) letters not visible from the road without binoculars. Begin up a blank wall and ascend a six-bolt ladder to the beginning of a splitter crack right of a prominent right-facing dihedral.

Paraphernalia: Standard desert rack; quickdraws.

Descent: Rappel the route.

DEATH BY HANDS Rating unknown, I, 1 pitch

First Ascent: Unknown.

Location and Access: *Death By Hands* comes into view from Long Canyon Road when the large cottonwood trees high on the right side of the canyon become visible. Rappel slings are visible from below.

Paraphernalia: Unknown.

Descent: Rappel the route.

SLITHER AND SCREAM I, 5.11, 1 pitch, 150 feet (46m)

First Ascent: Craig Luebben, Liza Grenard, March 1991.

Location and Access: *Slither and Scream* ascends a prominent 3-tiered corner/crack approximately 0.8 mile (1.2km) from the Potash Road. The climb may be identified by an obvious deep cut in the skyline to the left of the route. *Slither and Scream* involves an extended section of hand-stacking. Begin left of a flake and climb a 4-inch crack (10cm) as it widens to 8 inches (20cm). Pass a ledge and continue up a 7-inch crack (18cm) to a rappel ledge with double-anchors.

Paraphernalia: Friends (1) #4; Big Bros (3-4) #1, (5-6) #2, (3-4) #3, (1-2) #4.

Descent: Double-rope rappel the route.

HAND DELIVERY I, 5.11+, 1 pitch, 165 feet (50m), ★★★★★

First Ascent: Stuart Ruckman, Bret Ruckman, May 1988.

Location and Access: *Hand Delivery* is 0.8 mile upcanyon (1.2km) from Potash Road, right of *Slither and Scream*. There is a deep, long, narrow chimney from halfway up to the top of the Wingate wall. Below on the Chinle slope are two islands of cliff rock. Three crack systems right of the deep narrow chimney, on the right wall, rappel slings are visible at the top of the route. The climb begins with 5.10– stemming up a gap protected by wired nuts, then traverse into the next crack to the right when under a loose appearing block. Continue up a corner, but protecting in the crack to the left (therefore saving handsized units). Switch into the crack to the left at the last possible chance and climb 5.11+, then 5.10+ ending with 5.11– to a belay/rappel station with double-anchors.

Paraphernalia: Friends in ascending order: #3 at loose looking block. #3, #1.5, #2, #2, #2.5, #2.5, #3, #3.5; Small to medium nuts protect the beginning stem.

Descent: One 165-foot (50m) double-rope rappel from double-anchors above a ledge.

Lion's Back

Lion's Back is the south, middle wall region of Long Canyon, beyond a large recess right of Hand Delivery. The Lion's Back of scree runs from the Wingate wall to Long Canyon Road and is the approach for *Carnivore* and *Made in the Shade*.

CARNIVORE (aka Predator) I, 5.12b, 1 pitch, 60 feet (18m)

First Ascent: Jay Smith, Jo Smith, October 1991.

Location and Access: *Carnivore* is up Long Canyon above the lion's back scree formation of relatively fresh rockfall. It may be identified by a thin crack left of a deep chimney which goes to two crescent-shaped light-red overhangs. Climb a 0.75- to 1-inch crack (1.9-2.5cm) at 5.12b to a rappel station on the right wall.

Paraphernalia: TCUs (1) #0.4, #0.5, (6) #0.75, #1.

Descent: Rappel the route from cold shuts.

MADE IN THE SHADE I, 5.12, A1, 4 pitches, 260 feet (79m)

First Ascent: Mike Klein, Bob Novellino, John Rosholt, Summer 1993.

Location and Access: *Made in the Shade* is several yards right of *Carnivore*. The fifth pitch to the summit was not finished at the time of this writing.

Pitch 1: Climb a 5.8 offwidth 25 feet (7.6m) to a belay ledge.

Pitch 2: Move left on the ledge and climb 5.12 to a second belay ledge.

Pitch 3: Climb past a drilled piton, then up an offwidth at 5.11, finishing 5.10 hands at a bulge and a belay.

Pitch 4: Continue 5.9+ to a two drilled piton rappel station, 80 feet (24m).

Paraphernalia: Two sets of Friends with (3) #3.5, (1) #4; Camalot (1) #4; (1) 7" piece; (3) quickdraws.

Descent: Rappel the route.

Warrior

Warrior is a free-standing tower approximately 2 miles (3.2km) up Long Canyon. It is obvious on the left side of a prominent saddle or col on the canyon's south (left) side. From the saddle right of Warrior it is possible to look from Long Canyon down the other side to the potash mine. The gap in the Wingate buttress divides an otherwise solid barrier of sandstone into east and west flanks.

HAPPY HUNTING GROUND II, 5.12a, 3 pitches, 230 feet (70m), ★★★★★

First Ascent: Jim Olsen, Alan Hunt, 5.12–, A0, 29 October 1995. First free ascent: Steph Davis, 5.12a, Spring 1996.

Location and Access: *Happy Hunting Ground* starts on the north side of the tower and eventually turns around to the west, finally ending on the south side. Jim Olsen: "*Happy Hunting Ground* is one of the best climbs I have done in 15 years of desert climbing."

Pitch 1: Begin left of a corner on the Long Canyon side of the landform and climb in ascending order: fingers, hands, offwidth, chimney, and face, ending on a belay ledge at a white horizontal band of rock, 90 feet (27m).

Pitch 2: The 5.12a crux climbs a thin crack and a face to "rattley" fingers and thin hands, pinching back down to tight fingers, then bold face climbing. Move right around the corner and clip two bolts before reaching a bombproof belay, 110 feet (34m). Protect the stance with two #2.5 Friends. The first ascent team hung off hooks while placing the bolts of Pitch 2. Jim Olsen: "To free climb the tower one must heel hook the corner and commit to face climbing to the other side to bolts not visible until the move has been made, making for a perfect psychological drama!"

Pitch 3: Continue right to face climb the south side of the structure. Future ascents will need (1) ¾" piton for protection, 5.8, 30 feet (9m).

Paraphernalia: Friends (2) #1, (6) #1.5, (5) #2, (3) #2.5 (two of which are for the belay on Pitch 2), (2) #3, (1) #3.5, #4; Camalots (1) #4; TCUs (1) #0.4, #0.5, #0.75; Tri-cams (1) #0.5, #1; (4) quickdraws.

Descent: Rappel toward Long Canyon (north) to the top of Pitch 1, then to the ground from double anchors.

Maverick Buttress Right

Maverick Buttress is 3.4 miles (5.5km) up Long Canyon from Potash Road. The buttress is the prow of rock dividing Long Canyon into north and south branches. Long Canyon Road climbs the right branch at Maverick Buttress. Routes are listed left to right. Maverick Buttress Right routes are upcanyon above the road beyond Maverick Buttress proper. Routes are listed left to right.

NOTE: The area is a critical watering location for desert big horn sheep. Climbers are asked not to camp nearby. Be responsible!

SHOOT OUT I, 5.11, 1 pitch, 65 feet (20m)

First Ascent: Jay Smith, Jo Smith, October 1991.

Location and Access: *Shoot Out* is 100 feet (30m) right of Maverick Buttress. Climb hands passing a block on its right side and two pods. Continue up a thin crack to cold-shut anchors on the left wall.

Paraphernalia: Protection for a hands to thin/stem crack system; Friends in ascending order: #3, #0.5 (below the block), #2.5, #2, #1.5, #1; TCU (1) #0.4.

Descent: Rappel the route.

SHOW DOWN I, 5.11b, 1 pitch, 80 feet (24m)

First Ascent: Jay Smith, Jo Smith, October 1991.

Location and Access: *Show Down* is three cracks right of *Shoot Out*. Begin right of a right-facing corner. Climb past a block and an overhang. Continue up thin hands, then a finger/flare to cold-shut anchors on the left wall.

Paraphernalia: Protection for a thin crack; (2) each Friends #1 through #4; TCUs.

Descent: Rappel the route.

SHORT CRACK I, 5.11d, 1 pitch, 50 feet (15m)

First Ascent: Unknown. Second Ascent: Jay Smith, Jo Smith, 1994.

Location and Access: *Short Crack* is three cracks right of *Show Down*. Climb a splitter crack on bumpy rock with the crux at the top of the route.

Paraphernalia: Friends (2) #0.5, (1) #2.5, (3) #3.

Descent: Rappel the route.

UNKNOWN ROUTE Rating unknown, I, 1 pitch, 60 feet (18m)

First Ascent: Unknown.

Location and Access: *Unknown Route* is approximately 100 feet (30m) left of *Quarterhorse*. Climb a hand-and-finger crack to rappel slings visible from below.

Paraphernalia: Finger to handsize protection.

Descent: Rappel the route.

QUARTERHORSE I, 5.10d, 2 pitches, 80 feet (24m)

First Ascent: Mia Axon, Dougald MacDonald, Greg Davis, Rita Davis, Douglas Nethercutt, April 1990.

Location and Access: *Quarterhorse* is approximately 100 feet (30m) right of *Short Crack*.

Pitch 1: Begin up rotten rock and climb to steep hand-jamming/liebacking in a right-facing corner.

Pitch 2: Continue up a wide crack system to rappel anchors visible from below.

Paraphernalia: Protection for wide crack climbing.

Descent: Rappel the route.

EASY RIDER I, 5.10c, 1 pitch, 85 feet (26m)

First Ascent: Mia Axon, Dougald MacDonald, Greg Davis, Rita Davis, Douglas Nethercutt, April 1990.

Location and Access: *Easy Rider* is approximately 50 feet (15m) right of *Quarterhorse*. Climb a slab to an acute right-facing corner with a small roof at the top.

Paraphernalia: Unknown.

Descent: Rappel the route.

Maverick Buttress

Seven Best Routes (rated on quality of rock, most classic line, climbability at its grade, access, and safe protection):
(1) *Gunsmoke*, 5.11a splitter crack; (2) *Tequila Sunrise*, 5.10d splitter crack; (3) *Hot Toddy*, 5.10b right-facing crack system; (4) *Boothill*, 5.12b thin hands and off-fingers; (5) *Miss Kitty Likes It That Way*, 5.11d; (6) *Round-up*, 5.11a finger-to-fist splitter; (7) *Texas Two-Step*, 5.10 hand-to-fist crack.

On a more somber note, Lisa Hathaway cautions: "Beware of early spring malicious, malevolent, wo-man eating gnats!"

The routes are listed right to left.

RAWHIDE I, 5.11d, 1 pitch, 120 feet (37m), ★★★

First Ascent: Charlie Fowler, Jack Roberts, January 1987.

Location and Access: *Rawhide* climbs the right-most crack on the buttress. It is visible from the road right of *Miss Kitty Likes It That Way*. Begin up a 3.5-inch crack (8.8cm), then 3-inch (7.6cm) past a flake and a wide area. Continue past a bedding seam up a 1.5- to 2-inch crack (3.8-5cm) and on at 5.10 to rappel slings not visible from below.

Paraphernalia: Four set of Friends.

Descent: Double-rope rappel the route.

MISS KITTY LIKES IT THAT WAY I, 5.11d, 1 pitch, 80 feet (24m), ★★★★★

First Ascent: *Charlie Fowler, Jack Roberts*, January 1987.

Location and Access: *Miss Kitty Likes It That Way* is between *Gunsmoke* and *Rawhide*. The crux is a thin squeeze at the top of the route. A rappel chain is visible from below.

Paraphernalia: Two sets of Friends #1 through #2.5; TCUs (1) set.

Descent: Rappel the route.

GUNSMOKE I, 5.11a, 1 pitch, 110 feet (34m), ★★★★★

First Ascent: Charlie Fowler, Jack Roberts, January 1987.

Location and Access: *Gunsmoke* is the most perfect splitter crack on Maverick Buttress. It is one crack left of *Miss Kitty Likes It that Way*. Begin atop a large block and climb up rock right of the route's obvious crack system. Continue to rappel anchors at a bedding seam. The crux is a short section of thin moves at the top with a good rest before the commitment.

Paraphernalia: Friends (2) #0.75, (1) #1, (2) #1.5, #2, (5) #2.5, (1) #3; Camalot (1) #3.

Descent: Rappel the route with double-ropes.

GUNSMOKE DIRECT I, 5.11C, 1 pitch, 110 feet (34m)

First Ascent: Charlie Fowler, Jack Roberts, Top-rope, January 1987. First Lead: Linus Platt, 1990.

Location and Access: *Gunsmoke Direct* climbs the left side of a pillar.

Paraphernalia: A selection of Friends.

Descent: Rappel from *Gunsmoke* anchors.

BOOTHILL I, 5.12b, 1 pitch, 130 feet (40m), *****

First Ascent: Linus Platt, Jimmy Dunn, July 1991.

Location and Access: *Boothill* climbs a #2-size right-facing dihedral up thin hands to a perfect straight-in off-fingers crack up roofs and bulges to the right of *Clanton's in the Dust*. To approach, traverse left around a corner and pass through a notch in the rock. Make a dirty scramble to a fixed piton, then pull over a roof and protect with #1.5s in a splitter crack (the crux). Rappel slings are not visible from below.

Paraphernalia: Many #1.5, #2 Friends; (1) quickdraw.

Descent: Rappel the route.

CLANTON'S IN THE DUST I, 5.10+, 1 pitch, 90 feet (27m)

First Ascent: Jimmy Dunn, Jay Smith, October 1991.

Location and Access: *Clanton's in the Dust* is 10 feet (3m) left of *Boothill* on a left wall (*Boothill* is on a right wall). Climb offwidth up a right-facing dihedral. Rappel slings are visible from below.

Paraphernalia: Large pieces.

Descent: Rappel the route.

HIGH NOON I, 5.11b, 1 pitch, 40 feet (12m)

First Ascent: Unknown.

Location and Access: *High Noon* is the next crack system left of *Clanton's in the Dust*. Climb a double-crack in a right-facing dihedral to rappel slings visible from below.

Paraphernalia: One set of TCUs.

Descent: Rappel the route.

TEQUILA SUNRISE I, 5.10d, 1 pitch, 80 feet (24m), *****

First Ascent: Charlie Fowler, Jack Roberts, January 1987.

Location and Access: *Tequila Sunrise* is two cracks left of *High Noon*. Begin atop a small pillar and climb a left-angling splitter crack to rappel anchors at an offwidth section shared with *Hot Toddy*. The crux is at the start of the climb.

Paraphernalia: Friends in ascending order: (2) #1.5, (1) #2, (2) #2.5, (2) #3, (2) #3.5, (2) #4; Camalot (1) #4.

Descent: Rappel *Hot Toddy*.

NOTE: If *Tequila Sunrise* is climbed, one may top-rope *Hot Toddy*, or visa-versa.

HOT TODDY I, 5.10b, 1 pitch, 80 feet (24m), *****

First Ascent: Charlie Fowler, Jack Roberts, January 1987.

Location and Access: *Hot Toddy* is left of *Tequila Sunrise* in a large corner and climbs a right-facing crack system to rappel anchors shared with *Tequila Sunrise*.

Paraphernalia: Camalots (2) #3, (4) #3.5, (2) #4.

Descent: Rappel the route.

NOTE: The following three routes, *Texas Two-Step*, *Round-up*, and *Saddle Sores*, are all in a deep gully above a giant boulder field.

TEXAS TWO-STEP I, 5.10, 1 pitch, 70 feet (21m), ★★★★★

First Ascent: Chris Begue, Tim Begue, Kirsten Davis, Kent Wheeler, Spring 1988.

Location and Access: *Texas Two-Step* is 150 feet (46m) left of *Tequila Sunrise*, at the right side of an alcove in a left-facing corner, at a position one crack left of a prominent left-facing dihedral. Climb a hand-to-fist crack which begins in a right-facing corner then changes to a left-facing corner. Rappel slings are visible from the base of the route.

Paraphernalia: Friends #2 through #4 with extra #3, #3.5, #4.

Descent: Rappel the route.

ROUND-UP I, 5.11a, 1 pitch, 80 feet (24m), ★★★★

First Ascent: Mia Axon, Dougald MacDonald, Greg Davis, Rita Davis, Douglas Nethercutt, October 1989.

Location and Access: *Round-up* is in the alcove left of *Texas Two-Step*. It climbs a classic finger-to-fist crack splitting a smooth wall. Ascend finger-to-hands, to fist, to hands. The crux is the first 20 feet (6m) to a good handjam. Rappel slings are visible from below.

Paraphernalia: Units in ascending order: TCUs #0.75, #0.5, #0.4; Friends #1, #1.5, #2.5, #1.5, #2.5, #3, #3.5.

Descent: Rappel from a fixed hex.

SADDLE SORES I, 5.10, 1 pitch, 50 feet (15m)

First Ascent: Mia Axon, Dougald MacDonald, Greg Davis, Rita Davis, Douglas Nethercutt, April 1990.

Location and Access: *Saddle Sores* is on the left wall of the gully opposite *Round-up* and climbs perfect hands up a left-facing corner, then continues with unique hueco stemming and a squeeze chimney.

Paraphernalia: Hand-size protection.

Descent: Rappel the route.

NOTE: A plaque at the base of the route warns: "Bad Anchor."

MUSTANG MAN I, 5.11d/5.12a, 1 pitch, 70 feet (21m)

First Ascent: Galen Howell, John Lauretig, May 1994.

Location and Access: *Mustang Man* faces east and is left of a prominent gully with giant boulders. The route follows a discontinuous right crack to a left crack climbing fingers, then diagonally right to double drilled angle pitons. The crux is approximately 60 feet (18m) up the route at a point where a lieback negotiates the right side of a flake. Rappel anchors are visible from below.

Paraphernalia: Friends (2) #0.5, (4) #1, (2) #2, #2.5.

Descent: Rappel the route.

O.K. CORRAL I, 5.10b, 1 pitch, 80 feet (24m)

First Ascent: Charlie Fowler, Dan Mannix, Dr. Tom Dickey, Dr. Geoff Tabin, 1 December 1988.

Location and Access: *O.K. Corral* faces south and is right of *Doc Holliday* and 300 yards (91m) up the left canyon from *Mustang Man*. It may be identified by its position above a giant pillar leaning against the lower Wingate buttress. The route is clearly in view when one walks around the left corner from *Mustang Man* and views the south-facing wall of Long Canyon's left branch. Ascend from fingers-to-fist up the first corner left of a thin splitter (not the arête). Begin with a 5.9 lieback up a left-facing corner to 5.10b climbing. *O.K. Corral* is joined by *Doc Holliday* 70 feet (21m) up, then continues another 10 feet (3m) with 5.10a offwidth to double-rappel anchors visible from below. Rappel slings are visible from the left of the blocky pillar.

Paraphernalia: One set of Friends; Big Bro (1) #3 for the upper offwidth.

Descent: Rappel the route.

NOTE: *O.K. Corral* may be top-roped after climbing *Doc Holliday*, or visa-versa.

DOC HOLLIDAY I, 5.11a, 1 pitch, 70 feet (21m)

First Ascent: Charlie Fowler, Dan Mannix, Dr. Tom Dickey, Dr. Geoff Tabin, 1 December 1988.

Location and Access: *Doc Holliday* climbs a prominent arête using face holds left of *O.K. Corral*. Begin 5.11a and climb 5.10, then 5.11a and merge with *O.K. Corral* 70 feet (21m) up the route.

Paraphernalia: Unknown.

Descent: Rappel the route.

MYSTERY ROUTE Rating unknown

First Ascent: Mike Friedrichs.

Location and Access: *Mystery Route* is 300 yards (274m) left of the prominent leaning pillar left of *O.K. Corral* and *Doc Holliday*. *Mystery Route* climbs thin-hands up a left-facing dihedral straight-in on a left wall. Rappel slings are visible on the left wall.

Paraphernalia: Small units

Descent: Rappel the route.

Long Canyon Tower

Long Canyon Tower is above the road (left) farther up canyon from Maverick Buttress Right.

LONG CANYON TOWER Rating unknown, I, 2 pitches, 175 feet (53m)

First Ascent: Unknown

Location and Access: Long Canyon Tower is the westernmost of two prominent towers rising above Long Canyon Road west of Maverick Buttress Right.

Paraphernalia: Unknown.

Descent: Rappel slings are visible from the below.

Photo: Judy Ruckman

Brett Ruckman bouldering in Long Canyon

The late anthropologist, author, philosopher Loren Eisley asked "What is it we are a part of that we do not see?" For me, that question helps explain the meaning of the desert. I have experienced and related to the benign, empty desert. Its open spaces speak to me. In it I find time and room for intuition and insight to its beauty, and a sense of connectedness that delights and rewards me immensely.

The desert is a paradox. It is at once an experience of nurturing and discomfort, mystery and comprehension. The sounds of wind, earth, and sky fill my ears, but it is the powerful silence of the desert that tugs at my unconscious, inspires my imagination, until both the abstract and the real are perceived. . . .The sound, smell, clarity of air, and quality of light on the desert all invite my return.

David Muench, *Eternal Desert*

Photo: Lin Ottinger

The Bride

U.S. HIGHWAY 191 AND STATE HIGHWAY 313

Between Arches and Canyonlands National Parks, the Gemini Bridges area is a mesa bowed in its middle, incised by intricate canyons, and tilted just enough to drain into the Colorado River. It is rimrocked on three sides. . . . They were named by rockhound extraordinaire Lin Ottinger, who located them around 1961 on a tip from an understated cowboy. A decade went by before Lin could find them again, such were the uncertainties of backcountry travel in that day. Now, it isn't uncommon to hear of people playing hacky sack on them or wheeling across them (on a mountain bike). Before guidebooks were published and signs were erected, the Bridges were easily overlooked. One can nearly stand on top of them without appreciating the gravity (or potential of gravity) of the situation.

Todd Campbell, *Above and Beyond Slickrock*

U.S. Highway 191

U.S. Highway 191 is the artery running north/south from I-70 through Moab and Monticello (50 miles south of Moab). It gives access to State Highway 313 (Dead Horse Point State Park and Island-in-the-Sky District of Canyonlands National Park), the Gemini Bridges Trail (Little Canyon, Bride Canyon, Gooney Bird), Scenic Byway 279 (Potash Road, Wall Street, Culvert Canyon, Day Canyon, Long Canyon, Chimney Rock), Scenic Byway 128 (Colorado River Road, Castle Valley, Fisher Towers, Colorado National Monument), and south to State Highway 211 (Indian Creek and Needles District of Canyonlands National Park). Beyond, 191 connects to Monument Valley and Flagstaff Arizona.

For Cultural History, Flora and Fauna, Climate, Geology, Campgrounds, Moab Information Center, and Maps see page 7.

Powerline Crag

Powerline Crag is the maroon Cutler Formation cliff 3.3 miles (5.3km) before the junction of State Highway 313 and U.S. 191. To reach, drive 5 miles north (8km) from the Colorado River bridge (north of Moab) on U.S. 191. The crag will be obvious to the west.

FORGOTTEN FUN II, 5.10+, 4 pitches, 300 feet (92m)

First Ascent: Jimmy Dunn, Betsy McKittrick, lower pitches, August 1990. Jimmy Dunn, Betsy McKittrick, Kevin Chase to the summit, October 1994.

Location and Access: *Forgotten Fun* begins right of the obvious prow west of the highway and follows a crack systems to the summit.

Pitch 1: Climb 5.10+ to a small belay stance, 45 feet (14m). Continue past "the ear" (5.10+) to a good belay ledge. At this point it is possible to walk-off to the right.

Pitch 3: Continue at 5.10 to a belay ledge.

Pitch 4: Move right to a chimney which is climbed at 5.6.

Paraphernalia: Two set of Friends; (2) sets of TCUs. There are no bolts or fixed anchors on the climb.

Descent: Downclimb to the right of Pitch 4 ascent chimney (5.3) to where it is possible to walk-off right of the route.

Gemini Bridges Trail

Gemini Bridges Trail is designated on the Moab West map. It may be reached from the bottom at its junction with U.S. 191, or from the top of State Highway 313. To ascend from the lower entrance requires 4-wheel-drive, but 2-wheel-drive vehicles with high clearance should have no trouble descending the steep, and difficult hill encountered between State Highway 313 and U.S. 191.

The trail, especially popular with mountain bikers and 4-wheel-drivers, is the gateway to a vast region of relatively unexplored canyon country regulated by the Bureau of Land Management (BLM). There is an information kiosk at the lower entrance to the trail. For further information visit the BLM office in Moab: 82 East Dogwood Avenue, (801) 259-2196.

To reach from the bottom, drive 7.1 miles north (11.4km) from the Colorado River bridge on U.S. Highway 191 and turn west at an asphalt-paved left turn between Mile Post 135-136. This is beyond the emergence of the Denver and Rio Grande Western Railroad tracks from a 120-foot-deep (37m) trench, graded for the climb out of Moab Valley, and 1.2 miles (1.9km) before the turn onto State Highway 313. Cross the railroad tracks and continue on the dirt road which turns left onto the dirt embankment taken from the railroad grading and positioned to defer water runoff from flooding the tracks. At this left turn, continue straight on a smaller dirt road to reach the Putterman Cliffs, visible directly ahead (west). A short distance beyond the Putterman turn, the Gemini Bridges trail serpentines steeply upward toward Little Valley. Two miles (3.2km) beyond U.S 191 the trail crests, crosses a cattle guard, and descends into Little Valley Two miles (3.2km) farther is Bride Canyon, the box canyon housing The Bride, Frankenstein, and The Dowry. To reach, turn left a few feet beyond the point where the Gemini Bridges Trail comes closest to the Wingate Sandstone cliffs on the left. Three-fourths of a mile (1.2km) farther the road ends and The Bride's slender profile becomes apparent.

Aiguille du Putterman (Cliffs of Putterman)

To reach, see Gemini Bridges Trail approach. Aiguille du Putterman is the low maroon-colored Cutler Sandstone buttress in view directly west of the lower entrance to the Gemini Bridges Trail. A dirt road branches west (where the Bridges Trail makes a sharp south turn) and leads near the base of the cliff. The routes are listed left to right.

L'OFFWIDTH DU PUTTERMAN (Offwidth of Putterman) I, 5.9, 1 pitch

First Ascent: Cameron Burns, Luke Laeser, 13 November 1994.

Location and Access: *L'offwidth du Putterman* is left of *Putterman pour Tout*. Begin 5.7 up a wide crack system, past 5.8, then a 5.9 squeeze and an offwidth to 5.6 climbing to double rappel anchors.

Paraphernalia: Friends (2) #4, #5.

Descent: Rappel the route.

PUTTERMAN POUR TOUT (Putterman for All) I, 5.8, 1 pitch

First Ascent: Luke Laeser, Cameron Burns, 19 November 1994.

Location and Access: *Putterman pour Tout* is between *L'offwidth du Putterman* (left) and *Putterman en Primetemps* (right). Begin left of a horn of rock above a prominent bedding seam. Climb 5.6 up the left side of a large flaring slot. Pass a ledge on its left and continue 5.8 hands over a bulge and finally 5.7 fingers to double-rappel anchors.

Paraphernalia: One set of Friends with doubles helpful.

Descent: Rappel the route.

PUTTERMAN EN PRINTEMPS (Putterman in Spring) I, 5.10+, 1 pitch

First Ascent: Cameron Burns, Luke Laeser, 19 November 1994.

Location and Access: *Putterman en Primetemps* is right of *Putterman pour Tout*, around the right point of the buttress. Ascend a roof created by a weathered bedding seam, passing a bolt and several pockets in the rock. Continue up a 5.10a face, then climb into a 5.8 squeeze section which narrows and becomes 5.6 climbing. At the crack system's top, move right onto a 5.9 face, pass a bolt on its right and climb thin fingers, then hands 5.10+ to a single rappel bolt.

Paraphernalia: One set of Friends including #0.5 and ¾ sizes, plus (1) #5, #6 or equivalent; (2) quickdraw.

Descent: Rappel the route.

Little Valley

Little Valley is two miles (3.2km) from U.S. 191 and the lower entrance to the Gemini Bridges Trail.

ROUTE WITH A VIEW I, 5.9, 1 pitch, 100 feet (30m)

First Ascent: Kevin Chase, Lisa Hathaway, December 1995.

Location and Access: *Route with a View* faces toward the Gemini Bridges Trail (southeast) and climbs the left wall of a right-facing dihedral on the right (west) side of the trail. It is directly opposite (west) *Little Valley Private Mystery*. Climb a wide crack to rappel anchors above a large ledge. Rappel slings are visible from below.

Paraphernalia: Friends (2) #1 through #4.

Descent: Rappel the route.

CYCLOPS I, 5.10+, 1 pitch, 100 feet (30m)

First Ascent: Kevin Chase, Lisa Hathaway, December 1995.

Location and Access: *Cyclops* is on the same landform as *Route with a View*. It climbs a tower semi-detached from the Wingate wall behind it. The buttress is divided into thirds by horizontal fractures. *Cyclops* ascends to the second fracture, where rappel slings are visible on the wall to the right of the crack system. The climb faces

Photo: Eric Bjørnstad

Little Valley, *Route with a View*

Photo: Eric Bjørnstad

Little Valley, *Cyclops*

Photo: Eric Bjørnstad

Little Valley: Pinky Tower

northeast and ascends the right side up a right-facing dihedral. It may also be identified as the second crack system right of a slab/pillar formation leaning against the base of the cliff.

Paraphernalia: Friends (1) #0.5, #0.75, (2) #1 through #4.

Descent: Rappel the route.

PINKY TOWER—RING SIZER I, 5.10-, 2 pitches, 100 feet (30m)

First Ascent: Matt Laggis, Keith Reynolds, Bill Russel, 13 December 1995.

Location and Access: *Pinky Tower* is on the left (east) side of Little Valley and is designated on the Moab West map.

Pitch 1: The pitch faces northwest and climbs to the notch between Pinky Tower and the Wingate wall behind, 20 feet (6m). Begin up the left of two fracture systems climbing 5.10 big-hands to offwidth up double cracks.

Pitch 2: Walk through the notch to the east face, then face climb 5.10 past five fixed anchors around to a southwest-facing offwidth crack which is followed to the summit, 80 feet (24m). It is possible to 4th class to the notch from the opposite side of the tower and continue up Pitch 2 to the left. Long runners or double-rope technique will relieve rope drag.

Paraphernalia: Pitch 1: #3 Friends up to Big Dude 6"–8" size. Pitch 2: Friends (1) #0.75; TCUs to #4 Camalot; (5) quickdraws.

Descent: One 100-foot (30m) rappel to the ground from a soft summit rock.

EWE WHAT I, 5.10–, 1 pitch, 50 feet (15m)

First Ascent: Keith Reynolds, Peter Verchick, December 1995.

Location and Access: *Ewe What* is one crack left of *Pinky Tower.* Climb a 5.10– wide crack to the bedding seam at a level with the notch of Pinky Tower. Rappel slings are visible from below.

Paraphernalia: Friends (1) #2.5, #3, (2) #3.5, #4; Camalot (1) #4.

Descent: Rappel the route.

LITTLE VALLEY PRIVATE MYSTERY I, 5.10, 1 pitch, 60 feet (18m)

First Ascent: Unknown.

Location and Access: *Little Valley Private Mystery* is left of *Ewe What,* left of the first buttress to the east (left) as one drives south into Little Valley The route climbs a splitter crack up a very smooth wall to anchors visible from below.

Paraphernalia: Finger-size protection.

Descent: Rappel the route.

Photo: Eric Bjørnstad

Little Valley: Pinky Tower from the southeast

BENDER OVER CRACK I, 5.11a, A2, 2 pitches, 165 feet (50m)

First Ascent: Steve Mesdough, Chris Haaland, Doug Frost, 10 April 1988.

Location and Access: *Bender Over Crack* is left of *Little Valley Private Mystery.* The route ascends a prominent overlapping two-crack system on the second pinnacle of the first buttress complex on the left-hand side of Little Valley when viewing from the lower entrance to Gemini Bridges Trail. This is a point approximately 200 yards (183m) to the left of the approach road and a little beyond a deep chimney system. Some route finding will be required to locate the climb.

Pitch 1: Climb with finger jams and liebacks 60 feet (18m), 5.10, then 5.11a to A2. Continue A2 (will probably go free at 5.11+) for 20 feet (6m) to a semi-comfortable belay.

Pitch 2: Fist-jam at hard 5.10 to a platform with rotten weathered Wingate above and two fixed baby angles, 5.8+.

Paraphernalia: Two sets of Friends #1 through #4.

Descent: Rappel the route.

Photo: Eric Bjørnstad
Little Valley: *Little Canyon Private Mystery*

Bride Canyon: Frankenstein, The Bride, The Dowry

To reach Bride Canyon continue on the Gemini Bridges Trail through Little Valley. Turn left a few feet beyond the point where the trail comes close to the Wingate cliffs on the left. A short distance farther, the tall silhouette of The Bride comes into view. She is facing right and holding a bouquet of flowers.

The walls of Bride Canyon are weathered from Wingate Sandstone and are missing the usual protective Kayenta caprock. As a result of increased exposure to erosional elements, The Bride and other landforms within the canyon are rounded, and resemble weathering Navajo Sandstone rather than the usually angular Wingate. In addition, the natural cementing compounds and iron oxide coloring of the summit rock of The Bride and surrounding landforms have been leached out, causing the normally russet-colored Wingate to turn white and become very soft and friable.

Frankenstein is on the left (north) side of Bride Canyon 0.25 miles (0.4km) before The Bride is reached. The Bride is named on the Moab West map and is at the head of Bride Canyon, a short spur from Gemini Bridges Trail. The Dowry is opposite the Bride on the south side of the canyon.

FRANKENSTEIN IV, 5.9, A2+, 4 pitches, 300 feet (91m)

First Ascent: Mike Baker, solo, May 1992.

Location and Access: *Frankenstein* is a tower 0.25 miles (0.4km) before The Bride on the left (north) side of Bride Canyon.

Pitch 1: Begin on the left end of the wall facing the road. Climb mostly A2 with some 5.8 and 5.9 where the angle lessens.

Pitch 2: Continue from a belay stance up 5.8 to the base of a bolt ladder.

Pitch 3: Climb mostly A2+, with 5.9 free moves on good pockets and a wild overhang (A2+) with good protection.

Photo: Eric Bjørnstad

Bride Canyon: *Frankenstein*

Photo: Eric Bjørnstad

Bride Canyon: *The Bride, Shotgun Wedding*

Pitch 4: Climb up and right, traversing to a crack (5.8) on the main tower. Continue up blocks, then mantel the summit, 5.9.

Paraphernalia: Technical Friends (2) each through #1.5; Camalot (1) #0.5 through #3; TCUs (1) set; Tri-cams (1) set through #2.5; Stoppers (1) each #3 through #8; Angles (2) 0.5", (1) ⅝", 1"; quickdraws.

Descent: Rappel 25 feet (7.6m) to the top of Pitch 3, then rappel to 2 drilled angles 165 feet (50m) straight down, and a final rappel 110 feet (34m) to the ground.

The Bride

HONEYMOON III, 5.7, A3, 3 pitches, 300 feet (91m)

First Ascent: Fred Beckey, Eric Bjørnstad, Jim Huddock, May 1971.

Location and Access: The Bride is at the head of Bride Canyon only four miles northwest of Moab, as the raven flies.

Pitch 1: Begin approximately 150 feet (46m) left of the Bride tower. Climb an incipient crack with fixed bolts, 5.6, A1. Belay or continue to the saddle at the back side of the tower.

Pitch 2: Continue up an obvious crack system, A2, then A3 beginning on the right side of the tower and belay around the left edge.

Pitch 3: Climb A1, then (angling right) continue up loose 5.7 rock to the summit.

Paraphernalia: Friends (2) #3; (3) long pitons; many baby and regular angles; quickdraws.

Descent: Rappel 150 feet (46m) to the saddle, then 150 feet (46m) to the ground.

SHOTGUN WEDDING III, 5.11, A2, 3 pitches, 300 feet (91m)

First Ascent: Richard Harrison, Jay Smith, 1983.

Location and Access: *Shotgun Wedding* follows a crack system beginning on the left side of a detached pillar at the base of the west face.

Pitch 1: Begin up a 5.10 squeeze on the left side of a pillar at the west side of the tower. Above the pillar climb with hands a left-facing corner (5.11) past a fixed anchor, then finish 5.9 at a double-anchor belay station.

Pitch 2: Continue up the crack on the right passing two anchors and loose blocks, then climb 5.10+ ending with A2 to a belay ledge atop the Bride's flower bouquet obvious in her profile from the approach drive.

Pitch 3: Follow bolts, then turn the corner to the right and climb rotten rock to the summit.

Paraphernalia: Two sets of Friends # 0.5 through #4; hexes (1) #10, #11; (1) medium stopper; (1) 6" tube chock; quickdraws. No pitons are necessary.

Descent: Rappel *Honeymoon*.

COLD FEET II, 5.10, A3, 3 pitches, 300 feet (91m)

First Ascent: Keith Lober, Tim Hansen, Ingun Raastad, Eric Ming, 1983.

Location and Access: *Cold Feet* follows prominent cracks on the east face of the tower. All fixed anchors are drilled baby angles.

Paraphernalia: Standard desert rack; quickdraws. The first ascent party used a selection of pitons.

Descent: Rappel *Honeymoon*.

THE DOWRY II, 5.9+, A2, 2 pitches, 220 feet (67m), ★★★

First Ascent: Mike Baker, Leslie Henderson, 7 April 1992.

Location and Access: *The Dowry* is across the canyon from The Bride. Ascend a left-facing crack system. Begin up a right-facing broken area and climb to the top of a leaning pedestal, then traverse on a crackless wall up and right to a groove that continues into a vertical left-facing dihedral.

NOTE: All bolts but the first were retro-bolted by an unknown culprit. It is imperative that routes on the desert be climbed by the standard (or better) established by the first ascent party. Please be responsible, do not bastardize a route by lowering its standard.

Pitch 1: Climb 110 feet (36m) at 5.8, A2.

Pitch 2: Continue up a smooth light-colored left-facing dihedral 110 feet (36m) at 5.9+, then 5.8 to double-rappel anchors visible from below.

Photo: Eric Bjørnstad

Bride Canyon: The Dowry

Paraphernalia: Camalots for Pitch 1 #0.75, #1, #2; Camalots for Pitch 2 #0.5, #0.75, #1, (2–3) #2, #3; (4) Bugaboos; (2) knifeblades; (5) quickdraws.

Descent: Rappel the route.

Gooney Bird

Gooney Bird is named for the black-footed Albatross of the South Sea Islands and is designated on the Moab West map. It is perched at the northeast edge of Arths Pasture, which is the first valley south of Bride Canyon.

TEA PARTY III, 5.10+, 3 pitches, 250 feet (76m)

First Ascent: Keith Reynolds, Courtney Scales, Alan Stephenson, Mack Hester, John Weinberg, May 1995.

Location and Access: Begin up a right-facing corner which starts at the edge of the Gemini Bridges Trail.

Photo: Eric Bjørnstad

The Gooney Bird

Pitch 1: Climb an obvious crack at 5.10 to a belay from double-anchors (rappel slings are visible from below), 100 feet (30m).

Pitch 2: Continue up the crack at 5.10+ to a belay ledge with double-anchors at the neck of the bird, 100 feet (30m).

Pitch 3: Climb past a bolt, then traverse right to the opposite side of the tower, and continue to the summit, 5.9+, 50 feet (15m).

Paraphernalia: Two sets of Camalots through #3 with (1) #4; (2) sets of TCUs; (1) set of nuts; double-ropes; (1) quickdraw.

Descent: Rappel to the top of Pitch 2, then the top of Pitch 1, and finally to the ground.

Song of the Canyon Wren, Bull Snake, No Name

These remote climbs are near the junction of Dry Fork and Bull Canyon. To reach, continue up the Gemini Bridges Trail past the Gooney Bird, then exit Arths Pasture up a steep hill which requires 4-wheel-drive, although it can be reached with 2-wheel-drive from the upper Gemini Bridges turnoff at State 313. At a "Y" in the road, take the signed Bull Canyon south turn. Continue along the main (most used) trail, which turns right and climbs a steep, often difficult hill. At its crest, continue on the main road, not taking the spur branching to the left. A little farther a major fork appears. Follow the left branch as it descends toward Bull Canyon. Continue on the most used road (there are two smaller left branches), and eventually there is a wide intersection with a branch coming from the right. This is the wrong route (going to the bottom of Gemini Bridges). Continue straight up the left branch (Dry Fork) 0.1 mile (0.16km) to a branch joining from the right. This is the beginning of Bull Canyon. *Song of the Canyon Wren* is approximately 1.5 miles (2.4km) upcanyon. After a green livestock watering trough watch for a left branch in approximately 0.33 mile farther (0.5km). From this point *Song of the Canyon Wren* climbs the third crack system left of the right edge of the Wingate wall north (right) of the trail. Rappel slings are visible a little past the midway point up the wall. A small arch is salient on the skyline left of the route. *Bull Snake* is right and *No Name* is left of *Song of the Canyon Wren.*

SONG OF THE CANYON WREN I, 5.11a, 2 pitches, 155 feet (47m)

First Ascent: Jeff Widen, Tony Valdes, 27 November 1986. First Free Ascent: John Rosholt, 1994.

Location and Access: *Song of the Canyon Wren* is composed of Wingate Sandstone, although the walls bordering Bull Canyon on the approach do not have the protective Kayenta caprock and thus have eroded to rounded fins and gullies.

Pitch 1: Begin the climb with hands, past overhanging rock, then climb 5.10 offwidth to a belay ledge on the left wall, 75 feet (23m).

Pitch 2: Traverse right to another ledge before ascending a thin 5.11a handcrack, then fistcrack to a belay ledge with double-rappel anchors on the left wall, 80 feet (24m).

Paraphernalia: Friends (2) #2.5, #3.5, #4.

Descent: One double-rope rappel down the route.

BULL SNAKE I, 5.11a, 3 pitches, 400 feet (122m)

First Ascent: Keith Reynolds, John Rosholt, March 1994.

Location and Access: *Bull Snake* is 100 feet (30m) right of *Song of the Canyon Wren.*

Pitch 1: Climb a face/corner through roofs to a fist crack to a 2-bolt anchor, 5.10+.

Pitch 2: Continue up a corner fist crack to a second 2-bolt anchor, 5.10+.

Pitch 3: Climb the fistcrack to a pod, then exit left up a thin crack/face and traverse left to a 2-bolt anchor (the crux), 5.11a.

Paraphernalia: Standard desert rack with two sets of Friends and extra fist-size.

Descent: One double-rope rappel.

NO NAME I, 5.11a, 1 pitch, 100 feet (30m)

First Ascent: John Rosholt, 1984.

Location and Access: *No Name* is left of *Song of the Canyon Wren.* Climb a splitter crack to anchors visible from below.

Paraphernalia: Two sets of Friends.

Descent: One double-rope rappel.

State Highway 313

State Highway 313 branches west from U.S. 191, 8.3 miles (13.3km) north of the bridge over the Colorado River (at the north edge of Moab). A sign at the 313/191 junction reads "Dead Horse Point State Park, Island-in-the-Sky District of Canyonlands National Park."

Heat Wave

Heat Wave is the westmost of three Wingate buttes in view south (left) of the highway after the turn onto State 313 from U.S. 191. To approach, turn south (left) from State 313, 1.4 miles (2.2km) or two Reflector Posts before Mile Post 21, onto a dirt road and drive through a gate. Continue approximately 1 mile (1.6km) with a high-clearance vehicle until the road branches. Take the uphill (left) branch and park at the first switchback. To reach Heat Wave buttress scramble up, passing *Undertow* on its right. Take the line of least resistance through the Chinle cliff band above. A short black rope is fixed at a steep section to aid passage up an easy 5th class section. This approach arrives a little left of *The Swim*, the leftmost route on Heat Wave buttress. All routes are on a south-facing wall with rappel slings visible from below, and are listed left to right.

Photo: Eric Bjørnstad

State Highway 313, Heat Wave, from left to right: *The Swim, Pirates of the Desert, Surf This, Wave Bye-Bye, Don't Make Waves, Shark Bite*

UNDERTOW I, 5.11c, 1 pitch, 50 feet (15m), ★★★★

First Ascent: Dave Medara, John Merriam, May 1995.

Location and Access: *Undertow* is passed on the approach to *Heat Wave*. Hike directly up the Chinle slope above the parking area. Undertow is a left-facing, left-angling crack on a smooth overhanging wall at the top of a slope where an obvious dark-varnished Chinle cliff band is first encountered. The route is plaqued but there are no fixed anchors.

Paraphernalia: Friends (2) #1.5 through #3.5.

Descent: Walk-off to the right.

THE SWIM I, 5.9, 1 pitch, 70 feet (21m), ★★★

First Ascent: Dan McRoberts, Dave Medara, 12 February 1995.

Location and Access: *The Swim* is the farthest left route established on Heat Wave. Its is one crack left of *Pirates of the Desert*. Climb a right-facing corner with 5.9 hands to double-rappel anchors on the left wall. Kevin Chase: "Further progress up the dihedral is impeded by death blocks."

Paraphernalia: Friends (1) set with (2) #2, #3.

Descent: Rappel the route.

PIRATES OF THE DESERT I, 5.10a, 1 pitch, 50 feet (15m), ★★

First Ascent: Andrés Zegers (from Chile), Dave (from Denver), June 1995.

Photo: Eric Bjørnstad

State Highway 313, Heat Wave, from left to right: *Don't Make Waves, Shark Bite, Subway Mugging, Subway Murder, Summer of Love, Perfect Wave, Gumby Cracks*

Location and Access: *Pirates of the Desert* is one crack right of *The Swim* and one crack left of *Surf This*. Boulder to the crack system of the climb, then climb up a left-facing corner with perfect hands to rappel slings.

Paraphernalia: Two #1 through #3 Friends.

Descent: Rappel the route.

SURF THIS I, 5.12, 1 pitch, 140 feet (43m), ★★★

First Ascent: Dave Medara, belayed by Andrés Zegers, 1995.

Location and Access: Climb an easy chimney to a left-diagonaling splitter crack on light-colored rock. Dave Medara: "Long and demanding fingercrack with the crux at the top."

Paraphernalia: Two sets of Friends; extra small TCUs.

Descent: Double-rope rappel the route.

WAVE BYE-BYE I, 5.11d, 1 pitch, 80 feet (24m), ★★★★★

First Ascent: Jay Smith, Jo Smith, June 1995.

Location and Access: *Wave Bye-Bye* is approximately 50 feet (15m) right of *Surf This*. Begin up a right-trending arch (5.11c) and climb a steep right-angling, left-facing fingercrack up dark-varnished rock. Continue up a left-facing, then right-facing, crack with 5.11d fingers to double-rappel anchors on the left wall. The route is plaqued.

Paraphernalia: Many small cams: (1) #0.4, (1) #0.5, (5) #0.75, (2) #1; (5) quickdraws.

Descent: Descend the route from a rappel hanger.

DON'T MAKE WAVES I, 5.11d/5.12a, 1 pitch, 80 feet (24m), ★★★

First Ascent: Jay Smith, Jo Smith, Mark Baur, June 1995.

Location and Access: *Don't Make Waves* is one crack left of *Shark Bite*. Climb a right-facing, right-leaning thin handcrack to double-anchors on the left wall.

Paraphernalia: Friends (1) #0.5, (2) #0.75, #1, (3) #1.5, #2, (1) #2.5.

Descent: One rappel from double anchors.

SHARK BITE I, 5.10b, 1 pitch, 100 feet (30m), ★★★

First Ascent: Dave Medara, Dan McRoberts, 12 February 1995.

Location and Access: *Shark Bite* ascends a left-facing handcrack up steep rock. Climb 5.10 hands up a left-facing corner past a pod, 5.10b, then continue 5.9 over a bulge to double-rappel anchors. The crux is an offwidth pod visible halfway up the route.

Paraphernalia: Friends (1) #1.5, (3) #2.5, #3, (2) #3.5, #4.

Descent: Descend the route from a rappel hanger.

SUBWAY MUGGING I, 5.11c, 1 pitch, 90 feet (27m) ★★★★

First Ascent: Dave Medara, Bob Novellino, January 1995.

Location and Access: *Subway Mugging* is approximately 100 feet (30m) right of *Shark Bite*, or 30 feet (9m) left of *Subway Murder*. Climb a west face up a good splitter handcrack. Begin 5.10 hands and continue into a 5.10 lieback to a small stance. Finish up 5.11c fistjams (the crux), passing a small overhang on its right.

Paraphernalia: Standard desert rack with extra #4 Camalots.

Descent: Rappel the route from double anchors.

SUBWAY MURDER (Top-rope) I, 5.12, 1 pitch, 90 feet (27m), ★★★★

First Ascent: Dave Medara, Andrés Zegers, January 1995.

Location and Access: Top-rope from *Subway Mugging* anchors. *Subway Murder* is one crack right of *Subway Mugging*. Ascend face moves to a left-diagonal splitter handcrack which joins *Subway Mugging* just below its crux. There is a potentially dangerous block at the beginning of the route.

Paraphernalia: Top-rope.

Descent: Rappel from *Subway Mugging* double anchors.

SUMMER OF LOVE I, 5.10c, 1 pitch, 100 feet (30m), ★★★★

First Ascent: Dave Medara, Dan McRoberts, 13 January 1995.

Location and Access: *Summer of Love* is one crack right of *Subway Murder*. Begin up a boulder to a stance, then climb a steep right-facing corner (the crux) with 5.10c fist into 5.10 hands past a bulge. Finish with a lieback to double-rappel anchors.

Paraphernalia: Two sets of Friends; TCUs.

Descent: Rappel the route.

PERFECT WAVE I, 5.11a, 2 pitches, 210 feet (64m), ★★★★★

First Ascent: Dave Medara, Dan McRoberts, Pitch 1, 7 January 1995. Dave Medara, Bob Novellino, Kevin Chase, Pitch 2, 7 February 1995.

Location and Access: *Perfect Wave* is one crack right of *Summer of Love*.

Pitch 1: Begin up a left-facing corner, passing a block on its left, then climb to double anchors, 60 feet (18m).

Pitch 2: Move right to a left-facing crack, then continue up *Perfect Wave* (left-angling crack), up a steep 5.10 perfect handcrack. The pitch encounters a small overhang which is passed on its right (5.11a), then climbs 5.10 fingers to double-rappel anchors, 150 feet (46m). Dave Medara: "One of the best pitches on Heat Wave."

Paraphernalia: Standard desert rack without #4s; TCUs.

Descent: Rappel to the top of Pitch 1, then to the ground.

GUMBY CRACKS I, 5.6 to 5.9, 1 pitch, 70 feet (21m)

First Ascent: Unknown

Location and Access: *Gumby Cracks* are at the far right of Heat Wave. They are composed of several splitter cracks and may be climbed direct or top-roped.

Paraphernalia: Friends; long runners.

Descent: Walk-off.

Gnat's Landing

Gnat's Landing is on the south side of 313, west of the turn to Heat Wave, in an alcove across from Big Cave Valley

GNAT'S LANDING I, 5.8, 1 pitch, 80 feet (24m)

First Ascent: Dennis Kilker, Bego Gerhart, June 1991.

Location and Access: *Gnat's Landing* begins up a wide crack, traverses right, then continues up a wide system to double-rappel anchors.

Paraphernalia: Friends: (1) #1, #1.5, #2, (2) #2.5, #3, #3.5, (1) #4.

Descent: Rappel the route.

Photo: Eric Bjørnstad

State Highway 313: Cassidy-Wiggins-Paspal

Photo: Eric Bjørnstad

State Highway 313 East: Sunset Tower

State Highway 313 East

State Highway 313 East's two routes are along the right (north) side of 313 and are listed right to left beginning with *Cassidy-Wiggins-Paspal*, then *Sunset Tower* west from U.S. 191.

CASSIDY-WIGGINS-PASPAL I, 5.10, 2 pitches, 140 feet (43m)

First Ascent: Katy Cassidy, Earl Wiggins, Sonja Paspal, Spring 1988.

Location and Access: *Cassidy-Wiggins-Paspal* is one Reflector Post east of Mile Post 121, or 0.1 mile (0.16km) east (right) of Sunset Tower. Climb a hand-size to 5-inch (12.7cm) crack system to rappel slings visible from below 80 feet (24m). Pitch 2 continues to the summit, 60 feet (18m).

Paraphernalia: Friends #3s, #3.5s, #4s; 5" protection.

Descent: Rappel the route.

SUNSET TOWER I, 5.8 C2/C3, 2 pitches, 210 feet (64m), ★★★

First Ascent: Mike Baker, Leslie Henderson, November 1995.

Location and Access: *Sunset Tower* is left of *Cassidy-Wiggins-Paspal* 1.6 miles west (2.5km) on Highway 313 from its junction with 191 at the point where the Wingate wall on the right (north) first comes close to the roadway. Climb a steep fingercrack from bottom to top with little change in crack size.

Pitch 1: Begin 5.8, then climb C2 past a fixed piton. Continue up the left crack at C2/C3 to belay/rappel anchors visible from below, 130 feet (39m).

Pitch 2: Continue C2 past a small overhang and on at C2/C3 to a fixed anchor. It is then 5.8 to the summit, 80 feet (24m).

Paraphernalia: Two sets TCUs; Camalots (2) #0.5, #0.75, (1) #1, #2, #3; stoppers; (2) quickdraws.

Descent: Rappel the route.

Big Cave Valley: Leanie Meanie, Jag and Class Act

Big Cave Valley

Big Cave Valley is on the right (north) side of State 313, 1.7 miles west (2.7km) of U.S. 191 (left of Sunset Tower). It is named for a 100-foot-deep cave (30m) behind a large boulder at the northwest end of the valley. Routes are listed right to left.

CLASS ACT I, 5.11a, 2 pitches, 165 feet (50m) ★★★★★

First Ascent: Earl Wiggins, Katy Cassidy, Charlie Fowler, February 1987.

Location and Access: *Class Act* climbs the west face of the first landform around the corner left from Sunset Tower, and ascends a right-facing corner on the east wall of Big Cave Valley. Rappel slings are visible at the top of Pitch 1 from the highway.

Pitch 1: Climb a right-facing crack system with a 5.11a lieback, 80 feet (24m).

Pitch 2: Continue up the right-facing system with offwidth past a drilled Lost Arrow, then finish 5.10+ offwidth at rappel anchors atop a good bench, 85 feet (26m).

Paraphernalia: Pitch 1: Friends (3) #1, #2, (1) #2.5, #3; TCUs (1) #4; (1) #4 Friend for the belay; (1) quickdraw. Pitch 2: Friends (3) #4; (1) 6" Tube; Tri-cams.

Descent: Rappel the route.

LEANIE MEANIE OF THE DESERT I, 5.11, 1 pitch, 130 feet (49m)

First Ascent: Scott Cole, Jason Keith, May 1993.

Location and Access: *Leanie Meanie of the Desert* is on the left side of a large drainage gully north of (beyond) *Class Act*, and opposite a large tall boulder positioned

Photo: Eric Bjørnstad

Big Cave Valley: Leanie Meanie

at the entrance to the gully. The route becomes visible past a piñon pine at the gully's entrance. Approach from the left side of the boulder. The route faces south and ascends a right-facing right-leaning dihedral formed by the Wingate wall on the left and a leaning tower/flake system on the right. Begin with fingers and work up to hands. Rappel slings are visible from below.

Paraphernalia: Several #1.5, #2, #3, #3.5 Friends.

Descent: Rappel from a small stance at the top of the route.

JAG I, 5.10+, 1 pitch, 65 feet (20m)

First Ascent: Sonja Paspal, Katy Cassidy, Earl Wiggins.

Location and Access: *Jag* is two crack systems right of *Leanie Meanie of the Desert*. Climb the hands-wide jagged looking right side of a tower/flake formation to a good ledge with rappel slings visible from below.

Paraphernalia: Friends #3, #3.5, #4, #5.

Descent: Rappel the route from a ledge formed by the top of a tower/flake system.

BI-CLOPS—BLOW JOB I, 5.9–, 1 pitch, 100 feet (30m)

First Ascent: Jamie and Jake, 24 April 1991.

Location and Access: *Bi-Clops* is on the left (west) wall of Big Cave Valley. To reach, park beside the west edge of the valley, then hike north along a BLM closed road. The route is on the friction slab left of the big cave (hidden by a large boulder in front of it). Rappel slings and five drilled pitons are visible from below the climb.

Paraphernalia: Five quickdraws.

Descent: Rappel from the shelf at the left side of the right eye of Bi-Clops.

BI-CLOPS—BOBO I, 5.9, 1 pitch, 90 feet (27m)

First Ascent: Kyle Copeland, Mike, Sonja Paspal, 1 April 1990.

Location and Access: *BoBo* is left of *Blow Job*. Rappel slings and four pitons are visible from below.

Paraphernalia: Four quickdraws.

Descent: Rappel the route.

TODD DIDN'T MAKE LITTLE GREEN APPLES I, 5.10, 1 pitch, 65 feet (20m)

First Ascent: Kyle Copeland, Todd Gordon, April 1992.

Location and Access: *Todd Didn't Make Little Green Apples* is a few yards in from the highway on the west wall of Big Cave Valley, left of *Bi-Clops*. Begin up a chimney and climb broken rock below a desert-varnished slab with gun-shot graffiti. Continue up a thin crack on a right-facing dihedral. Climb around a wide roof, then traverse right to anchors visible from below.

Paraphernalia: Protection for a thin crack system.

Descent: Rappel the route.

State Highway 313 West

State Highway 313 West is a small area just left of Big Cave Valley (west) and right of Small Adventures Cliff.

ELVIS MEMORIAL CORNER I, 5.12c, I pitch, 80 feet (24m), ★★★★

First Ascent: Rob Slater, Jim Bodenhamer, December 1988. Second ascent: Alan Lester, January 1993.

Location and Access: *Elvis Memorial Corner* is right of a prominent right-facing dihedral forming the left side of a blind arch (arch-in-the-making).

Pitch 1: Start with stemming past five drilled baby angles (the crux) 5.12c., continue with hands to rappel anchors visible from below, 5.11b.

Paraphernalia: Two sets of Friends through #2.5, with extra #2, #2.5; (5) quickdraws.

Descent: Rappel the route.

SQUAWBERRY JAM I, A2, 1 pitch, 50 feet (15m)

First Ascent: Kyle Copeland, solo, 1987.

Location and Access: *Squawberry Jam* begins behind a squawberry bush left of *Elvis Memorial Corner* (left of the arch-in-the-making) at the left end of a small overhang formed by a bedding seam two feet (0.6m) above ground. Work up and right fifteen feet (4.5m) to a vertical crack system. One drilled piton, bolt, then another piton protect this right traverse. Continue up a splitter crack, past a bolt, a drilled angle, and three more bolts to belay anchors visible from below.

Paraphernalia: Eight quickdraws.

Descent: Rappel the route.

Small Adventures Cliff

Small Adventures Cliff is west (left) of Big Cave Valley just left of State 313 West climbs, along the same side of the highway. Jim Beyer: "Small Adventures Cliff is a bold climbing zone from a different planet." It is an area of obvious huecos (deep pockmarks in the rock). Most routes on Small Adventures Cliff require 15 long runners to tie off huecos, small wires to 4-inch cams and quickdraws.

SMALL ADVENTURE I, 5.11c S, 1 pitch ★★★★★

First Ascent: Jim Beyer, solo.

Photo: Eric Bjørnstad

State Highway 313 West: *Squawberry Jam, Elvis Memorial Corner* (arrow)

Location and Access: *Small Adventure* is right of *5.10 Warm Up*. Begin above a claret-cup cactus growing six feet (1.8m) out from the wall. Climb the hueco wall past four bolts to rappel anchors visible from below. Jim Beyer: "This is the best route in the area."

Paraphernalia: See introduction to Small Adventures Cliff.

Descent: Rappel the route.

5.10 WARM UP I, 5.10c, 1 pitch, ★★★

First Ascent: Jim Beyer, solo, January 1991.

Location and Access: *5.10 Warm Up* is between *Your Own Personal Snakefest* and *Small Adventure*. Climb past two bolts, then one piton to rappel anchors visible from below. Jim Beyer: "This is a well-protected warm-up route."

Paraphernalia: See introduction to Small Adventures Cliff.

Descent: Rappel the route.

YOUR OWN PERSONAL SNAKEFEST I, 5.11a, 1 pitch, ★★★

First Ascent: Jim Beyer, solo, January 1991.

Location and Access: *Your Own Personal Snakefest* is between *Roof Rout* and *5.10 Warm Up*. Climb past four bolts to anchors visible from below. Jim Beyer: "Scary and quality."

Photo: Eric Bjørnstad

Small Adventures Cliff, left to right: *Your Own Personal Snakefest, Warm-up, Small Adventures*

Paraphernalia: See introduction to Small Adventures Cliff.

Descent: Rappel the route.

ROOF ROUT I, 5.11 S, A0, 1 pitch

First Ascent: Jim Beyer, solo, January 1991.

Location and Access: *Roof Rout* is between *Master of Sport* and *Your Own Personal Snakefest.*

Paraphernalia: See introduction to Small Adventures Cliff.

Descent: Rappel the route.

MASTER OF SPORT I, 5.12, A0 S, 1 pitch

First Ascent: Jim Beyer, solo, January 1991.

Location and Access: *Master of Sport* is left of *Roof Rout*. Jim Beyer: "A hard loose fall zone."

Paraphernalia: See introduction to Small Adventures Cliff.

Descent: Rappel the route.

313 Slab

313 Slab is west (left) of Small Adventures Cliff. It is the location of short, quality friction routes that (with the exception of *Beach Party*) may be climbed direct or top-roped from

Photo: Eric Bjørnstad

Small Adventures Cliff, left to right: *Master of Sport, Roof Rout, Your Own Personal Snakefest*

"The Sidewalk," a shelf above the routes which is reached by 3rd class from the left edge of 313 Slab. Routes are listed right to left.

BEACH PARTY I, 5.11b, 1 pitch

First Ascent: Jim Beyer, Charlie Fowler, Spring 1991.

Location and Access: *Beach Party* climbs the lip above a right-curving blind arch (arch-in-the-making). Begin above a desert holly bush and climb past four drilled pitons to rappel slings visible from below.

Paraphernalia: Four quickdraws.

Descent: Rappel from top anchors.

SHAKE AND BAKE I, 5.11 R, 1 pitch, 85 feet (26m), ★★★★★

First Ascent: Kyle Copeland, Charlie Fowler, February 1991.

Location and Access: *Shake and Bake* is right of *Pigasus* and approximately 100 feet (30m) left of *Beach Party*, or directly below loose looking rocks on an otherwise smooth face. Begin atop a large boulder/dirt mound behind a single leaf ash tree. Climb past three drilled pitons, then angle left past a fourth piton and up to double-anchors left of the loose looking rocks. The crux is between the third and fourth anchor.

Paraphernalia: Four quickdraws.

Photo: Eric Bjørnstad

313 Slab: *Beach Party*

Descent: Rappel the route or traverse third-class to the left on "The Sidewalk" (a third-class shelf at the top of 313 Slab).

PIGASUS–THE WINGED PIG I, 5.10, 1 Pitch, 90 feet (27m)

First Ascent: Kyle Copeland, Charlie Fowler, February 1991.

Location and Access: *Pigasus–The Winged Pig* is between *Beyer Friction* and *Shake and Bake*. Begin behind a desert holly bush by a tall juniper tree and angle right. Continue past five drilled pitons to rappel slings shared with *Shake and Bake*.

Paraphernalia: Five quickdraws.

Descent: Rappel the route or traverse third-class to the left on "The Sidewalk."

BEYER FRICTION I, 5.9–, 1 pitch, 85 feet (26m)

First Ascent: Jim Beyer, Solo, Spring 1991.

Location and Access: *Beyer Friction* is 20 feet (6m) left of *Pigasus*. Begin behind a juniper tree on the left and a single leaf ash on the right. Climb up and right past three drilled pitons visible from below.

Paraphernalia: Three quickdraws.

Descent: Traverse third-class to the left on "The Sidewalk."

UNKNOWN I, 1 pitch, Rating unknown

First Ascent: Unknown.

Location and Access: *Unknown* is 15 feet (4.5m) left of *Beyer Friction*. Begin right of a juniper tree. Climb past a small alcove on the right of the route.

Paraphernalia: One quickdraw.

Descent: Traverse third-class to the left on "The Sidewalk."

OLD KOR ROUTE—OF-KORS I, 5.6, 1 pitch

First Ascent: Layton Kor, circa 1960.

Location and Access: *Of-Kors* is left of *Beyer Friction*. Begin right of a large juniper tree and climb past one fixed anchor to "The Sidewalk."

Paraphernalia: Quickdraws.

Descent: Traverse third-class to the left on "the sidewalk."

NOTE: There are numerous low-angle route possibilities left of *Old Kor Route*.

Putterman's Frisbee

Putterman's Frisbee is the prominent hoodoo high on the north side of the highway before the first switchback west of 313 Slab. The exposed hoodoo is best viewed from the top of the first switchback 6.5 miles (10km) from the junction of U.S. 191 and State Highway 313.

PUTTERMAN'S FRISBEE I, A1, 1 pitch, 50 feet (15m)

First Ascent: Cameron Burns with Paul Fehlan as rope anchor, 18 January 1990.

Location and Access: The tower was climbed by throwing a rope over it and prussiking to the top.

Paraphernalia: Rope; ascenders.

Descent: Rappel the route.

The trickiest moves on any climb are the mental ones, the psychological gymnastics that keep terror in check.

Jon Krakauer, *Outside Magazine*

The days of wandering alone in a lonesome land and calling topographical features what you please are gone . . . . I am not eager to splash names around the remaining few wild canyons, but once in a while a name helps a person find his way.

Kent Frost, *My Canyonlands*, 1971

Photo: Doug Cochran

Jeff Widen on Pitch 2 of *Echo Pinnacle*, Courthouse Pasture.

TUSHER CANYON, COURTHOUSE PASTURE AREA

Dehydration: the desert air sucks moisture from every pore. I take a drink from the canvas water-bag dangling near my head, the water cooled by evaporation. Noontime here is like a drug. The light is psychedelic, the dry electric air narcotic. To me the desert is stimulating, exciting, exacting; I feel no temptation to sleep or to relax into occult dreams but rather an opposite effect which sharpens and heightens vision, touch, hearing, taste, and smell. Each stone, each plant, each grain of sand exists in and for itself with a clarity that is undimmed by any suggestion of a different realm. Claritas, integritas, veritas. Only the sunlight holds things together. Noon is the crucial hour; the desert reveals itself nakedly and cruelly, with no meaning but its own existence.

Edward Abbey, *Desert Solitaire*

Tusher Canyon and Courthouse Pasture are adjacent areas approximately 10 air miles north-northwest (16km) of Moab, and may be reached with a 4-wheel-drive vehicle, mountain bike, or long hike. The landforms are composed of Entrada Sandstone, the same rock as most of the climbs in Arches National Park. They are identified on the Moab West map.

Tusher Canyon

To reach Tusher Canyon (from Moab), gateway to Courthouse Pasture, drive 13.5 miles north (22km) of the bridge over the Colorado River and turn west onto Mill Canyon Road, a dirt track north of Mile Post 141, approximately 4.5 miles north (7km) of State Highway 313. Cross the Denver and Rio Grande Western Railroad tracks, which are used only to haul potash from the plant 16 miles downriver (26km) from Moab. Approximately 0.6 mile (1km) from U.S. 191 a sign reads "Mill Canyon" (with an arrow indicating straight ahead) and "Tusher Canyon" (arrow to the right). Approximately 2.5 miles (4km) from State Highway 191 a sandy drainage is entered. Not far beyond, a 4-wheel-drive vehicle will be necessary. One-tenth of a mile (0.16km) farther there is a "T" in the road and a sign reading "Monitor and Merrimac Jeep Trail" (arrow pointing to the left), 4.6 miles (7.4km) from the turnoff at U.S. 191. This is the entrance to Tusher Canyon and the point from which mileage to the climbs in the canyon is measured, as well as distances to Courthouse Pasture. There are two projections from the south wall of Tusher Canyon. The first, a butte, is House of Putterman, and beyond (west) is Storm in Heaven.

House of Putterman, Storm in Heaven

House of Putterman is a butte with a tower formation at its top center, 0.5 mile (0.8km) into Tusher Canyon from the "T" with the "Monitor and Merrimac Jeep Trail" sign.

Storm In Heaven is 1 mile (1.8km) from the "T." Take left branches, keeping toward the south wall and park at the end of the road on a flat bench covered with white agate (chalcedony). If right branches are taken, the trail continues to the head of the canyon beyond the climb.

WALDEN'S ROOM II, 5.10c/d, 4 pitches, 230 feet (70m), ★★★★★

First Ascent: Cameron Burns, Brian Takei, 22 October 1994. First free ascent: Jon Butler, Cameron Burns, 22 October 1995.

Location and Access: *Walden's Room* climbs the east side of the obvious butte projecting from the south wall of Tusher Canyon.

Pitch 1: Begin up the left side of a large flake and climb 5.7, then 5.9+ hands to a ledge.

Pitch 2: Move right on the ledge to the center of a flake. Stem at 5.6 and continue up a 5.8 offwidth past a stance, then past a fixed piton. Make a "weird" mantle (5.9) and belay from easier ground.

Pitch 3: Continue up and right (2nd class), then 1st class to a 0.25" (0.6cm) crack near the center of the butte's tower.

Pitch 4: Climb past a second fixed piton and continue with fingers (5.10c/d, the crux), then 5.8 past two more fixed pitons to summit rappel anchors.

Photo: Cameron Burns

Tusher Canyon: House of Putterman, east face.

Paraphernalia: Friends #2.5, #3, #4; (1) offwidth piece (#7 Friend); (4) quickdraws.

Descent: Two double-rope rappels, one to the top of Pitch 2, the second to the ground.

STORM IN HEAVEN II, 5.8, A3, 3 pitches, 350 feet (107m), ★★★★★

First Ascent: Tom Sherman, Jim Angione, 3 April (Easter) 1994.

Location and Access: *Storm in Heaven* climbs a large right-facing dihedral above the parking area. The first ascent party climbed with aid, but suggests the route will go free with a variation to Pitch 3.

Pitch 1: Begin right of a huge boulder at the base of the wall. Climb a V-crack (formed by the dihedral and right wall) to a hanging belay below a loose looking block (potentially dangerous).

Pitch 2: Continue up the V-crack to a large ledge, passing the loose looking block on its right.

Pitch 3: Traverse left and continue up an arête past a large roof to the bench above. There are two fixed pitons on the right wall above the loose looking block before the ledge, but they are difficult to see from below without binoculars or a spotting scope.

Paraphernalia: Friends (1) set; (2) quickdraws.

Descent: Walk left (east) until it is possible to descend a talus cone to the canyon floor.

Photo: Eric Bjørnstad

Tusher Canyon: *Putterman's Outhouse* (arrow) **and *Puttterman's Pinkies.***

Putterman's Outhouse, Putterman's Pinkies

PUTTERMAN'S OUTHOUSE I, 5.10, A1, 1 pitch, 60 feet (18m)

First Ascent: Cameron Burns, Luke Laeser, 30 October 1994.

Location and Access: *Putterman's Outhouse* is a small tower to the right, 0.5 mile (0.8km) down the Monitor and Merrimac Jeep Trail (east) of the "T" in Tusher Canyon, before the east end of the canyon opens onto Courthouse Pasture (near Echo Pinnacle and Aeolian Tower). The route ascends the southeast side of the landform. Begin 5.5 and climb through 5.10, then A1 to a fifth-class, right-leaning ramp. Continue A1 up a 0.5-inch (1.2cm) crack to a mantel and a stance above it. Pass a hole, then surmount the caprock, passing a second hole and a fixed bolt. Continue, angling right to the summit.

Paraphernalia: Camalots (1)#3; large stoppers; (1) ⅜" bolt hanger may be needed; (3) ⅝" angle, (1) 1" angle; (15) carabiners; (1) quickdraw; long webbing for the rappel.

Descent: Rappel with one rope from a sling around the summit block.

PUTTERMAN'S PINKIES I, 5.10a, 1 pitch, 70 feet (21m), ★★★★★

First Ascent: Luke Laeser, Cameron Burns, Mel Macdonell, Ann Robertson, 30 October 1994.

Location and Access: *Putterman's Pinkies* is uphill to the right and behind *Putterman's Outhouse*. The route faces west and ascends a classic handcrack in a V-formation. Climb a clean lieback crack to a rappel ledge with slings visible from below. Begin 5.8 and continue 5.9, and finally 5.10a.

Paraphernalia: Friends (2) #0.5 through #2.5.

Descent: Rappel the route.

Courthouse Pasture

Courthouse Pasture is reached from the east end of Tusher Canyon 1.5 miles (2.4km) from the "T" where a sign reads: "Monitor and Merrimac Jeep Trail," 6.1 miles (9.8km) from the junction of Mill Canyon Road and State Highway 191.

Hashishabrum Tower, Run of the Mill

Hashishabrum Tower is north of Echo Pinnacle near the nebulous point where the south end of Mill Canyon becomes the north edge of Courthouse Pasture. Pass through the cattle gate at the entrance to Courthouse Pasture (from Tusher Canyon). The tower is obvious beside the rimrock wall to the north (left). *Run of the Mill* is approximately 1 mile north-northeast (1.6km) of the entrance to Courthouse Pasture from Tusher Canyon. To reach, hike an old road up Courthouse Pasture going north to Mill Canyon, then east to the prow of an unnamed buttress.

HASHISHABRUM TOWER II, 5.7, A2, 3 pitches, 160 feet (49m)

First Ascent: Cameron Burns, Luke Laeser, Jon Butler, 21 January 1995.

Location and Access: Begins on the northwest side of the tower.

Pitch 1: Climb 5.7, then continue A2 to A1 ending at a prominent ledge.

Pitch 2: Traverse 1st class through a window to the south side of the tower.

Pitch 3: Begin A1 and finish up a 5.5 chimney to the summit.

Paraphernalia: Two sets of Friends #1 through #5 (or equivalent); (5) Lost Arrows; (2) baby angles; (2) knifeblades.

Descent: One rope rappel down the south face.

RUN OF THE MILL (aka Mill Levy) II, 5.11, 3 pitches, 230 feet (70m)

First Ascent: Katy Cassity, Earl Wiggins, Dan Mannix, 1 December 1987.

Location and Access: *Run of the Mill* ascends an obvious line right of the prow of the unnamed buttress.

Pitch 1: Begin up a left-facing corner at 5.11 and climb 5.10 offwidth to a nut belay.

Pitch 2: Climb 5.10+ hands to a belay from double-anchors 155 feet (47m) above ground.

Pitch 3: Continue up an unprotectable offwidth, then 5.10 squeeze to double belay/rappel anchors, 75 feet (23m).

Paraphernalia: Friends (1) #0.75, (2) #1, #1.5, #2, #3, (1) #3.5, (2) #4; Tube Chock 3", 4", 5"; large stoppers.

Descent: Rappel the route.

Photo: Jeff Widen

Courthouse Pasture, Echo Pinnacle

Echo Pinnacle

Echo Pinnacle (and Aeolian Tower) is designated on the Moab West map, and also labeled "Determination Towers," the name given on the USGS map. Locally they are known as Airport Towers, being in view from U.S. 191 a short distance south of the Moab Airport. Echo is the first (northernmost) landform south as one enters Courthouse Pasture from Tusher Canyon. Aeolian Tower is the smaller landform south of Echo Pinnacle.

EAST FACE III, 5.7, A2, 2 pitches, 270 feet (82m)

First Ascent: Rick Horn, John Horn, Pete Carmen, April 1967.

Location and Access: Begin near the southeast corner of the tower and ascend a crack system to a ledge where the lower Dewey Bridge formation meets the upper Slickrock member of Entrada Sandstone. Traverse right (north) to a tower-like structure and belay. The second pitch climbs the chimney to the top of the tower and continues to the summit on aid up cracks protected with bolts.

Paraphernalia: Standard desert rack.

Descent: Two double-rope rappels down the west side of the tower, beginning near the southwest end of the summit.

WINDOW ROUTE III, 5.10+, A2, 3 pitches, 270 feet (82m)

First Ascent: Eric Bjørnstad, Ken Wyrick, Terry McKenna, 1974.

Location and Access: *Window Route* is unique in that it climbs the east face of the tower, traverses through a natural tunnel to finish up the west face. Begin up the Dewey Bridge member of Entrada and climb to the obvious 5-foot-high (1.5m) window, 5.7, A2, 120 feet (37m). The window is eroded at the bedding seam between the Dewey Bridge and Slickrock members of Entrada. Walk through the window to the west side of the tower. Continue 70 feet (21m) at 5.10+ with thin hands in a corner, then belay from slings (#10 Hex). The summit pitch climbs 60 feet (18m) at 5.10 up a squeeze chimney, then third class to the highest point. Airy views through the split in the tower makes the climb memorable.

Paraphernalia: Friends (1) #1, (3) #2, (2) #2.5, (3) #3, (2) #4; (1) #10 Hex; medium to large stoppers.

Descent: Two double-rope rappels from the southwest end of the tower, the first 130 feet (40m) free to the south end of a ledge level with the window, the final rappel is 120 feet (37m) to the ground.

WINDOW ROUTE FREE VARIATION III, 5.10+, 3 pitches, 270 feet (82m)

First Ascent: Unknown.

Location and Access: The *Free Variation* allows a free ascent of *Window Route* by climbing Pitch 1 (5.9) to the window from the west rather than east, then join Pitch 2 (5.10+) of the original route.

Paraphernalia: Standard desert rack.

Descent: Same as *Window Route*.

NO REPLY III, 5.9, A2+, 4 pitches, 270 feet (82m), ★★★★

First Ascent: Mike Baker, Leslie Henderson, April 1992.

Location and Access: *No Reply* climbs the far right side of the west face. No pitons or hammer are necessary after Pitch 1. Mike Baker: "The route may go free at 5.11/5.12. Good rock."

Pitch 1: Begin 5.8 and continue A2 to A2+. An expanding flake to the right is off-route. Pass a fixed piton and climb to a belay ledge at the bedding seam, 100 (30m).

Pitch 2: Climb A2, then behind a flake at 5.9, passing two fixed pitons. Belay atop the flake, 40 feet (12m).

Pitch 3: Climb a 2–3" (5-7.6cm) crack A2. Pass an A2 roof and reach a belay stance, 100 feet (30m).

Pitch 4: Continue A2 up a 3" (7.6cm) then 4" (10cm) crack to the top, 30 feet (9m).

Paraphernalia: One set of technical Friends; Camalots (2) #0.5 through #3 plus (1) #4; Tri-cams (2) #0.5; (1) medium long Lost Arrow; (2) 0.5" angles; (1) ⅝" angle, (2) ¾" angles; (3) quickdraws.

Descent: Same as *Window Route*.

Aeolian Tower

Aeolian Tower is the smaller tower south of Echo Pinnacle. See Echo Pinnacle page 149.

SOUTHWEST CORNER III, 5.9, A3+, 2 pitches, 295 feet (90m)

First Ascent: Peter Gallagher, Peter Williams, 1980.

Location and Access: *Southwest Corner* follows grooves up rotten rock on the southwest corner to a ledge. Pitch 2 traverses east and ascends the first crack to the summit.

Paraphernalia: Standard desert rack.

Descent: Two double-rope rappels from the south end of the tower.

LAWNCHAIR LIZARD III, 5.8, A3, 3 pitches, 295 feet (90m)

First Ascent: Art Wiggins, Earl Wiggins, Katy Cassidy, 10 April 1988.

Location and Access: *Lawnchair Lizard* was the second ascent of Aeolian Tower. Climb the north ridge diagonally up and right to a belay, then up a straight-in crack which splits the caprock.

Pitch 1: Begin up an A1 seam, then climb 5.8 up a left-facing corner to a belay ledge at the bedding seam between the lower Dewey Bridge and upper Slickrock member of Entrada Sandstone, 140 feet (43m).

Pitch 2: Ascend a right-leaning thin crack to the south shoulder of the tower, A3, 120 feet (37m).

Pitch 3: Continue right to the highest point, 5.8, 35 feet (11m).

Paraphernalia: Three sets of Friends; many Lost Arrows; baby angles and ¾" angles.

Descent: Two double-rope rappels off the south end of the tower.

PROJECT Rating unknown, I, 1 pitch, 140 feet (34m)

First Ascent: Unknown.

Location and Access: *Project* is an unfinished aid line climbing past seven bolts and ending at an overhanging knifeblade crack 50 feet (15m) left of *Howling Winge*.

Paraphernalia: Seven quickdraws.

Descent: Rappel the route with a double-rope.

HOWLING WINGE III, 5.8, A3+, 5 pitches, 395 feet (90m)

First Ascent: Dave Goldstein, Dougald MacDonald, March 1995.

Location and Access: This first ascent of the east face of Aeolian Tower climbs a zig-zagging line beginning near the right side of the tower. Dougald MacDonald: "Desperate drilling in Dewey Bridge stone inspired us to place only three (poor) bolts in 5 pitches. The first pitch took 7.5 hours to climb, with the summit reached after three long days of marginal aid."

Pitch 1: Climb with hard aid past a bolt to a belay stance and a second poor bolt, 70 feet (21m).

Pitch 2: Angle up and left at A2 to a ledge and a poor bolt, using a RURP, Pecker, and angles with good Friends and wires, 70 feet (21m) from the ground.

Pitch 3: Continue past an overhang and angle right up "The Real Thing," a very overhanging crack using Peckers and knifeblades. Pass a pod and climb 5.8 to a belay stance.

Pitch 4: Traverse A1, then 5.8 left to a belay at a crack system (no fixed anchors).

Pitch 5: Climb a right-angling crack, passing an overhang on its left, then continue angling right up a rotten face to the top, A3+.

Paraphernalia: Friends; wires; RURPs; Peckers; knifeblades; angle pitons; selection of large units; (3) quickdraws.

Descent: Same as *Southwest Corner*.

Monitor and Merrimac Buttes

The Monitor and Merrimac Buttes, named for the iron-clad Civil War battleships, are in view approximately 20 miles south (32km) from I-70 (in the area of Ranch Exit 173) between Green River and Crescent Junction. The two massive landforms are in reality mesas, for a true butte is taller than it is broad, but the word butte has become a widely used catch-all term for small mesas with vertical sides. The Monitor and Merrimac are also in prominent view from many points along U.S. 191 as it descends south to Moab from the Interstate, and they are a commanding sight from State Highway 313 (gateway to Dead Horse Point State Park and Island-in-the-Sky District of Canyonlands National Park). They are named on the Moab West map.

To reach, approach as for Courthouse Pasture; the buttes are positioned at its southern end. At the entrance to Tusher Canyon there is a "T" in the road and a sign reading "Monitor and Merrimac Jeep Trail" (with a arrow pointing to the left). The junction of Tusher Canyon and Courthouse Pasture is 1.5 miles (2.4km) down this dirt track where a wire fence and cattle gate are encountered. Please leave it open or closed as found. One mile (1.6km) farther is a "Y." Keep left. Two-tenths of a mile (0.32km) beyond is a symbol sign on a brown fiberglass post (carsonite) with a jeep, ATV, and motorcycle. One-tenth mile (0.16) farther is a symbol sign of a mountain bike. Go straight (not right). Three-tenths mile (0.48km) farther is a "Y." Keep right. Approximately 1 mile (1.6km) beyond is a 4-way junction with a sign facing west (away from your approach) reading "Monitor and Merrimac Jeep Trail" with an arrow to the left and "Spur to Buttes" with an arrow to the right. This is approximately 2.6 miles (4km) from the cattle gate at the juncture of Tusher Canyon and Courthouse Pasture. From this location, the right turn ends in 0.6 mile (0.95km) at Wipe Out Hill, a popular 4-wheel machismo exercise during the Moab Easter week jeep safari. Go straight (the Spur to Buttes Road). The trail follows along the east face of the Merrimac Butte, with the smaller Monitor Butte in view straight ahead (south). Approximately 0.3 mile (0.48km) from the 4-way intersection make a sharp right up onto the Navajo Sandstone bed occupied by the two buttes. Three-tenths of a mile (0.48km) farther one will be opposite the northeast corner of Merrimac, and *Hyper-crack on the Anchor Chain* will be obvious. Three-tenths of a mile (0.48km) farther is the col between the two buttes and the south edge of Courthouse Pasture. This is the approach for routes on Monitor. South facing routes on Merrimac may be reached by continuing to drive west along its southern edge.

Merrimac Butte

Routes are listed right to left beginning on the east buttress, then south and finally west buttress.

Photo: Eric Bjørnstad

Merrimac Butte, east face, from left to right: ***Without a Net, Merrymaker, Hyper-Crack on the Anchor Chain.***

HYPER-CRACK ON THE ANCHOR CHAIN II, 5.11, 2 pitches, 200 feet (61m)

First Ascent: Jimmy Dunn, John Bouchard, Eric Bjørnstad, Lin Ottinger, with Jeff Widen working on Pitch 1, 22 September 1985.

Location and Access: Ascend the northeast corner of the butte.

Pitch 1: Four anchors protect the first lead, which climbs an overhanging lieback before switching to an overhanging jamcrack ending at 2-bolt and one drilled angle belay station where the rock begins to lean back a few degrees, 5.11.

Pitch 2: Begin with a 40-foot (12m) offwidth (strenuous 5.11) protected by two drilled angles. The lead continues another 80 feet (24m) up a tight chimney leading to the summit.

Paraphernalia: Large and extra large Friends and Tri-cams. The beginning of Pitch 1 is protected with a standard selection of stoppers; quickdraws.

Descent: Two double-rope rappels down *Merrymaker.*

MERRYMAKER II, A3, 2 pitches, 200 feet (61m)

First Ascent: Ron Olevsky, Dave Mondeau, Dan McGee, May 1986.

Location and Access: *Merrymaker* climbs the first crack system left of *Hyper-Crack on the Anchor Chain.*

Paraphernalia: Many angles and thin pitons.

Descent: Rappel to the ledge at the top of Pitch 1, then to the ground with two 165-foot (50m) ropes.

WITHOUT A NET II, 5.8, 4 pitches, 200 feet (61m), ★★★★★

First Ascent: Charlie Fowler, Sue Wint, April 1991.

Location and Access: *Without a Net* is left of *Merrymaker* and right of *Stand and Deliver*.

Pitch 1: Begin on the right side of a large leaning round pillar (Paddle Wheel) and climb 5.6 offwidth to a belay stance.

Pitch 2: Continue diagonally up and left belaying behind Paddle Wheel, 5.8.

Pitch 3: Continue 5.8 behind Paddle Wheel.

Pitch 4: Angle right to the top. Charlie Fowler: "The route is a classic offwidth chimney."

Paraphernalia: Friends #1 through #3 for belays; (1) set of stoppers.

Descent: Two double-rope rappels down *Merrymaker*.

STAND AND DELIVER II, 5.11, A0, 2 pitches, 200 feet (61m)

First Ascent: Katy Cassidy, George Hurley, Earl Wiggins, 27 March 1988.

Location and Access: *Stand and Deliver* ascends a right-facing flake/crack system in the middle of the east face. This is the first crack left of the rounded pillar Paddle Wheel dominating the wall along the approach trail. Earl Wiggins: "The route will go free in the future. The first ascent team pulled on a couple of Big Bros at the beginning of the second pitch to clear the lip of the roof." Rappel slings are visible from below.

Photo: Eric Bjørnstad

Merrimac Butte, from left to right: *Prow, U-Slot, Stand and Deliver.*

Pitch 1: Climb overhanging thin hands for 40 feet (12m), then a short offwidth to a steep thin flake. Proceed to a fixed drilled piton, then do a tricky face traverse left a few feet to a 4-inch crack (10cm) leading to a belay under a roof, 5.11, 150 feet (46m).

Pitch 2: Climb a wide crack (6-inch, 15cm) to the top, 5.10, A0, 50 feet (15m).

Paraphernalia: Two sets of Friends with extra #3, #3.5, #4; Big Bros (2) #1, #2, #3; (1) quickdraw.

Descent: Rappel the route or *Merrymaker*.

U-SLOT Rating unknown

First Ascent: Unknown.

Location and Access: *U-Slot* is left of *Stand and Deliver* at the south end of the east face. Rappel slings are visible at the top of Pitch 1.

Paraphernalia: Unknown.

Descent: Rappel the route.

PROW II, 5.10, 2 pitches, 240 feet (73m)

First Ascent: Earl Wiggins, Katy Cassidy, 1991.

Location and Access: *Prow* is one crack left of *U-Slot*. Rappel slings are visible at the top of Pitch 1

Paraphernalia: Standard desert rack.

Descent: Rappel the route.

Photo: Eric Bjørnstad

Merrimac Butte, *Albatross*

ALBATROSS I, 5.11c, 2 pitches, 240 feet (73m), ★★★★

First Ascent: Stuart Ruckman, Bret Ruckman, 23 May 1991.

Location and Access: *Albatross* is 200 feet (61m) left of the butte's southeast prow on a west-facing wall, and begins 30 feet (9m) right of a rappel point. The right side of the south face is west-facing (Pitch 1 is west-facing and Pitch 2 south-facing).

Pitch 1: Begin right of a broken corner in a 2.5-inch crack (6.3cm) which curves left and narrows first to 2-inches (5cm), then 1.5-inches (3.8cm). The crux is at the end of the pitch, before the belay ledge.

Pitch 2: Climb a chimney protected by gear placed in a thin crack to its right. Continue past a chockstone protected with a #1.5 Friend, then make a 5.9 grunt past an overhang and up to a ledge. Move left for the rappel.

Paraphernalia: Friends (1)#1, (4) #1.5, (5) #2, (4) #2.5, (1) #3. Pitch 1 is protected with Friends in the following order: #2.5, #2.5, #2, #1.5, #1.

Descent: Rappel 140 feet (43m) from a ledge below the top and to the left of the route, to a ledge with double anchors, then 100 feet (30m) to the ground.

WHEELCHAIR RAMP Rating unknown

First Ascent: Peter Gallagher and party.

Location and Access: *Wheelchair Ramp* climbs an obvious right-to-left diagonal ramp on the south face of the butte.

Paraphernalia: Unknown.

Descent: Rappel *Merrymaker*.

KEEL HAULING II, 5.9, 3 pitches, 360 feet (110m)

First Ascent: Katy Cassidy, Peter Gallagher, Earl Wiggins, 25 February 1988.

Location and Access: *Keel Hauling* ascends a left-leaning crack system on the south face, left of *Wheelchair Ramp*.

Pitch 1: Climb a 5" crack (13cm) in a corner, up and left for 55 feet (17m) to a large roof. Squeeze through the roof and continue up an offwidth to a ledge, 5.9, 150 feet (46m).

Pitch 2: Follow a left-leaning system to a ledge below a vertical 5" crack (13cm) leading to another large roof, 5.8, 60 feet (18m).

Pitch 3: Climb a steep crack to a roof and face climb right at 5.6, around the roof, then continue to the summit, 5.9, 150 feet (46m).

Paraphernalia: A few medium nuts; many large nuts; protection for a 5–6" crack (13–15cm).

Descent: Scramble east from the summit to near the southeast corner of the rock. Two rappels down the south face end on the ground.

WET CLEAN UP AISLE #9 I, 5.10+, 1 pitch, 75 feet (32m)

First Ascent: Kyle Copeland, Pete Gallagher, 24 April 1991.

Location and Access: *Wet Clean Up Aisle #9* is right of *Mutate or Die* on the butte's west face. Begin hands up a left-facing corner. Continue right of a prominent V-slot to double-rappel anchors visible from below.

Paraphernalia: Friend (1) #2.

Descent: Rappel the route from double anchors.

Photo: Eric Bjørnstad

Merrimac Butte, left to right: ***Keel Hauling*** **and** ***Wheelchair Ramp.***

Photo: Eric Bjørnstad

Merrimac Butte, ***Wet Clean Up Aisle #9***

Photo: Eric Bjørnstad

Merrimac Butte, *Mutate or Die*

MUTATE OR DIE I, 5.11, 1 pitch, 80 feet (24m)

First Ascent: Kyle Copeland, Peter Gallagher, 24 April 1991.

Location and Access: *Mutate or Die* is left of the center of the west prow, left of *Wet Clean Up Aisle #9*. Climb a roof protected with a #0.75 TCU, and continue with a lieback, then hands-to-fist and finally offwidth into a pod. Continue offwidth to a ledge with rappel slings visible from below.

Paraphernalia: Friends (1) #1, #2, #3, (2) #3.5; TCUs (2) #0.75; Camalots (4) #4; Tri-cams (2) #7; Big Bros.

Descent: Rappel the route.

Monitor Butte

Monitor Butte is designated on the Moab West map. It is the smaller butte southeast of the Merrimac. Routes are listed left to right.

SONJA-WIGGINS II, 5.11, 2 pitches, 240 feet (73m)

First Ascent: Sonja Paspal, Earl Wiggins, 1991.

Location and Access: *Sonja-Wiggins* climbs the prominent fracture system left of the right prow of the Monitor as it is approached from the east buttress of the Merrimac. The climb faces north and is left (around the corner) from *Plunge*. There are rappel slings visible above a broken block at the lower end of the route. Above, the crack widens to an obvious chimney.

Paraphernalia: Standard desert rack with extra larger sizes; (1) quickdraw.

Descent: Rappel *Plunge*.

Photo: Eric Bjørnstad

Monitor Butte, *Sonja-Wiggins*

Photo: Eric Bjørnstad

Monitor Butte, from left to right: *Plunge* (arrow), *Nameless Route* (arrow) and *Plank*.

Photo: Eric Bjørnstad

Monitor Butte, left to right: *Plunge* and *Nameless Route*.

PLUNGE II, 5.12a, 3 pitches, 240 feet (73m), ★★★★★

First Ascent: Ron Olevsky, Dave Mondeau, 5.7, A2, May 1986. First free ascent: Peter Gallagher, Katy Cassidy, Earl Wiggins, 15 February 1988.

Location and Access: *Plunge* is the free ascent of the unnamed original route on Monitor Butte. The climb follows an obvious right-facing dihedral at the southwest corner of the landform. There are two aid bolts near the top of the second pitch placed by the first ascent team. The third pitch is a bouldering move onto the summit block. The first free ascent team recommends the climb as one of the finest in the Moab area.

Pitch 1: Climb up and left into the crack on a ledge about 15 feet (4.5m) off the ground. Continue up the thin fingercrack and around a small roof, 5.11. The crack gets steadily bigger until it is hands leading into a hanging belay, 5.12a, 130 feet (40m).

Pitch 2: Climb the offwidth above, 5.11, for 60 feet (18m) to the top of the crack.

Pitch 3: Third-class to the summit with a bouldering move to the highest point.

Paraphernalia: Three complete sets of Friends with extra #1.5, #2; many TCUs; (2) quickdraws.

Descent: Two rappels down the route.

NAMELESS ROUTE Rating unknown, II, 2 pitches, 240 feet (73m)

First Ascent: Unknown.

Location and Access: The first crack system right of *Plunge*.

Paraphernalia: Standard desert rack; (2) quickdraws.

Descent: Rappel *Plunge*.

Photo: Eric Bjørnstad

Monitor Butte, *Plank*

PLANK (aka Gang Plank) II, 5.10, A0, 3 pitches, 240 feet (73m)

First Ascent: Earl Wiggins, Katy Cassidy, 27 January 1988.

Location and Access: *Plank* climbs a large tower (right side) up an offwidth chimney left of center on the south side of the Monitor.

Pitch 1: Start on loose rock and work up and left onto a ledge (rappel slings are visible) at the base of the tower, 5.8, 90 feet (27m).

Pitch 2: Climb an overhanging offwidth into a chimney and proceed to a fixed belay on a large ledge, 5.9 (no protection), 100 feet (30m).

Pitch 3: Here the chimney is about 8 feet (2.4m) wide. One aid bolt was used by the first ascent team to move from the belay. They suggest the move could be done free by a tall person. Continue to the top of the rock up an unprotected bomb bay chimney, 5.9, A0, 50 feet.

Paraphernalia: One set of Friends in even sizes; (1) ⅝" angle to place in an extra hole at the top of the second pitch belay.

Descent: Third-class to the top of the rock, then work west to *Plunge*. Two fixed rappels bring one to the ground.

Photo: Dan Norris

Tusher Canyon, Courthouse Pasture Area

HOLLIS ROUTE I, 5.10, A1, 1 pitch

First Ascent: Jason Keith, Hollis McCord, 1995.

Location and Access: *Hollis Route* is the shortest climb to the summit of the Monitor. Begin on the lower east end of the butte. Boulder into a cave-like structure and aid out of it, continuing up the obvious crack system to the summit.

Paraphernalia: One set of Friends; TCUs.

Descent: Rappel the route or traverse west and rappel *Plunge*.

I love wild canyons–dry, fragrant, stone-walled, with their green choked niches and gold-tipped ramparts.

Zane Grey

[T]ravelling into unfamiliar territory is like turning a kaleidoscope ninety degrees. Suddenly, the colors and pieces of glass find a fresh arrangement. The light shifts, and you enter a new landscape in search of the order you know to be there.

Terry Tempest Williams, *An Unspoken Hunger*, 1994

Photo: Mike Baker

Match Stick

ISLAND-IN-THE-SKY MESA

At first it seems like geologic chaos, but there is method at work here, method of a fanatic order and perseverance: each groove in the rock leads to a natural channel of some kind, every channel to a ditch and gulch and ravine, each larger waterway to a canyon bottom or broad wash leading in turn to the Colorado River and the sea.

Edward Abbey, *Desert Solitaire*, 1968

The Island-in-the-Sky Mesa is a high plateau bordered by precipitous walls two thousand feet (610m) above the Green River west and the Colorado River east. It is the magic land of northern Canyonlands National Park, Dead Horse Point State Park, and Horse Thief Trail which leads to the breathtaking hairpin switchbacks descending to the northwest beginning of the White Rim Trail, Moses and Zeus in Taylor Canyon, and the desolate region of Hell Roaring Canyon.

Seven Mile Canyon Area

Seven Mile Canyon Area is the region west of Putterman's Frisbee, and is reached from State Highway 313. It is designated on the Moab West map.

Pigskin Parade, Petticoat Gumption

There is a paved overview of the Monitor and Merrimac Buttes, with BLM information kiosk, on the north side of 313 before Mile Post 18. *Pigskin Parade* and *Petticoat Gumption* are on the Navajo Sandstone west (left) of the viewing area and are behind a 12-foot-high (4m) boulder of the same rock formation. The two routes may be top-roped by approaching from the back side of the landform.

PIGSKIN PARADE I, 5.10a, 1 pitch, 25 feet (8m)

First Ascent: Ron Olevsky, Richard Pietro, 1985.

Location and Access: *Pigskin Parade* is right of an obvious overhanging wall, visible from the highway, and is fifteen feet (4.5m) left of *Petticoat Gumption*. The route is protected by three drilled angles.

Paraphernalia: Three quickdraws.

Descent: Walk-off the back.

PETTICOAT GUMPTION I, 5.9, 1 pitch, 25 feet (8m)

First Ascent: Ron Olevsky, Richard Pietro, 1985.

Location and Access: *Petticoat Gumption* is fifteen feet (4.5m) right of *Pigskin Parade*. Climb straight up using three drilled angle pitons for protection.

Paraphernalia: Three quickdraws.

Descent: Walk-off the back.

Joker, Match Stick, Blind Faith

The short canyon housing *Blind Faith* is in view from Mile Post 16, north from State Highway 313. To reach, take the first dirt road west of the Mile Post and follow the most traveled trail until one comes to the mouth of the canyon. There is about a ten-minute walk to the route located before an obvious tower on the left side of the canyon. *Blind Faith* is hidden from view until one is almost directly under the route. *Match Stick* may be viewed looking north from Mile Post 16. It is a slender stick-like formation against the far cliffs. *Joker* is beyond *Match Stick*. Drive 0.5 mile (0.8km) on a dirt road north from 313 to a point where the road becomes 4-wheel drive. Contour around the end of the mesa north approximately 200 yards (183m). Two splitter fingercracks are visible on what appears to be the mesa wall to the west. However, they ascend a tower separated from the mesa. The rightmost crack is *Submission* and the left *Dominance*. Routes are listed left to right.

Photo: Leslie Henderson

Blind Faith

JOKER—DOMINANCE I, 5.9, 1 pitch, 100 feet (30m), ★★★★

First Ascent: Mike Baker, Leslie Henderson, June 1996.

Location and Access: *Dominance* is left of *Submission*.

Paraphernalia: One set of TCUs; (2) sets of stoppers.

Descent: One double-rope rappel down *Submission*.

JOKER—SUBMISSION I, C1, 1 pitch, 100 feet (30m),★★★

First Ascent: Mike Baker, Leslie Henderson, June 1996.

Location and Access: Right of *Dominance*.

Paraphernalia: Camalots (2) #0.5, #0.75, (1) #1, #2, #3; (2) sets of TCUs.

Descent: One double-rope rappel down the route.

MATCH STICK I, 5.10, A2+, 3 pitches

First Ascent: Mike Baker, Leslie Henderson, February 1996.

Location and Access: *Match Stick* is north of State 313 opposite Mile Post 16.

Pitch 1: Climb the center corner of the tower.

Pitch 2: Continue up the left side.

Pitch 3: Chimney behind the tower and onto the top.

Paraphernalia: Standard desert rack; (2) Big Bros; (2) Lost Arrows; (2) 0.5" angles.

Descent: Rappel the route.

BLIND FAITH I, 5.10+, 2 pitches

First Ascent: Mike Baker, Leslie Henderson, February 1996. First free ascent: Mike Baker, Chris Decker, Leslie Henderson, Karen Ward, 5.10+, May 1996.

Location and Access: Begin up a right-facing dihedral and climb to rappel anchors, 5.9. Pitch 2 climbs 5.10+ to the top of the landform.

Paraphernalia: Standard desert rack.

Descent: Two double-rope rappels down the route.

Spring Canyon Point Road

Spring Canyon Point Road is remote and seldom visited, although the area is a beautiful place to camp and climb.

The region is west of State Highway 313 on the way to Dead Horse Point and Island-in-the-Sky District of Canyonlands National Park. To reach, drive 8 miles (13km) west from U.S. 191 on State Highway 313. Turn right at Mile Post 14 (Spring Canyon Point Road), a few yards past a paved pullout on the left, where there are restrooms and a BLM information kiosk. Although Moab is mislocated on the kiosk map, other information is accurate and worth taking the time to read.

An alternate approach is from I-70 east of Green River. This route may require 4-wheel drive. It was taken by the first ascent of the Tombstone party, but is far less direct than the State 313 approach. Take Ranch Exit 173, the only exit between Green River and Crescent Junction, and proceed north to Dubinky Well, then follow directions for the State 313 approach.

Tombstone (aka High Rise) Rest in Peace, Shallow Burial

Tombstone, a butte, is noted on the Moab West map with clear road markings, which may be essential to reaching the landform. Even then some route finding may be required. Tombstone can be seen from many points on the Island-in-the-Sky Mesa and also when looking south from I-70 approximately 15 miles (24km) east of Green River. It is 9 miles (14.4km) to Tombstone from the Spring Canyon Point Road turnoff. To reach, take the second possible right turn (the Dubinky Well Road), then after crossing the second cattleguard (before coming to Dubinkey Well–a windmill and bovine watering pond) take the first left road (Canyon Point) which will go directly to the butte. *Rest in Peace* and *Shallow Burial* are approximately 0.75 mile (1.2km) northwest of Tombstone.

CAUTION: Be wary of deep sand. The approach is generally passable with 2-wheel-drive but may vary with each passing storm. Some seasons deep sand may prevent even a 4-wheel-drive approach. Always carry a map, extra fuel, water, and a shovel.

TOMBSTONE—TRES GATOS II, 5.11, A0, 3 pitches, 370 feet (113m)

First Ascent: Katy Cassidy, Earl Wiggins, 13 March 1988.

Location and Access: *Tres Gatos* was the second route established on Tombstone. The climb is at the far right side of the west face and climbs a shallow left-facing corner leading to a large roof.

Pitch 1: Approach through the Dewey Bridge member of Entrada Sandstone, 5.9, 70 feet (21m), then climb a left-facing corner, 5.11, 150 feet (46m).

Pitch 2: Continue 20 feet (6m) to a large roof which is turned on its right side (2 points of A0). Climb a steep right-facing corner to a belay ledge on a ridge, 5.9, A0, 100 feet (30m).

Pitch 3: Face climb to the top, 5.8, 120 feet (37m).

Paraphernalia: Two sets of Friends through #3 with (1) #3.5, #4; small wires; quickdraws.

Descent: Rappel *Epitaph*.

TOMBSTONE—EPITAPH III, 5.10+, 3 pitches, 280 feet (85m)

First Ascent: Brian Smoot, Jonathan Smoot, 1981. Second ascent: Earl Wiggins, Katy Cassidy, 20 December 1987.

Location and Access: *Epitaph* follows a crack inside an oblique chimney on the extreme north ridge of the butte.

Pitch 1: Begin from a saddle on the north edge of the rock. The saddle may be reached by climbing a sand dune and traversing from the north end of a ledge level with the saddle or by making a few bouldering moves up 15 feet (5m) of overhanging rock. Climb a hand-and-fistcrack 75 feet (23m) to a bolt belay, 5.10+.

Pitch 2: Above the belay is an offwidth and squeeze chimney that narrows to a handcrack. Ascend past an overhang, then continue to a good ledge with bolts. This lead begins 5.10 at the overhang and is 5.9 in the chimney.

Pitch 3: An 80-foot (24m) 4th class pitch leads to the top, which has a 10-foot (3m) pit filled with sand. There was a cairn but no register left by the first ascent team.

Paraphernalia: Standard desert rack.

Descent: Double-rope rappels down the route.

REST IN PEACE I, 5.10a, 1 pitch, 70 feet (21m)

First Ascent: Dave Medara, Bob Novellino, Jorma Hayes, Bret Sutteer, May 1995.

Location and Access: *Rest in Peace* is the next landform, approximately 1 mile (1.6km), north of Tombstone. The route faces west and is approximately 120 feet (37m) left of *Shallow Burial*. Climb hands-to-fist to rappel anchors not easily seen from below.

Paraphernalia: Standard desert rack.

Descent: Rappel the route.

SHALLOW BURIAL I, 5.10d, 1 pitch, 70 feet (21m)

First Ascent: Dave Medara, Bob Novellino, Jorma Hayes, Brett Sutteer, May 1995.

Location and Access: *Shallow Burial* is approximately 120 feet (37m) right of *Rest in Peace*. Climb thin-fingers-to-hands to offwidth. Rappel anchors are visible from below the route.

Paraphernalia: Standard desert rack.

Descent: Rappel the route.

Dead Horse Point State Park

Dead Horse Point State Park offers one of the most magnificent views found on the Colorado Plateau. It is 22 miles (15km) up State 313 from its junction with U.S. Highway 191 north of Moab.

Dream of Dead Horses

Dream of Dead Horses climbs to the rimrock of the Canyonlands National Park Overlook at Dead Horse Point State Park. To approach the climb from the top, rappel the northeast slabs (a buttress just north of a watertank camouflaged by a rock wall) at Dead Horse Point, then traverse left to the base of the climb. The rappel ends next to the mouth of a large bivouac cave. To approach the climb from the bottom, descend the Shafer Road north of the Island-in-the-Sky District of Canyonlands National Park visitor center (4.5 miles beyond Dead Horse Point turn on State 313), then from the White Rim at the bottom of the Shafer Road. Difficult route finding will be required through the lower bands of Cutler and Moenkopi Sandstone before the Wingate stratum (and the climb) is reached.

DREAM OF DEAD HORSES IV, 5.7, A3, 7 pitches, 450 feet (130m)

First Ascent: Ron Olevsky, solo, February 1978. Second ascent: Ron Olevsky, Pat Miller, September 1979.

Location and Access: *Dream of Dead Horses* climbs a fracture system on the south-southeast buttress for four pitches before traversing left to avoid "Great Barrier Roofs" at the top of the wall. Olevsky previewed the upper 165 feet (50m) of the route and pried off several large loose blocks.

Paraphernalia: Friends up through #3.5; (2) knifeblades; (5) Lost Arrows.

Descent: Walk to car if approach was from the top, or, as the first ascent team did, mountain bike back to the bottom via the Shafer Road.

Crow's Head Spires

Crow's Head Spires, composed of Wingate Sandstone, are in a small box canyon northwest of Deadhorse Point State Park Overlook. They may be viewed by traversing the rimrock west of the overlook, or (at a distance) from the Colorado River Overlook or the Walking Rocks, located (with signs) on the White Rim Road south of the Shafer Trail off the Island-in-the-Sky Mesa. To reach, turn east on a dirt road south of the turn to Deadhorse Point on State 313. Drive 2.5 miles (4km) to the mesa rim. Look for a cairn with a long, pointed top rock. This will be the nearest viewpoint from the mesa top. Make three rappels into the canyon, leaving ropes fixed for the return, then hike the short distance to the base of the towers. Crow's Head Spires may also be reached via a long hike upcanyon from the White Rim Road. Routes are listed right to left.

Luminous Being Spire

NORTH FACE (aka North Crow's Head Spire) II, 5.10+, 2 pitches, 250 feet (76m)

First Ascent: Robert Warren, Jeff Web, 1983.

Location and Access: *North Face* is right of *Lizard Action.*

Pitch 1: Ascend an obvious crack system on the north face, then traverse left and join *Lizard Action.*

Pitch 2: Follow *Lizard Action* to the summit.

Paraphernalia: Standard desert rack.

Descent: Rappel to the notch between the spires, then to the west.

LIZARD ACTION II, 5.10+, 2 pitches, 250 feet (76m)

First Ascent: Robert Warren, Steve Wood, Jeff Web, Spring 1983.

Location and Access: *Lizard Action* ascends the tower from the northeast.

Paraphernalia: One set of Friends.

Descent: Rappel to the notch, then to the west.

HECKLE AND JECKLE II, 5.10, A1, 2 pitches, 250 feet (76m)

First Ascent: Jason Keith, Greg Bimmesteffer, May 1993.

Location and Access: *Heckle and Jeckle* ascends the south ridge of the north spire.

Paraphernalia: Standard desert rack; selection of pitons.

Descent: Rappel to the notch, then to the west.

THE NOTCH I, 5.12, 1 pitch, 140 feet (43m)

First Ascent: Robert Warren, Steve Wood, Jeff Web, Spring 1983.

Location and Access: *The Notch* climbs from the west to the notch between the north and south spires. The summit of the spires was not reached.

Paraphernalia: One set of Friends.

Descent: Rappel the route.

Don Juan Spire

LITTLE SMOKE (aka South Crow's Head Spire) II, 5.9, 2 pitches, 250 feet (76m)

First Free Ascent: Robert Warren, Steve Wood, Jeff Web, Spring 1983.

Location and Access: Ascend the southeast side of Don Juan Spire.

Paraphernalia: One set of Friends.

Descent: Rappel to the notch between the spires, then to the west.

YESTERDAY'S NEWS II, 5.9, A3, 4 pitches, 250 feet (76m)

First Ascent: Bill Ellwood, Bryan Ferguson, 26 May 1984.

Location and Access: Climb the south ridge of Don Juan Spire, not in view from the mesa rim rappel point.

Paraphernalia: TCUs up to #3.5 Friends.

Descent: Rappel to the notch between the spires, then to the west.

YESTERDAY'S NEWS VARIATION II, 5.10– A3, 4 pitches, 250 feet (76m)

First Ascent: Jason Keith, Greg Bimmesteffer, May 1993.

Location and Access: This variation is to the 2nd and 3rd pitches of *Yesterday's News*. From the top of Pitch 1 veer left up a left-facing crack ascending first on aid, then 5.9. Continue over the left side of a roof, 5.10–, up a wide crack system, 5.9, to the top of Pitch 3 of the original route.

Paraphernalia: Standard desert rack; small selection of pitons.

Descent: Rappel to the notch, then to the west.

DON JUAN II, 5.11+, 1 pitch, 250 feet (76m)

First Ascent: Ken Trout (and party), 5.10, A1. First Free Ascent: Jeff Web, Robert Warren.

Location and Access: Climb a left-facing corner up the left edge of the west face to the notch between the two spires, then to the summit of Don Juan Spire.

Paraphernalia: Standard desert rack.

Descent: Rappel to the notch, then to the west.

Tones of color, shades of light, drifts of air... These are the most sensuous qualities in nature... and wherever you go, by land or by sea, you shall not forget that which you saw not but rather felt the desolation and the silence of the desert.

Frank Waters, *Eternal Desert*

Photo: Dave Medara

***Warlock*, southwest face**

GREEN RIVER AREA

The river becomes a way of thinking, ingrained, a way of looking at the world. I listen to its commentary on the rocks and willows that block its way, feel cooled by the touch of spray, and smell all of the odors that emanate from it. Judgment and recognition of odors depend so much on familiar reference smells that it is difficult to describe a new smell without recourse to them. The river, of course, often smells of off-river odors: an aloof and elusive smell, soft, faintly like clean clay or like wet wash hanging out on a windy day. It is neither sweet nor sharp, acrid nor aromatic, nor distinctly anything ever smelled before or elsewhere unless one has had a river in his or her childhood. It is a smooth, tentative smell. It is light and deep, cool, it comes in curling tendrils and sometimes it is difficult to pick out from other smells. But it is there. And, once smelled, it become easier to recognize and soon there is almost a sense of river in the landscape even when it cannot be seen.

Ann Zwinger, *The Canyonlands of Southeastern Utah*

Climbs in the Green River area are on Wingate Sandstone and are north of the switchbacks that descend to Horsethief Bottom and the northwest beginning of the White Rim Road north of Canyonlands National Park. To reach, drive 9 miles (14.5km) north of Moab on U.S. 191. Turn left (west) on State Highway 313 where a sign reads "Island-in-the-Sky District of Canyonlands National Park" and "Dead Horse Point State Park." Just before Mile Post 10 (12.3 miles, 19.8km from U.S. 191) turn right (west) onto the dirt Horsethief Trail; 13.2 miles (21.2km) farther, the trail descends 2000 feet (610m) in 1.5 miles (2.4km) via spectacular switchbacks to Horsethief Bottom at the Green River. This is the western beginning of the White Rim Road. Turn right (north, upriver) and drive to the BLM river put-in/take-out, where there is an information kiosk, river sign-in box, and restrooms. During the summer season there is also a camp host.

Mineral Bottom

Climbs at Mineral Bottom are on the Wingate buttress above the BLM put-in/take-out, and the buttress north of the entrance to Mineral Canyon.

Taint Much, Moaner Lisa, Shadow Nose

Taint Much is on the south-facing wall a few yards south of (before) the BLM put-in/take-out. *Moaner Lisa* is left of *Taint Much* on the west facing portion of the wall before the river station. It climbs the right side of a pillar formation in the center of the face. *Shadow Nose* is left on the north-facing wall left of *Moaner Lisa*.

TAINT MUCH II, 5.10c, 2 pitches, 165 feet (50m)

First Ascent: Jay Smith, Jo Smith, 1991.

Location and Access: Begin up a left-facing dihedral left of two parallel cracks (5.10c) and climb to a belay ledge. Switch to the right (continuous) crack, 3-4-inches wide (7.6-10cm) and climb 5.10b to poor anchors at a rappel station.

Paraphernalia: Three sets of Friends through #4.

Descent: One double-rope rappel down the route.

MOANER LISA—LISA'S FAT BUTTRESS I, 5.12a, 1 pitch, 80 feet (18m), ★★★★★

First Ascent: Linus Platt, Kyle Copeland, Eric Johnson, Lisa Hathaway, 1990.

Location and Access: *Lisa's Fat Buttress* climbs a fingercrack in a right-facing dihedral to a snaking handcrack.

Paraphernalia: Friends through #3.

Descent: Rappel the route.

SHADOW NOSE III, 5.9, A1, 4 pitches, 425 feet (130m)

First Ascent: Dave Mondeau, Ron Olevsky, June 1984.

Location and Access: Left of *Moaner Lisa*.

Pitch 1: Climb a long aid crack of variable size to a hanging belay from two bolts, 135 feet (41m).

Pitch 2: Continue up the crack system another 80 feet (24m) and belay at the base of a chimney. Protect with many #2.5 Friends.

Pitch 3: Climb the chimney at 5.9, then aid in a left-facing dihedral, 100 feet (30m).

Pitch 4: Climb A1 over a roof to a belay on a ledge with two bolts, 110 Feet (34m).

Paraphernalia: One set of Friends with several extra of the larger sizes, including many #2.5; TCUs; selection of pitons (Rock 'n Rollers can probably replace a few piton placements); quickdraws.

Descent: Double-rope rappel the route.

NOTE: Rappel slings are visible on an unknown route on the west-facing wall right of the canyon above the BLM river station.

Pretty Much, Too Much, KC Route

These routes are approximately 1 mile upriver(1.6km) from the BLM river station, on the first buttress (west facing) beyond Mineral Canyon. Opposite the buttress and upriver is an airstrip with a wind-flag visible between the road and the river.

PRETTY MUCH I, 5.11c, 1 pitch, 135 feet (41m), ★★★★★

First Ascent: Jay Smith, Jo Smith, October 1991.

Location and Access: *Pretty Much* climbs the second projecting buttress upriver from Mineral Canyon (north of the BLM river station). The first buttress may be identified by its being the scene of relatively recent rock fall (pink cliffs rather than desert varnished). The two buttresses are separated by a shallow bowl. Begin at the highest point of the talus cone one crack right of a pillar formation. Climb the right side of a block, then thin hands (5.11a) up a right-facing dihedral. Finish with liebacking up a left-facing corner to a double-bolt rappel station at a stance on the left wall.

Paraphernalia: Friends (1) #1.5, (6) #2, (5) #2.5, (2) #3.

Descent: One double-rope rappel down the route from slings visible from below.

TOO MUCH I, 5.11d, 2 pitches, 165 feet (50m)

First Ascent: Jay Smith, Jo Smith, October 1991.

Location and Access: *Too Much* is between *Pretty Much* and *KC Route*. Begin up a block on the right side of a right-facing crack system.

Pitch 1: Stem (5.11d) past a fixed anchor to a ledge with a bolt, 80 feet (24m).

Pitch 2: Continue past a wide section and finish 5.10 hand-and-fist at a 2-bolt rappel station on the left wall, 85 feet (26m).

Paraphernalia: Friends #0.4 through #4 with many #2.5, #3; RPs; wires.

Descent: Rappel the route.

KC ROUTE I, 5.11c, 1 pitch, 100 feet (30m)

First Ascent: Kyle Copeland, 1991.

Location and Access: *KC Route* is on the left side of the buttress (north-facing), left of *Too Much*. Climb a splitter crack to a rappel station at the Kayenta caprock. A pod is visible half-way up the route.

Paraphernalia: Friends (6) #1.5, (8) #2, (2) #2.5.

Descent: Rappel the route from slings right of the crack system. Visible from below.

Hell Roaring Canyon Area

Hell Roaring Canyon is approximately 3.5 miles upriver (5.6km) from the BLM river station, or 3 miles upriver (4.8km) from Mineral Canyon, which is the major canyon 0.5 mile (0.8km) above the BLM river put-in/take-out. It is generally driveable with a high-clearance vehicle. The canyon was named by Major John Wesley Powell when he came upon it in flood stage during the historic first descent of the Green and Colorado Rivers in 1869.

Near the mouth of Hell Roaring Canyon, it is worth visiting the historic inscription of "D. Julien 1836" on the south wall approximately 1000 feet (305m) from the river. This is the best known and most accessible of several inscriptions left by the French-Canadian fur trapper.

Vena Cava, Warlock, Cauldrons, Witch, Corner Tower

Vena Cava is the distinct free-standing tower in view on the west side of the river approximately halfway between Mineral and Hell Roaring Canyons. To reach Vena Cava, drive toward Hell Roaring Canyon and cross the river by boat or raft to a point directly below the tower. A 10-minute hike up the talus will take one to the base of the East Face (longest) of the tower.

Warlock, Cauldrons, and The Witch are Wingate towers in a cirque on the south side of Hell Roaring Canyon approximately 3 miles (4.8km) from the river. An old 4-wheel-drive mining road is blocked by a rock slide about 2 miles upcanyon (3.2km). Thus, approximately a one-mile hike (1.6km) is required to reach the landforms.

Corner Tower stands at the north side (south-facing) of the mouth of Hell Roaring Canyon. A 20-minute hike up the talus cone is necessary from the river to reach the base of the tower.

VENA CAVA—VENTRICULAR TACHYCARDIA III, 5.11, A2, 2 pitches, 280 feet (85m), ★★★★

First Ascent: James Garrett, Mike Pennings, 26 February 1995.

Location and Access: The route climbs the right side of the east face.

Pitch 1: Begin up an obvious right-facing corner. The crack begins wide (6-7-inches, 15–18cm) with some free climbing. It soon narrows and steepens to fingers with some aid to a 2-bolt belay, 5.10, A1, 130 feet (40m).

Pitch 2: Continue up and left through difficult free climbing, 5.11, then small hands to an offwidth section, 40 feet (12m), 6-7-inches, (15–18cm). Follow a thin crack which diagonals up and right through an overhanging headwall, leading to some tricky hooking to a bolt that lends access to the summit caprock, 110 feet (34m).

Paraphernalia: Two 200-foot (60m) ropes; (2) sets of Friends; many medium to small wired nuts; a few big pieces of protection for the offwidth sections; a selection of hooks; quickdraws.

Descent: Rappel with two 200-foot (60m) ropes from bolts to the north, then easy scrambling to the start of the climb.

WARLOCK III, 5.9, A3, 6 pitches, 350 feet (107m)

First Ascent: Ron Olevsky, Dave Mondeau, Dale Kruse, April 1985.

Location and Access: Begin on the north side of the tower, then halfway up tunnel through the rock and finish the ascent on the southeast side of the tower.

Paraphernalia: Standard desert rack; wires.

Descent: Rappel the route.

Photo: James Garrett

Vena Cava: *Ventricular Tachycardia*

Photo: James Garrett

Mike Pennings climbing first pitch of *Vena Cava*.

WARLOCK—DUDE, THAT'S NOT FUNNY III, 5.11+, C2, 3 pitches, 385 feet (117m), ★★★

First Ascent: Mike Pennings, Dave Medara, 19 February 1995.

Location and Access: *Dude, That's Not Funny* follows a varnished splitter crack on the southwest face of the tower. It is easily recognized by a rectangular offwidth pod at the 160-foot level (49m). No bolts were placed, and only one piton was used to avoid blocks in the top of a chimney on Pitch 2.

Pitch 1: All but 15 feet (5m) were climbed free (5.12b top-rope) by the second team member, 5.11, C2 on lead, 190 feet (58m). An optional belay is possible at a yellow horizontal band below a 5.11+ offwidth.

Pitch 2: Ascend the left of two cracks (5.11), then continue (5.10) with hands passing a chimney and a fixed piton and ending with 5.11 at a belay stance with no fixed anchors. Climbed free by the second at 5.11. Lead at 5.10, C1, 160 feet (49m).

Pitch 3: Finish up an easy crack and chimney to the summit, 5.7, 35 feet (11m).

Paraphernalia: Three sets of Friends; (3) sets of TCUs; (1) set of nuts; quickdraws.

Descent: Rappel *Warlock*.

CAULDRONS—EYE OF NEWT II, 5.10–, A1, 3 pitches, 260 feet (79m)

First Ascent: James Funsten, Mike Wood, Davin Lindy, 13 April 1993.

Location and Access: Cauldrons is the tower left of The Witch and right of The Warlock. The route ascends a crack system dividing the twin summits on the south face. Climb to the notch on the southwest face, then right to the highest point.

Pitch 1: Begin 5.7 up a right-facing then left-facing system to a belay ledge, 80 feet (24m).

Pitch 2: Climb a wide crack section past a fixed anchor (5.9), then end with A1 at a belay ledge, 85 feet (26m).

Pitch 3: Continue up a V-slot (5.7), then left of a roof at A1 and on (past a loose block) to the left summit of the landform, 95 feet (29m).

Paraphernalia: Two sets of Friends #0.4 through #0.75, (3) sets #1 through #3.5; (1) #6; (1) set of Rocks; (1) Big Bro.

Descent: Rappel 180 feet (55m) to the top of Pitch 1, then to the ground or make a rappel to the top of Pitch 2 and a 165-foot (50m) rappel to the ground.

WITCH—MIDNIGHT RIDER III, 5.11d R, 4 pitches, 415 feet (126m), ★★★★★

First Ascent: Ron Olevsky, solo, 31 October 1984, 5.7, A1. Second ascent: James Funsten, Davin Lindy, Mike Wood, 12 April 1993, 5.7, C2. First Free Ascent: Ken Sims, Mark Hesse, Maura Henning, October 1994, 5.11d.

Location and Access: *Midnight Rider* climbs to the prominent right shoulder of the southwest face of the tower, then to the summit up an obvious crack system. Begin the ascent behind a large boulder with a drilled angle piton.

Pitch 1: Climb up a perfect handcrack behind a large flake leaning against the wall of Witch, 5.10b, bolt anchors, 75 feet (23m).

Pitch 2: Climb an obvious fingercrack. Protect with many #0, #1 TCUs, 5.11d, bolt anchors, 140 feet (43m).

Pitch 3: Continue up an obvious crack to near the shoulder, then make a 5.9 left traverse to avoid a dangerous flake above, 5.10, bolt anchors, 140 feet (43m).

Pitch 4: Climb from anchors to the top up a nice arête to 3 bolts, protect with a fixed nut, 60 feet (18m).

Paraphernalia: Friends (3) #1, #2, #3; (1) set of Camalots; (4) #0,#1 TCUs; several #11 hexes; ball nuts; cheater stick; 200-foot (60m) ropes; (6) quickdraws.

Descent: Rappel to the top of Pitch 3, then double-rope rappel to the top of Pitch 1, and a final rappel to the ground.

CORNER TOWER—COMBUSTION CHAMBER III, 5.11c, 2 pitches, 350 feet (107m), ★★★★

First Ascent: Mike Pennings, James Garrett, 27 February 1995.

Location and Access: On Pitch 1 of *Corner Tower* the second team member has to move up before the leader can reach belay anchors. James Garrett: "You feel like you are about to explode in those offwidths, thus the name *Combustion Chamber*." A summit register was left by the first ascent team.

Pitch 1: Climb with fist-to-offwidth-to-hands a long and obvious crack that splits a strenuous overhanging block at the start of the route. The pitch is 30 feet (9m) right of an aid climb by an unknown party, which was probably the first ascent of the

Photo: James Garrett

Corner Tower

landform. Pitch 1 shares the same 2-bolt belay with the aid route's Pitch 2 belay, 5.11c, 215 feet (66m).

Pitch 2: From the belay ledge climb right (offwidth) to a chimney. The pitch is shared with the aid route. A few drilled angles are passed on the way to a lower summit of the landform. The route continues to the higher summit by jumping to a small ledge and climbing to the top, 5.10, 135 feet (41m).

Paraphernalia: Two sets of Friends with triples on the larger sizes; (1) set of TCUs; (4–5) large pieces to 9"; quickdraws.

Descent: Two long rappels to the ground, or three shorter rappels following the aid route.

To see a world in a grain of sand and a heaven in a wild flower, hold infinity in the palm of your hand and eternity in an hour.

William Blake

It's a warm wind, the west wind, full of birds' cries; I never hear the west wind but tears are in my eyes.

John Masefield

Photo: Randall Weekley

Frosty Weller climbing *Sandcastle*, southwest face.

SAN RAFAEL SWELL AREA

We simply need that wild country available to us, even if we never do more than drive to its edge and look in. For it can be a means of measuring ourselves and our sanity as creatures, a part of the geography of hope.

Wallace Stegner, *The Sound of Mountain Water*

We abuse land because we regard it as a commodity belonging to us. When we see land as a community to which we belong, we may begin to use it with love and respect... There is no other way for land to survive the impact of mechanized man.

Aldo Leopold, *A Sand County Almanac*

The San Rafael Swell is a great domed anticline in southeastern Utah, due south of Price, west of Green River and Canyonlands National Park, and north of Capitol Reef National Park. This large tract of public land is managed by the Bureau of Land Management. It is one of the largest and least known of the high deserts of the vast Colorado Plateau, a land of incomparable beauty. Earlier this century it was recommended as a national park and once again is under consideration for national park status. Seven Wilderness Study Areas are now included within its boundaries. The Swell's annual precipitation averages only six inches. Its highest elevation is 7921 feet (2414m) at the San Rafael Knob. The lowest point is 4200 feet (1280m) at the bottom of the San Rafael River in the Mexican Bend area. The Swell is 80 miles long (129km), 35 miles wide (56km), and resembles an elongated bowl turned upside down. The east/west I-70, completed in 1970, crosses and divides the Swell into north and south territories. The Swell has always been one of the most remote and isolated regions on the Colorado Plateau and now the fenced freeway isolates it even more. Before it was bisected, the Swell's central section was far more accessible. There were numerous branches from the old road which are now cut off by freeway fences.

The San Rafael Swell began to form 40 to 60 million years ago as tectonic forces deep within the earth's crust resulted in an intense period of mountain building. As the land rose the region was severely attacked by erosion as water ran from higher elevations, resulting in this million-acre area (2000 square miles) of deep vertical-walled canyons, mesas, buttes, towers, spires, and stone arches.

The Swell's south and east escarpment compose the San Rafael Reef, a saw-toothed ridge of giant flatirons rising 1200 feet (366m) above the San Rafael Desert to the east. Although the San Rafael Swell appears to be rough barren desert, it is the home of a fragile, easily damaged desert ecology. Cryptobiotic soil here as elsewhere on the Colorado Plateau is critical to its health. Please travel on established roads, paths, slickrock, or in drainages. It is unfortunate that cattle grazing is still permitted on lands that belong to all of us equally;

however, the subject is a Pandora's box of contention not appropriate for this guide. As for the bovine and its ubiquitous presence, I am reminded of Steve Allen's caution in his book *Canyoneering–The San Rafael Swell*: "Roads can change overnight. It is best to be wary. If in doubt, walk through suspect sections of road first. Do not drive the roads at night. A black cow on a black road on a black night will not be seen."

River Gorges

There are two major canyons carved by rivers of the San Rafael–one by the Muddy River and one by the San Rafael. Each chasm has a dendritic pattern of tributary drainages which have cut numerous smaller yet often spectacular gorges. Both the Muddy and the San Rafael rivers originate in the high land of the Wasatch Plateau to the west. The Muddy joins the Fremont north of Hanksville where they become the Dirty Devil River and drain into the Colorado at the southern region of Cataract Canyon. The San Rafael River enters the Green south of the town of Green River and meets the Colorado near the geographic heart of Canyonlands National Park.

History

The San Rafael Swell was named by early explorers traveling the Old Spanish Trail, which traverses a portion of its northern region. The Barrier Canyon Culture occupied the San Rafael from approximately 7000 to 1500 years ago. Their pictographs are found at many locations from Buckhorn Wash north to the Temple Wash south. More recent inhabitants include the Fremont Indians, dating from approximately 750 to 1300 years ago, and later the Ute Indians who acquired the horse brought to the southwest by the Spaniards. The Swell is rich in antiquities in the form of stone granaries, campsites, petroglyphs, and pictographs left by both the Fremont and the Ute. Early travelers through the Swell were Mexican slave runners, wild horse traders, military mappers and geographers, Mormon missionaries, railroad builders, sheepherders, cattlemen, prospectors, miners, and outlaws. The San Rafael is noted as the hideout for Butch Cassidy and other bank robbers and cattle rustlers. In 1921 oil companies built the road over Buckhorn Flat and through Buckhorn Draw (Wash). The San Rafael River Bridge and the improved road to Temple Mountain were the work of the Civilian Conservation Corps (CCC) in the 1930s and the best access to the Swell until the 1970 opening of I-70, The 400-foot-high bridge (122m) over Eagle Canyon is one of the most spectacular in Utah and upon its completion won a Bridge of the Year award.

Small amounts of gold, silver, copper, lead, and zinc were mined in 1883. Uranium claims were staked at Temple Mountain in 1898 and vanadium produced a few years later. Oil was first drilled for in the 1890s, and sulphur and gypsum mined in 1911. The Swell boomed in the '50s when Uranium mining was subsidized by the government and thousands of claims were staked, and seemingly countless roads bulldozed.

Flora and fauna

With the wide range of elevations in the San Rafael (approximately 4000 to 8000 feet–1219 to 2438m) there is a corresponding abundance of flora and fauna. The Swell is home to

Utah's largest herd of desert bighorn sheep, and one may expect to see evidence of coyotes, deer, antelope, bobcats, skunks, and prairie dogs, as well as the usual desert variety of rodents, reptiles, et cetera, and a surprising number of ornithological species including eagles and owls. The vegetation of the Swell echoes most of the high deserts of the Colorado Plateau. There are juniper and piñon dwarf woodlands and a few yellow pines in areas enriched with water. Cottonwood trees are ubiquitous along stream beds. Greasewood, sagebrush, and rabbit brush are prolific along washes and roadways, and sparse grass and prickly pear are scattered here and there. As elsewhere on the plateau there is a surprising abundance of wild flowers, usually in peak bloom the last week of April to the second week of May.

Geology

The San Rafael Swell, a kidney-shaped geographic feature in the northwest part of the Colorado Plateau, began to form 40 to 60 million years ago as pressures deep within the earth's crust created a massive uplift, or anticline. Erosion has since removed thousands of feet of sediments, leaving us with a window into the endless geologic creation of deep canyons, massive buttes, and delicate spires.

Photo: Lin Ottinger

San Rafael Reef.

Formations of sandstone in the Swell today were deposited 100 to 230 million years ago. Many are the same type found in Canyonlands and Capitol Reef National Parks, with Wingate the dominant rock on which climbing routes are established. The following is a brief discussion of the stratum (oldest to youngest) most likely to be encountered on a climbing visit to the San Rafael. See rock strata sequence chart, page 10

Moenkopi Formation: Four hundred feet thick (122m) and Triassic in age (age of the dinosaurs), Moenkopi is widespread throughout the Colorado Plateau, forming vertical walls or steep slopes. It was deposited over a long span of time and influenced by tidal variations. The rock is a shale and one of the most recognizable stratum in the southwest desert. Of mudflat deposition it often resembles a chocolate layer cake with shades of maroon (deposited above water and oxidized) sandwiched between light greens (either formed under water or organic in origin). At the time it was deposited, the Moenkopi was a 200-mile (322km) flat, level floodplain stretching from present-day Colorado to western Utah. In the San Rafael, Moenkopi is up to 900 feet thick (274m), and although no climbs are established on it, it is sometimes encountered on approaches. Both Assembly Hall and Window Blind Peaks sit atop 700 feet (213m) of the stratum. Ripple rock commonly corrugates the surfaces of Moenkopi, petrifying wave marks of an ancient seashore.

Chinle Formation: One hundred fifty feet thick (46m) and Triassic in age (age of the dinosaurs), pronounced "Chin-lee," this layer forms steep slopes and cliffs below vertical Wingate walls. It is the most colorful rock on the desert, with hues of red, brown, purple, green, and gray. Extensive exposures are found throughout the Colorado Plateau. It is a petrified wood and uranium-bearing stratum composed of stream deposited mud, silt, sand, and gravel up to 850 feet deep (259m). At the south entrance to Buckhorn Wash the layer is up to 265 feet thick (81m). Although rare, silver and dinosaur bones have been found in the Chinle.

Wingate Sandstone: Four hundred feet thick (122m), Wingate is now accepted as Triassic in age (age of the dinosaurs). It is listed as Jurassic on maps dated before 1954 when geologist Dr. Lee Stokes discovered a fossil in northern Arizona which classified the sandstone as Triassic. Together with the Kayenta Formation and Navajo Sandstone this layer is a member of the Glen Canyon Group, so named for its spectacular exposures in the Glen Canyon of the Colorado River–it is up to 400 feet (122m) thick and the densest rock found there. Of aeolian or wind-blown deposition, it is vertically fractured, buff or reddish orange to light red in color, and often streaked with desert varnish (dark vertical lines of manganese-oxide). Wingate is the rock that has made desert climbing famous. It is found at Colorado National Monument, Indian Creek, Castleton Tower, Moses, Canyonlands, Capitol Reef, and the San Rafael to name but a few of its fortuitous locations.

Kayenta Formation: One hundred feet thick (30m) and Triassic in age (age of the dinosaurs), this stratum is red to brown in color, up to 320 feet thick (98m), and is part of the Glen Canyon Group (see Wingate description). The Kayenta was formed by stream-deposition and is composed of siltstone, sandstone, shale, and limestone–sediments cemented together with calcite and silica–making it one of the most resistant rocks on the Colorado Plateau. It forms benches between the cliff-forming Wingate and Navajo Sandstone. Dinosaur tracks are more often found (and better preserved) in the bedding planes of the Kayenta

Formation than any other sedimentary layer on the Colorado Plateau. Kayenta is also the caprock on Wingate, forming the resistant layer at Colorado National Monument on which are located Rimrock Drive, the campground, visitor center, and the visitor center at Dead Horse Point State Park.

Navajo Sandstone: Five hundred feet thick (152m) and late Triassic to early Jurassic in age. The Navajo is aeolian in deposition. It is up to 815 feet thick (248m) and is a member of the Glen Canyon group (see Wingate description). Navajo cliffs often spall-off in rounded arch forms (conchoidally), giving comparatively few vertical fracture lines for the climber to work with; thus there are few routes on this layer in the Swell. It is, however, the dominant rock of Zion National Park and Wall Street near Moab. It appears both as cliffs and petrified sand dunes and is white to light red in color.

Price, Green River

Price and Green River are north and east of the San Rafael respectively. Price is the home of the College of Eastern Utah (CEU) and has many of the amenities of a large town. It is worth visiting the excellent Prehistoric Museum and stopping by the San Rafael Resource Area office at 125 South 600 West, (801) 363-3600, for information on the Swell. Green River is home of the wonderful John Wesley Powell River History Museum at 855 East Main, (801) 564-3526, well worth a stop.

Climbing Season

The best months for climbing in the San Rafael are March through May and September through November. Most routes are on Wingate Sandstone at an average elevation of 5400 feet (1646m). The weather is generally warmer than in Price or Moab. If climbing in the Swell during summer months it is not unwise to consume two gallons of water in a twelve hour period. Though clouds are welcome on hot summer days, they may be harbingers of lightning and thunderstorms as well as impassable roads. Caution is advised.

NOTE: When estimating distances it may be helpful to remember that one-tenth of a mile (805km) is approximately 500 feet.

A Brief History of Climbing in the San Rafael Swell by James Garrett

In the original *Desert Rock* (1988) the San Rafael Swell and a mere half-dozen known climbing routes were mentioned under the chapter of "isolated areas." The remote San Rafael comprises an area eighty miles long and thirty-five miles wide, and is a land where giant flatirons, buttes, and towers fill a landscape lying less than half the driving distance to Zion or Canyonlands from Salt Lake City, the home to many desert climbers.

Most of the prominent buttes had been climbed as mountaineering objectives, summits to be attained, without much emphasis on aesthetics. Jim Langdon climbed both Window Blind and Bottleneck Peaks during this period in the early '70s. George Hurley and Bill Forrest spotted the White Knight along I-70 and climbed it. Paul Horton, Hal Gribble, Steve Walker, Joe Demarsh and Bert Stolt were active on towers beyond Mexican Mountain Road.

But where were the usually omnipresent desert legends Beckey, Carter, and Kor? Apparently the San Rafael had been passed over.

People like Chris Begué and Kent Wheeler visited and established a few climbs, but it was not until 1989–when Dave Anderson led a small group of friends from Salt Lake City into the Swell–that climbing and route development began in earnest. This group included Mike Friedrichs, James Garrett, Will Gilmer, George Jamison, Keith Royster, and Lynn Wheeler. Together they explored a seemingly infinite number of unclimbed Wingate cliffs and found little evidence of previous ascents. Certainly the Anasazi had 4th-classed many buttes in search of food and game. Rustlers and robbers known as the wild bunch had ridden with Butch Cassidy and outlaw Joe Walker into the deep, mysterious gulches of the San Rafael after bank and payroll heists in Price and Castledale. Withdrawing to the Swell, these groups knew it for what it was to become in the '90s for Dave and his friends–an almost mystical yet accessible retreat offering quiet and solitude from the burgeoning sport climbing taking place elsewhere.

As the number of climbs established on any given weekend between 1990-92 superseded all previous activity, statistician Mike Friedrichs began gathering data. Fittingly, he named his bootleg guidebook *Bad Obsession* and swore all to a vow of secrecy. Benjamin Franklin had quipped much earlier: "Three may keep a secret, if two of them are dead," so before long, copies of copies were noticed clutched in the hands of new visitors to the Dylan Wall, until then the exclusive domain of Friedrichs. Increasingly, visitors returned to "discover" and climb additional routes throughout the Swell from 1992 to the present.

While some pursued towers and multiple-pitch routes with all the various wall tactics employed, others concentrated on ever harder crack climbs. Difficult one-pitch free climbs still stand out as the most popular and most frequently climbed routes. The Navajo Sandstone found at the northern entrance to Buckhorn Wash piqued some interest and lent itself to rap-and-drill style face climbs, a source that has hardly been tapped and which offers enormous amounts of sport style red rock climbing.

Herein lies the threat to the San Rafael. Without the dreaded rules and regulations so often found in our National Parks, future climbers, mountain bikers, campers, hunters, cattle and sheep herders must take responsibility for the welfare of the land and the rock. We need to bring in our own firewood rather than gather it. It is a limited resource. Climbers should refrain from squeezing and fabricating routes just for the sake of "another line." We must walk softly around the desert flora and fauna to keep this special place as close as possible to what took us there in the first place. We must learn to respect the rock and respect each other.

J.G.

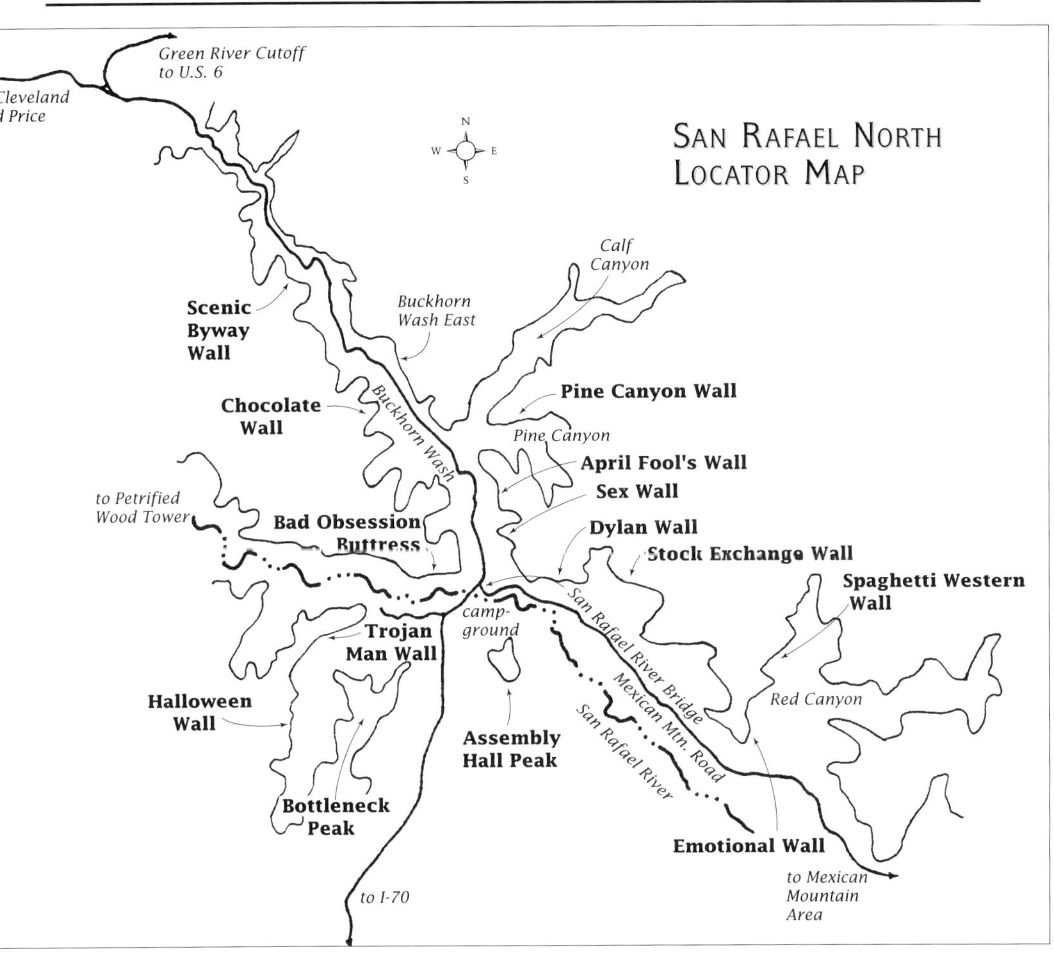

San Rafael North

South approach: I-70 divides San Rafael north and south. To reach San Rafael north, approaching from the south, drive 29 miles (47km) west on I-70 from Green River to Ranch Exit 129. The exit road turns east and parallels the freeway for 3.6 miles (5.7km), then makes a left (north) turn toward the San Rafael River and Buckhorn Wash. From the freeway exit it is 20 miles (32km) to the river and south entrance of Buckhorn Wash over a scenic, well-maintained dirt road (Cottonwood Wash Road). At the river there is a BLM-maintained campground with tables, toilets, firegrills, and information kiosk. North across the river from the campground, the Mexican Mountain Road begins to the east. Straight ahead (north) is the beginning of 10-mile-long (16km) Buckhorn Wash. Five miles (8km) up the wash is one of the Colorado Plateau's best Barrier Canyon Culture pictograph panels. This rock canvas of haunting beauty is believed to be 2000 years or older. These ancient people were hunters and foragers who did not have pottery but used stone and bone tools with atlatls for hunting. In an intensive six-week effort (part of the 1996 Utah Centennial Celebration), the panel was restored from past carvings, paint, chalk, and bullet hole vandalism. The antiquities of Buckhorn Wash are listed on the National Historic Register. Please respect this heritage for the generations yet to view them.

North approach: To reach the North San Rafael Swell from Salt Lake City, drive south on I-15 then State Highway 6 to Price via Soldier Summit. From Price continue toward Castledale via State Highway 10. Turn left on State Highway 155 toward Cleveland (6.1 miles, 9.8km). Cleveland is the last stop for gas and food before entering the Swell. Continue straight after a 4-way stop sign and drive to a "T" in the road. A sign 1.6 miles (2.5km) farther reads: "Dinosaur Quarry 14, Cedar Mountain Recreation Area 15, I-70 46, Lawrence 5." [**NOTE:** Some of the following intersections have multiple signs and many roads do not intersect at 90-degree angles. Mentioned are only the signs facing the approach road.] Veer left, and 0.2 mile (0.3km) farther begin a dirt road. Continue to a sign which reads: "Cleveland Lloyd Dinosaur Quarry 13.7, Buckhorn Wash 14.5, Cedar Mountain Picnic Area 18.7." Turn right and pass a sign: "Road may be impassable due to storms." From here follow signs to reach Buckhorn Wash and the San Rafael River Campground. A short distance farther a sign reads: "San Rafael Campground 22, Highway 50-6 39, I-70 42." This is the famed Green River Cutoff Road. The Buckhorn Well pumphouse and watertank are obvious. Bear left then turn right at the next main road. A little farther a sign reads: "The Spanish Trail 1800 to 1850." Still farther the Buckhorn Reservoir becomes visible to the west. At the next intersection the sign reads: "Buckhorn Wash, Wedge Overlook 6.1, Fuller Bottom 6.5, Cleveland 14 miles" (back to the north). Turn right at a sign which reads: "San Rafael Campground 10, I-70 30, Highway US-6 29." This is the beginning of Buckhorn Wash. At 0.5 mile (0.8km) from the turnoff a sign reads: "Navajo Sandstone." At 1.3 miles (2km) a dirt road branches east up Furniture Draw. Three-tenths of a mile beyond (0.48km), at the south end of a bench on the east side of the road, there is a perfect dinosaur footprint. Please replace the rock that covers and protects it.

NOTE: I recommend to all visiting the Swell a detour to Wedge Overlook for a breathtaking view of the Little Grand Canyon. It is one of the most dramatic scenes on the Colorado Plateau. On the return drive to Price or Green River, it is worth turning east at the north junction of Buckhorn Wash and following the scenic Green River Cutoff (Old Spanish Trail) to US Highway 6, then north to Price or south to Green River.

Buckhorn Wash

Buckhorn Wash descends north to south from younger to older strata of sedimentary rock. It begins with Carmel Sandstone (the equivalent of the Dewey Bridge at Arches National Park), then passes through successive layers of Navajo, Kayenta, Wingate, and Chinle. Climbs on the Wingate are of the excellent quality of Indian Creek (near the Needles District of Canyonlands National Park), but with a much greater variety of definition. For example, one might find a route requiring a variety of protection pieces rather than a splitter type crack requiring 8 to 10 #2 Friends. This added variety often makes for a more interesting and pleasurable climb. Upper Buckhorn Wash is the area from Scenic Byway Wall to Home Haunt.

Scenic Byway Wall

Routes on Scenic Byway Wall climb Navajo Sandstone facing northeast, and are shaded during hot summer afternoons. The climbs are on the west side of the road, are listed left to right, and have a 2-minute approach. Rappel slings are visible on all routes.

North approach: Scenic Byway Wall is 2.5 miles south (4km) of the entrance to Buckhorn Wash. **South approach:** The wall is 7.5 miles north (12km) of the San Rafael River.

NOTE: One-tenth mile north (0.16km) of Scenic Byway Wall, on the east side of the road, is a short trail leading to a panel of Fremont Indian Petroglyphs.

SCENIC BYWAY II, 5.10, 4 pitches, 400 feet (122m), ★★★★

First Ascent: James Garrett, Franziska Garrett, 1992.

Location and Access: *Scenic Byway* climbs to the rim and is in the center of a black wall with two chains visible at the top of Pitch 1. Rappel slings are visible at the top of Pitches 2, 3, and 4. Mike Friedrichs: "Pitch 1 is the best 5.9 handcrack in the swell."

Pitch 1: Ascend an obvious handcrack to a 2-bolt belay, 5.9, 90 feet (27m).

Pitch 2: Continue up a 5.10 offwidth crack (crux) on a right-facing dihedral past a bolt, to where it is possible to traverse left, then 25 feet (8m) of easy climbing to a belay ledge. Do not go to the obvious 2 bolts below the ceiling to the right. Protect the belay with (2) #1 Friends, 5.10, 90 feet (27m).

Pitch 3: The pitch ascends an upside-down "Y" formation with face and grooves over lighter-colored rock, then right to a 2-bolt belay, 5.7, 130 feet (40m).

Pitch 4: Traverse right and continue up a left-facing dihedral to a black patina face behind a small horn. Pass a bolt to a 2-bolt belay on the rim of the landform, 5.8, 90 feet (27m).

Paraphernalia: Standard desert rack; (1) set of TCUs; #1.5 through #3 Friends for Pitch 1; #6 Friend for the offwidth of Pitch 2; (2) quickdraws.

Descent: Rappel the route.

METACARPAL ROAD MAP I, 5.9, 2 pitches, 180 feet (55m), ★

First Ascent: James Garrett, Franziska Garrett, 1992.

Location and Access: *Metacarpal Road Map* ascends hands-to-fingers to a roof.

Pitch 1: Begin as for *Scenic Byway*, then climb 20 feet (6m) and traverse right to a bush.

Pitch 2: Continue up the large obvious left-facing dihedral to the right. Rappel chains are visible from below. Carpal bones are hand bones, thus the name.

NOTE: The route can join *Scenic Byway* below its Pitch 2 anchors, thus bypassing the Pitch 2 offwidth of *Scenic Byway*.

Paraphernalia: One set of Friends with double #1 through #3.5.

Descent: Rappel the route.

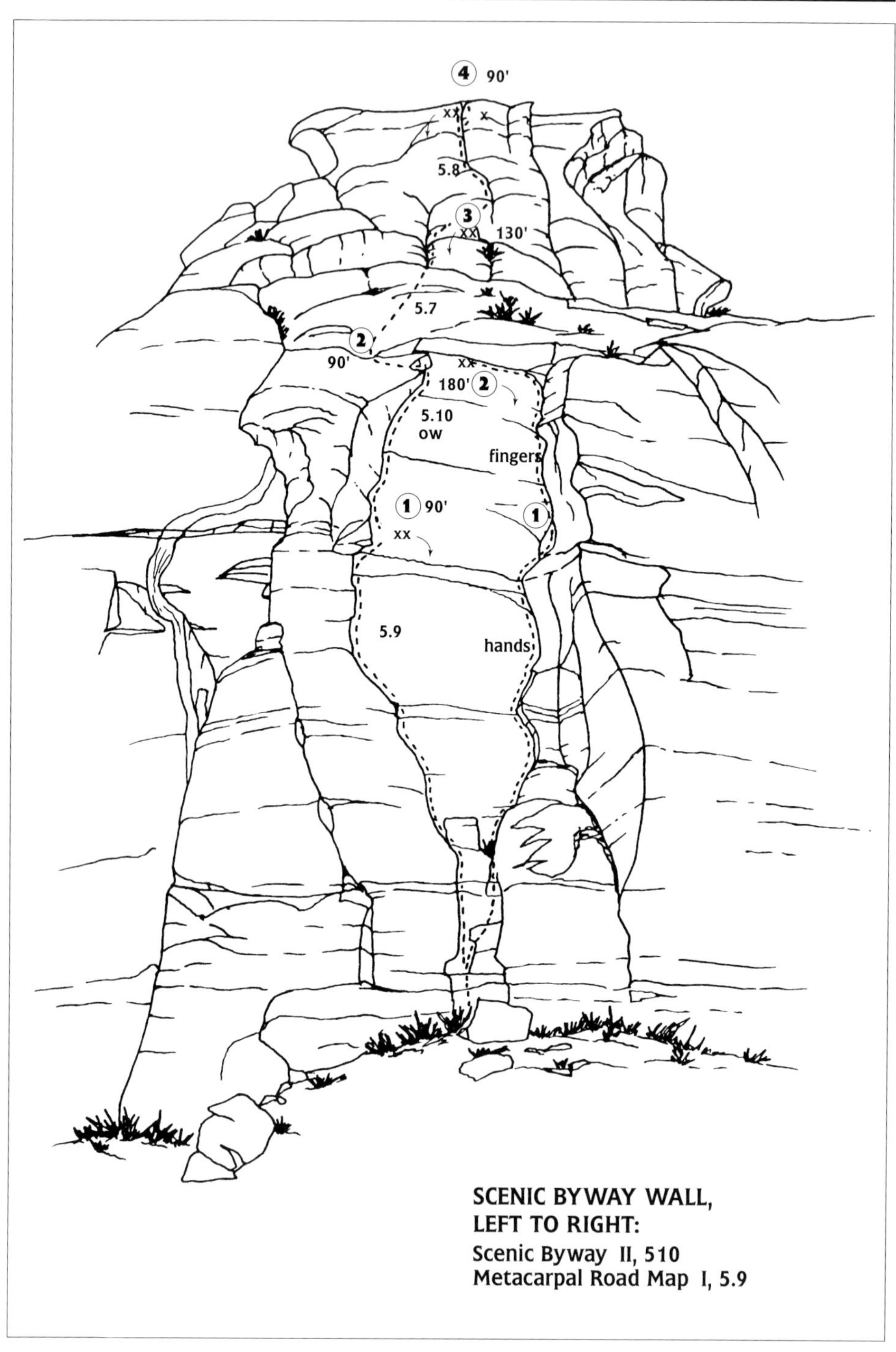

**SCENIC BYWAY WALL,
LEFT TO RIGHT:**

Scenic Byway II, 510
Metacarpal Road Map I, 5.9

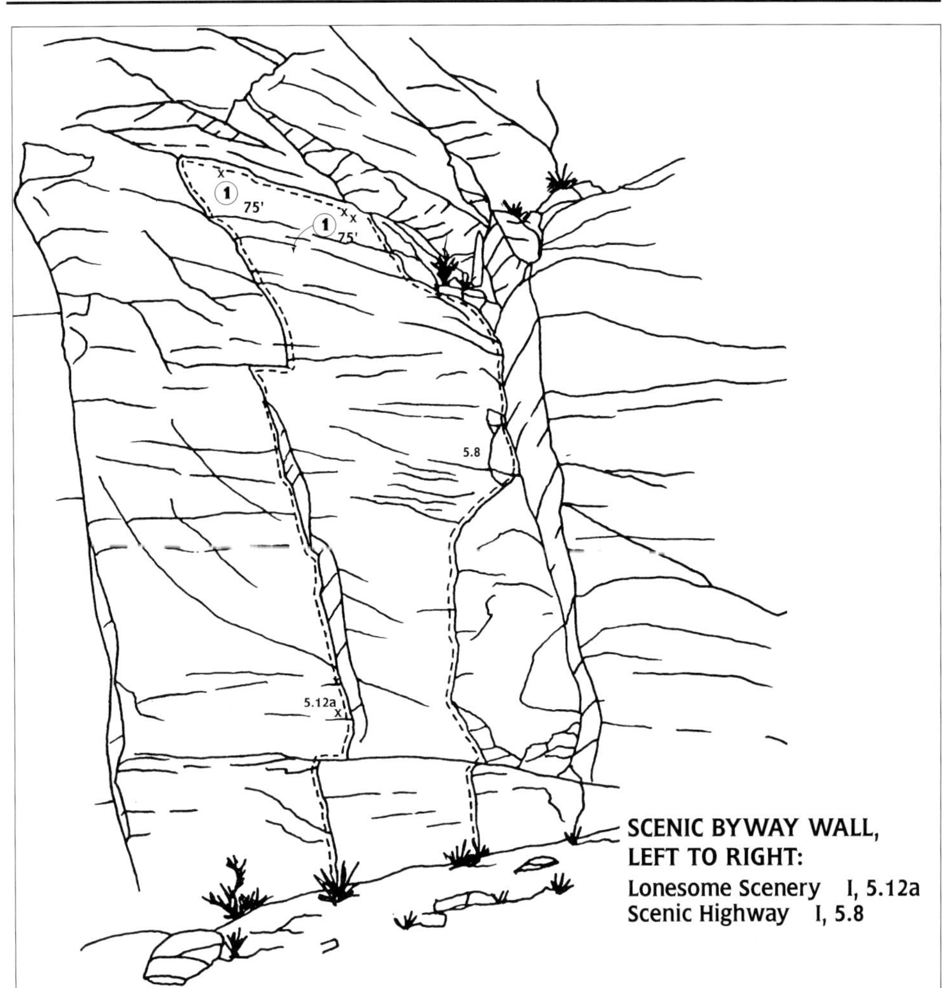

LONESOME SCENERY I, 5.12a, 1 pitch, 75 feet (23m)

First Ascent: Mike Friedrichs, Joe Cupps, 1993.

Location and Access: *Lonesome Scenery* is 15 feet (4.5m) left of *Scenic Highway*. The route climbs to a bolt, then traverses right to the top of *Scenic Highway*. Rappel slings are visible from below.

Paraphernalia: TCUs; small nuts; (1) quickdraw.

Descent: Rappel the route.

SCENIC HIGHWAY I, 5.8, 1 pitch, 75 feet (23m), ★

First Ascent: James Garrett, Franziska Garrett, 1992.

Location and Access: *Scenic Highway* is 15 feet (4.5m) right of *Lonesome Scenery*. It curves up a flake with a handcrack that ends at a ceiling and a 2-bolt anchor.

Paraphernalia: Standard desert rack.

Descent: Rappel the route.

Anti-Swell, Bradley Mountain Wear

Anti-Swell is on the west side of Buckhorn Wash, 0.2 mile south (0.3km) of Scenic Byway Wall. *Bradley Mountain Wear* is 0.5 mile south (0.8km) of *Anti-Swell* on the east side of the road. Both routes climb Navajo Sandstone.

ANTI-SWELL I, 5.10b, 1 pitch, 60 feet (18m)

First Ascent: Mike Friedrichs, Todd Leeds 1995.

Location and Access: *Anti-Swell* is a sport route beginning above a good-sized talus cone/boulder field. Climb the left wall of a large left-facing dihedral on the west side of the road. Face climb to rappel anchors visible from below.

Paraphernalia: Eight quickdraws.

Descent: Rappel the route from double-bolts.

BRADLEY MOUNTAIN WEAR I, 5.11d, 1 pitch, 165 feet (50m)

First Ascent: Mike Friedrichs, Todd Leeds, February 1995.

Location and Access: This sport climb is left of a chimney system above large boulders positioned on a talus slope at the right end of a buttress on the east side of Buckhorn Wash, south of *Anti-Swell*. Park on the west side of the road. Climb the left wall of a right-facing dihedral to rappel chains visible from below. The route is dedicated in memory of Sean Bradley.

Paraphernalia: Fifteen quickdraws.

Descent: One double-rope rappel from three bolts.

Outhouse Tower, Home Haunt

Approximately 2.4 miles (3.8km) toward the San Rafael River from the Scenic Byway Wall a sign reads: "Wingate Sandstone–Triassic Age, 180,000,000 years old." Outhouse Tower is the obvious landform on the east side of the road 2.7 miles south (4.3km) of Scenic Byway Wall, approximately 200 feet (61m) south of a BLM public outhouse. The only other facility in the area is at the San Rafael River Campground 5.1 miles south (8km).

OUTHOUSE TOWER—CHOPPED SAND I, 5.8, A0, 1 pitch, 160 feet (49m)

First Ascent: James Garrett, solo, 1990.

Location and Access: *Chopped Sand* begins beyond the left profile of the landform when viewed from the road, then climbs a ridge and finally a large summit block (Outhouse Tower). On the lower portion of the route follow steps carved by a previous unknown party.

Paraphernalia: One set of Friends.

Descent: Rappel the route.

NOTE: There are Petroglyphs on the upper wall near a cave left of the outhouse. A sign reading: "Chinle Formation" is 6.8 miles south (11km) of Scenic Byway Wall.

HOME HAUNT I, 5.10, A1, 3 pitches, 160 feet (49m)

First Ascent: James Garrett, Franziska Garrett, 9 October 1996.

San Rafael Swell, Assembly Hall Peak

Location and Access: *Home Haunt* is the next landform south of Outhouse Tower, 200 feet (61m). The landform is 25 feet (7.6m) from the east side of the road. Climb the northwest face of a pillar beginning up a left-facing dihedral.

Pitch 1: Climb past a fixed piton, a wide section, and two bolts to a double-anchor belay at a stance, 135 feet (41m).

Pitch 2: Continue up a right-facing corner (#4 Camalot) to an alcove and double-anchor belay.

Pitch 3: Climb 5.9 past a fixed anchor to the summit.

Paraphernalia: Standard desert rack; a few Lost Arrows; (4) quickdraws.

Descent: Walk-off to the left approximately 1500 feet (457m).

Middle Buckhorn Wash

Approximately 0.6 mile south (0.9km) of Outhouse Tower a sign reads: "Buckhorn Wash Pictograph Panel–Drive Slowly 500 feet." There is an unknown route on the east side of the wash across from the sign. Ascend a left-facing corner where three sets of rappel slings are visible at a bedding seam. The pictograph panel (around the corner) was restored from extreme vandalism in 1995–96. An interpretive kiosk, a rail fence, and viewing path were built to aid in the protection and appreciation of what is certainly one of the most beautiful rock art panels on the Colorado Plateau. Please visit with reverence and respect.

Photo: Eric Bjørnstad

Buckhorn Wash North, left to right: *Street Legal, BBQ Bomber, Ladies of the '80s.*

At a location 1.6 miles south (2.5km) of Outhouse Tower a sign reads "Chinle Formation." Middle Buckhorn Wash climbs begin 1.8 miles south (2.8km) of Outhouse Tower and are listed left to right.

STREET LEGAL I, 5.11, 1 pitch, 80 feet (24m), ★★★★★

First Ascent: Mike Friedrichs, Mary Ellen Gage, Gene Roush, 1990.

Location and Access: *Street Legal* is 15 feet (4.5m) left of *BBQ Bomber*. The route climbs a right-facing dihedral to rappel slings visible on the left wall below a prominent overhang.

Paraphernalia: Friends (1) #2.5; TCUs.

Descent: Rappel the route.

BBQ BOMBER I, 5.11, 1 pitch, 155 feet (47m), ★★★★★

First Ascent: Names withheld by request of first ascent party. The following route information was obtained by independent field research.

Location and Access: *BBQ Bomber* is plaqued with the date 3/90. Begin in a left-facing dihedral left of a large fallen pillar. Climb to a ledge right of a prominent ceiling with a 1.5-inch (3.8cm) crack system.

Paraphernalia: Friends (2-3) #0.5, (2) #1, (5) #1.5, (3) #2, (1) #2.5, #3, (2-3) #3.5, (3) #4.

Descent: Rappel the route from the top of the climb or traverse 30 feet (9m) right and rappel from slings visible from below.

Photo: Eric Bjørnstad

Left to right: ***Ladies of the '80s, Vertical Smile.***

LADIES OF THE '80s I, A2+, C1, 1 pitch, 130 feet (40m)

First Ascent: Rob McKeracher, Matt Fetbrod, 29 April 1996.

Location and Access: *Ladies of the '80s* climbs a uniform 0.25-inch (0.6cm) splitter crack right of a fallen pillar (right of *BBQ Bomber*) to a three-piton rappel station. The crux is 15 feet (4.5m) off the ground above a fixed Leeper Z-ton.

Paraphernalia: For clean aid (to avoid excessive nailing, especially on the first 30 feet-9m) bring (5-10) large Lowe Balls; (10) #0 TCUs, a few Blue Aliens; (1) medium Leeper Z-ton; quickdraws.

Descent: One double-rope rappel down the route.

NOTE: The first ascent party requests that future climbers repeat the start of the climb with clean aid and not desecrate the very straight and beautiful line by nailing it.

VERTICAL SMILE II, 5.7, A2+, 2 pitches, 310 feet (94m)

First Ascent: Rob McKeracher, Matt Fetbrod, 3-5 May 1996.

Location and Access: *Vertical Smile* follows the next crack system right of *Ladies of the '80s*, right of the south end of the buttress facing the road. The first ascent team climbed 70 feet (21m) of a third pitch before encountering large, very loose blocks and turning back. They suggest a more experienced (or brave) party may be able to push the 130-foot (40m) third pitch to the top.

Pitch 1: Begin at a 6-inch (15cm) sharp flare 6 feet (11m) above ground (in a roof right of the buttress facing the road). Continue up the crack system through various difficulties to an A1 crack which leads to three fixed pitons, 5.7, A2+.140 feet (43m). The crux is 15 feet (4.5m) off the ground past a fixed Leeper Z-ton.

Pitch 2: Continue up the same crack system past various flares, pods, and blocks through a chimney to a double-piton anchor on good rock to the right, 5.7, A1+, 170 feet (52m).

Paraphernalia: Two sets of Friends to #6; #5 Camalots; (2) sets of TCUs/Aliens to Friend sizes; #0.5 through #7 Tri-cams; (1) set of wires; small selection of long Lost Arrows, knifeblades, Bugaboos 0.5" to ⅝"; angles; 60m ropes; quickdraws.

Descent: Rappel the route 170 feet (52m), then 140 feet (43m).

PRIVATE PIZZA I, 5.9, 1 pitch, 70 feet (21m), ★★★★

First Ascent: Will Gilmer, 1990.

Location and Access: *Private Pizza* is 0.2 mile south (0.3km) of *Vertical Smile* on the south side of the drainage south of *Vertical Smile*. Climb a double-crack system up a left-facing dihedral (up light-colored rock) to rappel anchors visible from the road.

Paraphernalia: Friends #1 through #4.

Descent: Rappel the route.

Chocolate Wall

Chocolate Wall is north and across from Pine Canyon, on the right side of the second drainage north of *Kent's Hand Crack*. Routes are listed left to right.

BLONDE ON BLONDE I, 5.10, 1 pitch, ★★

First Ascent: Joe Statler, Mike Friedrichs, 1990.

Location and Access: Climb a right-facing dihedral to the top of a pillar formation. Rappel slings are visible from the road.

Paraphernalia: Protection for a 1-4" (2.5–10cm) crack system.

Descent: Rappel the route.

JAMISON ENGINEERING I, 5.10c, 1 pitch, ★★

First Ascent: George Jamison, Mary Ellen Gage, Mike Friedrichs, 1990.

Location and Access: *Jamison Engineering* is around the corner from *Short Stack*. Climb a steep crack leading to a ledge 15 feet (4.5m) above ground. Mike Friedrichs: "Continue up an undulating crack to fingers as the route arches left. Fun."

Paraphernalia: Standard desert rack.

Descent: Rappel the route.

SHORT STACK I, 5.10d, 1 pitch, 60 feet (18m), ★★★★★

First Ascent: Names withheld by request of first ascent party. Information on this route was obtained by independent field research.

Location and Access: Begin up a wide crack system, then continue with a 1.5-inch crack (3.8cm) to rappel anchors visible from below.

Paraphernalia: Protection for 1.5" crack (3.8cm).

Descent: Rappel the route.

Pine Canyon Wall

Pine Canyon Wall is reached from a 4-wheel-drive track 0.5 mile east (0.8km) up Pine Canyon from Buckhorn Wash. The mouth of the canyon is obvious 0.2 mile south (0.3km) of Chocolate Wall or approximately 2 miles north (3km) of the San Rafael River Bridge. Rappel slings are visible with binoculars from Buckhorn Wash Road. Routes are listed left to right and are one pitch except for the two-pitch *Once is Enough*.

BURGERDIER GENERAL I, 5.11, 1 pitch, 140 feet (43m), ★★★★

First Ascent: Names withheld by request of first ascent party. The following route information was obtained by independent field research.

Location and Access: *Burgerdier General* climbs a splitter crack on the wall's west face. It is approximately 100 feet left (30m) of *Once is Enough*. Rappel slings are visible from below.

Paraphernalia: Standard desert rack, with several #1, #2 Friends.

Descent: Rappel the route.

ONCE IS ENOUGH I, 5.10, 2 pitches, 130 feet (40m), ★★

First Ascent: Names withheld by request of first ascent party. The following route information was obtained by independent field research.

Location and Access: *Once is Enough* is approximately 100 feet right (30m) of *Burgerdier General* and climbs a left-facing dihedral with "KR" deeply inscribed at its base. It is the most prominent wide crack on the wall with desert varnish on both sides of the route. Rappel slings are visible from below.

Pitch 1: Climb to a small stance.

Pitch 2: Continue to anchors on the right wall of a dihedral.

Paraphernalia: Several #4 through #6 Friends.

Descent: Rappel the route.

LITE NOT SOLID I, 5.10d, 1 pitch, 155 feet (47m), ★★★★★

First Ascent: Mike Friedrichs, Mary Ellen Gage, 1991.

Location and Access: *Lite Not Solid* is 10 feet left (3m) of *Rabid Muslim*. Mike Friedrichs: "Climb up and left, clip 2 bolts, and surmount a wild roof to start. Follow corner and move right when the crack in the corner seams out. Follow splitter to double-bolt belay."

Paraphernalia: Many #1 and #2 Friends with (2) #3.5; TCUs; (2) quickdraws.

Descent: Rappel the route.

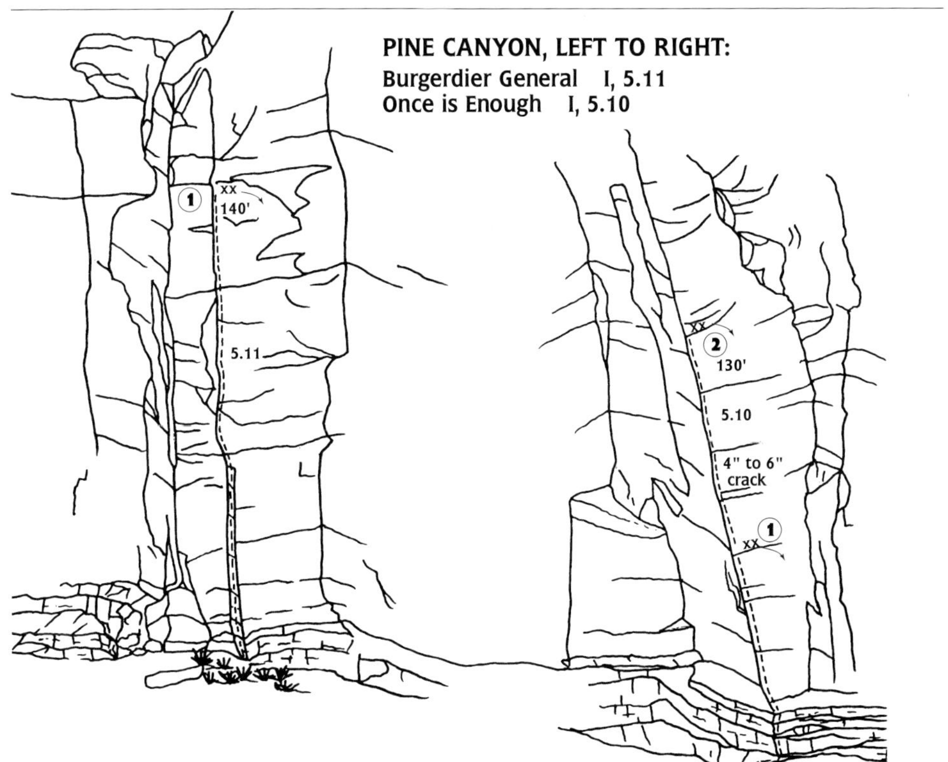

RABID MUSLIM I, 5.11, 1 pitch, 140 feet (43m), ★★★★★

First Ascent: Names withheld by request of first ascent party. The following route information was obtained by independent field research.

Location and Access: *Rabid Muslim* climbs a block about 10 feet (3m) right of *Lite Not Solid*. Pass a roof on its right side and continue to rappel slings visible from below. Dave Medara: "Awesome!"

Paraphernalia: Several #1 through #3.5 Friends.

Descent: Rappel the route.

OLD BUSHMILLS I, 5.10, 1 pitch, 70 feet (21m), ★★★

First Ascent: Kent Wheeler.

Location and Access: *Old Bushmills* is right of *Rabid Muslim*. Lieback in a shallow corner to rappel slings visible from below. The route is named for an Irish Whiskey.

Paraphernalia: Friends #2, #3.5, #1.5

Descent: Rappel the route.

ANCHORS FROM HELL I, 5.10c, 1 pitch, 75 feet (23m), ★★★★

First Ascent: Names withheld by request of first ascent party. The following route information was obtained by independent field research.

Location and Access: *Anchors from Hell* is 20 feet right (6m) of *Old Bushmills* and climbs to anchors in a pod and visible from below.

Paraphernalia: A selection of Friends with several #1.

Descent: Rappel the route.

UNNAMED ROUTE I, 5.12b, 1 pitch, ★★★★

First Ascent: Mike Friedrichs. First free ascent: John Merriam, April 1997.

Location and Access: *Unnamed Route* climbs the corner/arête (past 2 bolts) to the top of the wall.

Paraphernalia: Two quickdraws and small cams.

Descent: Rappel the route.

Lower Buckhorn Wash

Lower Buckhorn Wash climbs are on east and west walls south of Pine Canyon.

KENT'S HAND CRACK I, 5.11–, 1 pitch, 80 feet (24m), ★★★★

First Ascent: Kent Wheeler, Chris Begué, 1980s.

Location and Access: Kent's Hand Crack is on the west side of Lower Buckhorn Wash approximately 0.2 mile south (0.3km) of a sign reading "Mossback Formation." It is also obvious as a straight-in crack at the far left edge of the west (right) wall when looking south from the entrance of Pine Canyon. *Kent's Hand Crack* climbs a straight-in crack at the far left corner of a green lichen wall. Rappel slings are visible from below.

Paraphernalia: Two sets of Friends from #3 with extra #3.5, #4; Camalots (1) #4; Tri-cam (1)#7.

Descent: Rappel the route.

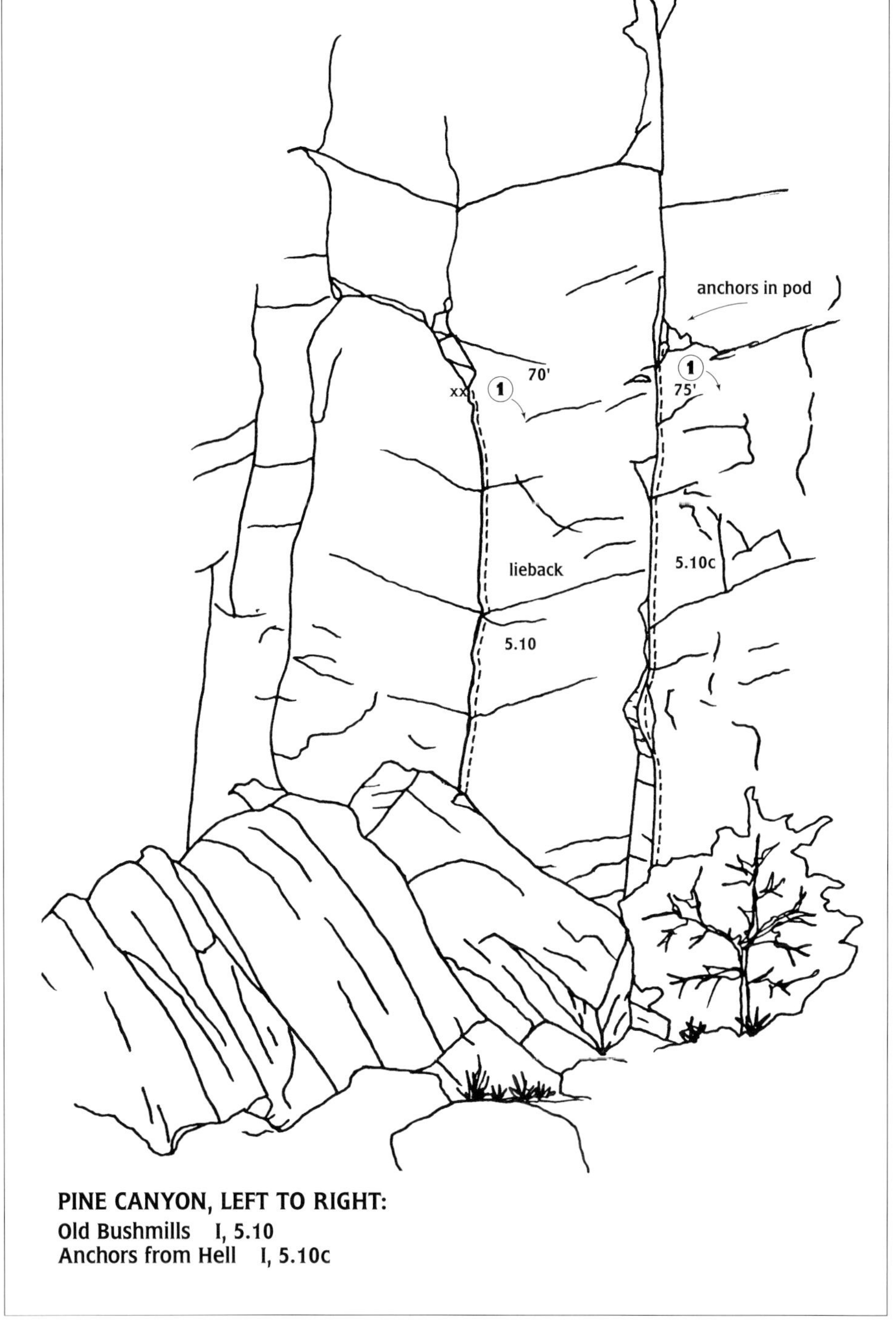

PINE CANYON, LEFT TO RIGHT:
Old Bushmills I, 5.10
Anchors from Hell I, 5.10c

April Fool's Wall

Approximately 0.5 mile south (0.8km) of *Kent's Hand Crack* a sign reads: "Moenkopi Formation." From this vantage there is an excellent view of James's Tower and Wisdom Tooth on the west side of Buckhorn Wash; on the east side and to the south are April Fool's Wall and Sex Wall, and further south Assembly Hall and Window Blind Peaks. April Fool's Wall is approximately 0.2 mile south (0.3km) of the Moenkopi Formation sign. Many routes are around the corner right from the portion of the wall facing the road, but the easiest approach to the buttress is from the far left. When approached from the San Rafael River, the climbs are on the next buttress north of Sex Wall (approximately 0.3 mile, 0.5km). The wall is named for its first ascent on April Fool's Day 1990. Routes are listed left to right.

MEAN WEENER I, 5.11b, 1 pitch, 90 feet (27m), ★★★★★

First Ascent: Names withheld by request of first ascent party. The following route information was obtained by independent field research.

Location and Access: *Mean Weener* is a splitter crack at the far left (west) end of the wall.

Paraphernalia: Several #1.5, #2 Friends.

Descent: Rappel the route.

FOOL'S GOLD I, 5.10b, 1 pitch, 80 feet (24m)

First Ascent: Dave Anderson, Keith Royster, James Garrett, Will Gilmer, 1 April 1990.

Location and Access: *Fool's Gold* is right of *Mean Weener*. Begin with hands and continue up a chimney to anchors visible from below.

Paraphernalia: Fist-to-offwidth protection; Friends #3.5 through #6.

Descent: Rappel the route.

FOOLS RUSH IN I, 5.10a, 2 pitches, 60 feet (18m), ★★

First Ascent: James Garrett, Will Gilmer, 1 April 1990.

Location and Access: *Fools Rush In* is approximately 100 feet south (30m) of *Fool's Gold* and climbs a right-leaning handcrack through a roof on a wall with dark desert varnish. Anchors are not visible from below.

Pitch 1: Begin with a 5.9 handcrack under a ceiling (block wedged in a crack).

Pitch 2: Climb over the block and up the face.

Paraphernalia: Standard desert rack.

Descent: Rappel the route.

Sex Wall

Sex Wall is the buttress south of April Fool's Wall on the same (east) side of Buckhorn Wash. When approached from the bridge over the San Rafael River, Sex Wall is north of the first drainage on the east walls of Buckhorn Wash, approximately 0.5 mile (0.8km) from the river. Routes are listed left to right.

PROSTATE PROBLEM I, 5.10d, 1 pitch, 140 feet (43m)

First Ascent: Dave Anderson, Keith Royster, James Garrett, April 1990.

Location and Access: *Prostate Problem* is left of *Safe Sex* and climbs a crack system through a ceiling to rappel anchors visible from below.

APRIL FOOL'S WALL:
Fool's Gold I, 5.10b
1
80'
wide
5.10b
chimney

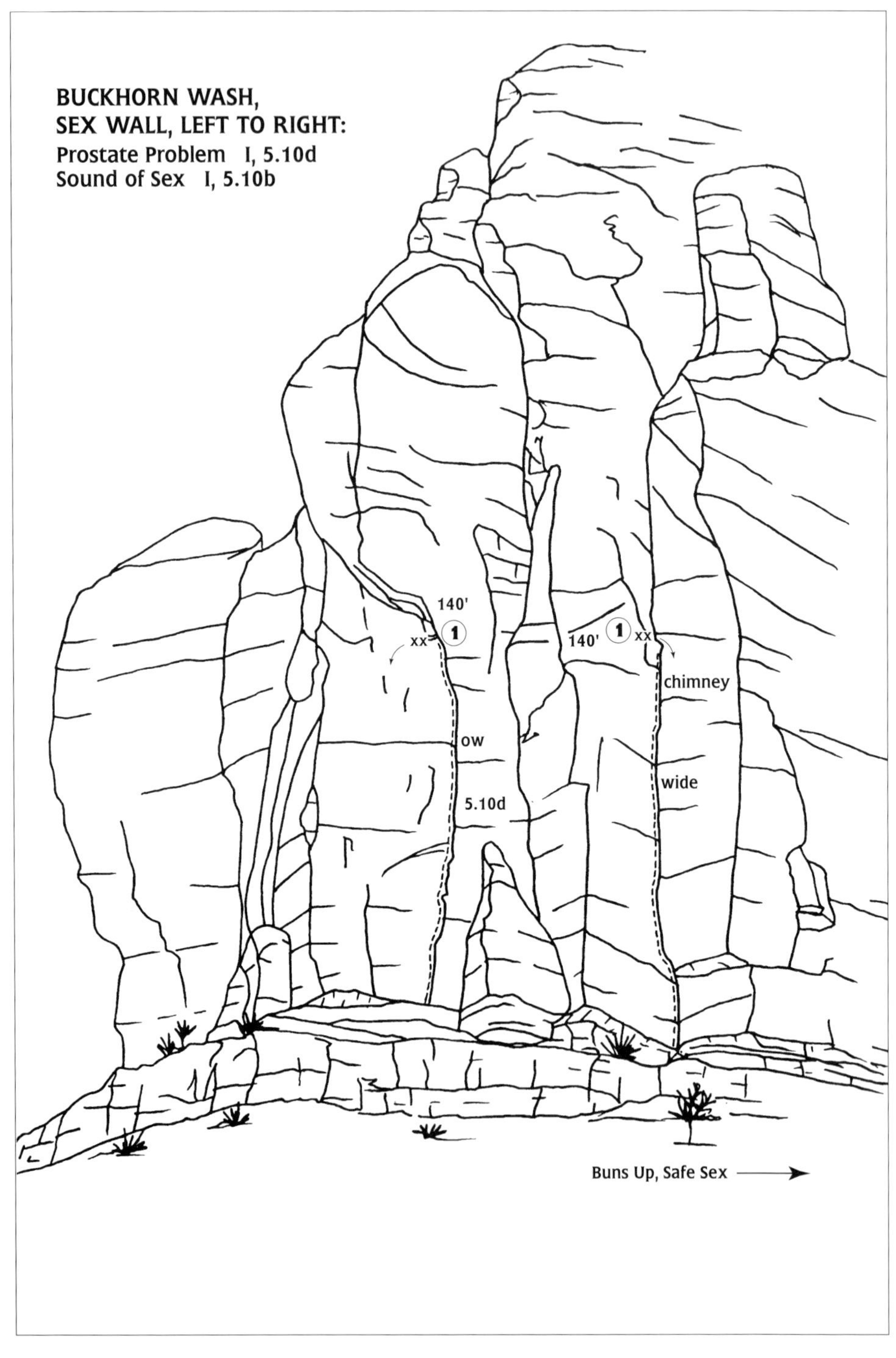
BUCKHORN WASH,
SEX WALL, LEFT TO RIGHT:
Prostate Problem I, 5.10d
Sound of Sex I, 5.10b
140'
xx
1
ow
5.10d
140'
1
xx
chimney
wide
Buns Up, Safe Sex

Paraphernalia: Standard desert rack.

Descent: Rappel the route.

SOUND OF SEX I, 5.10b, 1 pitch, 140 feet (43m), ★★★

First Ascent: Dave Anderson, James Garrett, Will Gilmer, 1990.

Location and Access: *Sound of Sex* is three cracks right of the prow and one crack right of an obvious tower. The route climbs a wide crack to a chimney.

Paraphernalia: Large Friends.

Descent: Rappel the route.

BUNS UP I, 5.11a, 1 pitch, 120 feet (37m), ★★

First Ascent: Names withheld by request of first ascent party. The following route information was obtained by independent field research.

Location and Access: *Buns Up* ascends a long offwidth crack on the right side of a tower-like structure right of *Sound of Sex*.

Paraphernalia: Standard desert rack.

Descent: Rappel the route.

SAFE SEX I, 5.12a, 1 pitch, 165 feet (50m), ★★★★★

First Ascent: Mike Friedrichs, James Garrett, 1990.

Location and Access: *Safe Sex* climbs right of a light brown wall six cracks right of the left prow of the landform, approximately 70 feet right (21m) of *Sound of Sex*. Rappel anchors are visible from the road.

Paraphernalia: Standard desert rack with many #1 Friends.

Descent: Rappel the route.

Lower Buckhorn Wash West

Lower Buckhorn Wash West routes are on the west side of Buckhorn Wash south of *Kent's Hand Crack*.

ATTENTION SPAN I, 5.11, 1 pitch, 165 feet (50m)

First Ascent: Mike Friedrichs, George Jamison, 1990.

Location and Access: *Attention Span* is around the corner (south) from *Kent's Hand Crack*, ten crack systems from the right prow of the buttress. When approached from the south a sign reads: "25 mph" (with a left-curving arrow). Rappel anchors are visible from the road. Climb a left-facing dihedral. Mike Friedrichs: "Wild liebacking and underclinging through rotten rock takes one to a nice clean crack up a corner to belay anchors. The crux is at the undercling. A fixed stopper at the lip is to prevent rope hassles."

Paraphernalia: Medium Friends; TCUs.

Descent: Rappel the route.

WISDOM TOOTH—CRYPTOGAMIC FOREST III, 5.11b, 2 pitches, 225 feet (69m), ★★★★★

First Ascent: Pitch 1: Mike Friedrichs, George Jamison, 5.11b, 1990. Pitch 2: Dave Medara, John Merriam, 5.9+, April 1996.

Location and Access: Wisdom Tooth is the stout tower on the south side of the canyon north of James's Tower. *Cryptogamic Forest* climbs the north face of the landform.

Pitch 1: Begin up a 1-inch (2.5cm) splitter crack which widens to 3-inches (7.6cm) and ends on a large ledge, 5.11b, 165 feet (50m).

Pitch 2: Continue to the top of the tower (wide), 5.9+, 60 feet (18m).

Paraphernalia: Friends #1 through #4.

Descent: Two double-rope rappels.

WISDOM TOOTH—TOOTHACHE I, 5.12c, 1 pitch, 120 feet (37m), ★★★★★

First Ascent: Dave Medara, John Merriam, 3 May 1996.

Location and Access: *Toothache* climbs the dihedral facing Buckhorn Wash Road. Follow three bolts to an overhanging corner. Dave Medara: "Incredible."

Paraphernalia: Three sets of Friends through #2; Camalots (1) #0.5; (3) quickdraws.

Descent: Rappel the route.

RED CORNER I, 5.11a, 1 pitch, 80 feet (24m), ★★★★★

First Ascent: Mike Friedrichs, George Jamison, 1990.

Location and Access: *Red Corner* is across from April Fool's Buttress. From James' Tower traverse 0.2 mile north (0.32km) around a bowl of broken light-colored rock to the next vertical cliff line. The route is around the corner (south) from Wisdom Tooth on the buttress facing Buckhorn Wash Road. Right of *Jet Pilot* climb a right-facing dihedral on red rock to double-bolt rappel anchors visible from below.

Paraphernalia: One set of Friends with many #1s.

Descent: Rappel the route.

JET PILOT I, 5.11R, 1 pitch

First Ascent: George Jamison, Mike Friedrichs, 1990.

Location and Access: *Jet Pilot* is left of *Red Corner* and begins from the same bench as *James' Tower.*

Paraphernalia: Unknown.

Descent: Rappel the route from anchors visible from below.

JAMES' TOWER (aka The Lightbulb) II, 5.10, A1, 2 pitches, 170 feet (52m), ★★★★

First Ascent: James Garrett, solo, 25 April 1990.

Location and Access: James' Tower is the obvious top-heavy spire 300 feet north (91m) of *Bat Dreams*. The tower's geographic location is 0.8 mile north (1.2km) of the San Rafael River, directly opposite Sex Wall. The approach is approximately 30 minutes from Buckhorn Wash Road. Begin the climb on the far right or northern edge of the landform and continue around to the south side.

Pitch 1: The first pitch is free and climbs fingers-to-hands-to-fists (dirty, sandy) wrapping around to the left and a good ledge (watch for rope drag).

Pitch 2: Ascend 11 bolts up the inverted bulb.

Paraphernalia: One set of Friends; (11) quickdraws; large cams.

Descent: One double-rope rappel.

Photo: Eric Bjørnstad

James' Tower **(aka** ***The Lightbulb*****) far right**

NOTE: There is an arch in the ridge right of James' Tower seen when the landform first comes into view when approaching from the south.

CAVE CRACK I, 5.9, 1 pitch, 150 feet (46m), ★★

First Ascent: Mike Friedrichs, Will Gilmer, 1990.

Location and Access: *Cave Crack* is near the south entrance to Buckhorn Wash, 0.5 mile north (0.8km) of the bridge over the San Rafael River. Watch for a black culvert running under the road for the approach point directly below the climb. Some route finding may be necessary. *Cave Crack* ascends a right-facing dihedral which becomes wide at its top.

Paraphernalia: Protection for a wide crack system.

Descent: Rappel from anchors in a cave-like formation.

BAT DREAMS I, 5.11a, 1 pitch, 150 feet (46m), ★★★★★

First Ascent: Will Gilmer, Mike Friedrichs, Gene Roush, 1990.

Location and Access: *Bat Dreams* is a prominent left-facing dihedral left of *Cave Crack* with rappel slings visible from below. The crux is steep liebacking up a #1.5 Friend crack at the top of the route.

Paraphernalia: Friends #1.5 through #2.5.

Descent: Rappel the route.

Mexican Mountain Road

Mexican Mountain Road begins just north of the bridge over the San Rafael River and runs east for approximately 14 miles (23km).

Bad Obsession Buttress

Bad Obsession Buttress is the south-facing wall above the San Rafael River west of the bridge at the south entrance to Buckhorn Wash, just west of the beginning of Mexican Mountain Road. *Bad Obsession* climbs the best looking crack system on the dark varnished wall left (west) of a large light-colored area of broken rock. *Bad Obsession* is the apt name Mike Friedrichs chose in 1990 for his private climbing guide to the San Rafael Swell. He quotes Guns N' Roses (rock and roll band): "I can't stop thinking about doin' it one more time. It's a bad obsession, always messin', always messin' my mind."

BAD OBSESSION III, 5.11d, 3 pitches, 305 feet (93m), ★★★★★

First Ascent: Mike Friedrichs, Gene Roush, October 1991.

Location and Access: Mike Friedrichs: "First pitch is thin corner (TCUs and #1s) to short overhanging splitter (#1.5s). After a rest, continue up splitter (#2s and #2.5s), jog left and up to bolts on face, 165 feet. The second pitch begins with hands and goes into a clean corner with aesthetic stacking, 5.10a, 140 feet. A short fourth-class pitch takes one to the top of the buttress."

Paraphernalia: Friends through #2.5; TCUs.

Descent: Rappel the route.

Dylan Wall

For years Dylan Wall has been the private sanctuary of a small fraternity of climbers who furtively visited this Wingate Shangri-la. It was inevitable that leaks would occur, and a young guidebook writer succumbed to the temptation of revealing its secrets. When this happened, Mike Friedrichs, who is the principal developer of Dylan Wall, agreed to provide *Desert Rock* with details of climbs there.

Dylan Wall is the south-facing buttress above the San Rafael River, right (east) of the bridge at the south entrance to Buckhorn Wash. To reach, scramble up the obvious boulder field breaching the Chinle cliffs at the left (west) end of the wall, then traverse to the far east where the established routes lie. A more popular and direct approach is from the east from Mexican Mountain Road, which begins north of the bridge over the San Rafael River. Drive 1.8 miles (2.9km) to the top of the first hill and turn left (north) on a dirt track which, in 0.4 mile (0.6km) ends at a drainage below the eastern end of Dylan Wall. Hike the wash until a scramble through the Chinle cliffs is feasible. Once on the broad shelf below the wall the climber approach trail should be followed to minimize destruction to the fragile topsoil and other aesthetic degradations. When familiar with the routes, climbers may approach Dylan Wall directly from the center of the buttress (by easy fifth class) at a point directly below *Changing of the Guard*. Routes are listed right to left.

TWEETER AND THE MONKEY MAN
I, 5.10c, 1 pitch, 155 feet (47m), ★★★

First Ascent: Steve Roach, Mike Friedrichs, Anne Yeagle.

Photo: Eric Bjørnstad

Dylan Wall, from left to right: *Watching the River Flow, Bob Can't Climb, Tweeter and the Monkey Man.*

Location and Access: *Tweeter and the Monkey Man* is four crack systems right of *Bob Can't Climb*. Rappel anchors are visible from below.

Paraphernalia: Friends #0.5 through #4.

Descent: Rappel the route.

BOB CAN'T CLIMB I, 5.10b, 1 pitch, 155 feet (47m), ★★★

First Ascent: Mary Ellen Gage, Mike Friedrichs, 1992.

Location and Access: *Bob Can't Climb* is at the far right (east) end of the south-facing wall. Climb a shallow right-facing dihedral to double-bolt rappel anchors visible from below.

Paraphernalia: One set of Friends with several #1.

Descent: Rappel the route.

WATCHING THE RIVER FLOW I, 5.11c, 1 pitch, 110 feet (34m), ★★★

First Ascent: Mike Friedrichs, solo, 1992.

Location and Access: Begin up a shallow right-facing corner past three bolts which lead to a good ledge low on the route. The climb is approximately 75 feet left (23m) of *Bob Can't Climb.*

Paraphernalia: Friends #2.5, #3.5; TCUs; stoppers; (3) quickdraws.

Descent: Rappel the route from anchors visible from below.

ISIS I, 5.12b/c, 1 pitch, 130 feet (40m), ★★★★

First Ascent: Mike Friedrichs, Keith Royster, Mary Ellen Gage, 1992. First Free Ascent: Jonny Woodward.

Location and Access: *Isis* is left of *Watching the River Flow* and climbs a left-facing dihedral with rappel slings visible from below. There is a bolt at the lip to keep ropes from jamming.

Paraphernalia: Several #1 and #2 Friends; TCUs for the top of the climb; (1) quickdraw.

Descent: Rappel the route.

SIMPLE TWIST OF FATE I, 5.11b, 1 pitch, 125 feet (38m), ★★★★★

First Ascent: Mike Friedrichs, solo, 1992.

Location and Access: Climb a thin deep crack with several pods, two cracks left of *Isis*, past two bolts to rappel slings visible from below.

Paraphernalia: A selection of small through large cams; (3) purple #0 TCUs; (2) quickdraws.

Descent: Rappel the route.

OBVIOUSLY 5 BELIEVERS I, 5.10c, 1 pitch, 135 feet (41m)

First Ascent: *Mike Friedrichs, Mary Ellen Gage*, 1992.

Location and Access: *Obviously 5 Believers* is one crack system (around a prow of rock) left of *Simple Twist of Fate*. Begin behind and right of a large detached boulder. Mike Friedrichs: "Anticlassic!"

Paraphernalia: A selection of Friends.

Descent: Rappel the route from slings visible from below.

ONE MORE CUP OF COFFEE I, 5.10d, 1 pitch, 165 feet (50m), ★★★★★

First Ascent: Mike Friedrichs, Mary Ellen Gage, 1991.

Location and Access: *One More Cup of Coffee* was the first route established on Dylan Wall. It climbs a left-facing dihedral one crack left of *Obviously 5 Believers*, to a small ledge and rappel anchors visible from below. Mike Friedrichs: "Unquestionably one of the best routes on the Dylan Wall."

Paraphernalia: TCUs to large Friends with several #1 and #1.5; large stoppers.

Descent: Rappel the route.

POSITIVELY 4TH STREET I, 5.11a, 1 pitch, 155 feet (47m), ★★★★

First Ascent: Mike Friedrichs, Mary Ellen Gage, Gene Roush, 1992.

Location and Access: Left of *One More Cup of Coffee*. Climb past three bolts to rappel slings not visible from below.

Paraphernalia: Many #1 through #2 Friends with extra #1.5; TCUs; small stoppers;#1 through #3 Rocks; (3) quickdraws.

Descent: Rappel the route.

LIKE A ROLLING STONE I, 5.11b, 1 pitch, 165 feet, (50m), ★★★

First Ascent: *Mike Friedrichs, Gene Roush*, 1992.

Location and Access: Left of *Positively 4th Street*, and left of two crack systems approximately 10 feet (3m) apart, a fixed bolt is visible above an overhanging deep pod low on the climb. The route is four cracks left of *One More Cup of Coffee*.

Paraphernalia: Many #1.5, #2.5 and a #4 Friend; TCUs; medium stoppers. Mike Friedrichs: "In order place #0.75 and #1 tech-friend after the bolt"; (1) quickdraw.

Descent: One full double-rope rappel from triple anchors.

Photo: Eric Bjørnstad

Dylan Wall, from left to right: *Like a Rolling Stone, Positively 4th Street, One More Cup of Coffee, Obviously 5 Believers, Simple Twist of Fate, Isis.*

BLOOD ON THE TRACKS I, 5.12b, 1 pitch, 80 feet (24m), ★★★★★

First Ascent: Mike Friedrichs, Gene Roush, 1992. Second ascent: Tim Coats.

Location and Access: Climb a thin crack in a smooth left-facing dihedral left of *Like a Rolling Stone*. Mike Friedrichs: "Unbelievably good."

Paraphernalia: Friends (1) #1, #1.5, #2.5; TCUs (3) #0, (7) #1.

Descent: Rappel the route.

BLOWIN' IN THE WIND I, 5.10b, 1 pitch, 130 feet (40m), ★★★

First Ascent: Anne Yeagle, Mike Friedrichs.

Location and Access: *Blowin' in the Wind* climbs a right-facing corner one crack left of *Blood on the Tracks*.

Paraphernalia: Standard desert rack with many hands-size units.

Descent: Rappel the route.

IDIOT WIND I, 5.11c, 1 pitch, 80 feet (24m), ★★★★★

First Ascent: Mike Friedrichs and party, 1991.

Location and Access: One crack left of *Blowin' in the Wind*. Mike Friedrichs: "The quintessential Wingate thin crack."

Paraphernalia: Friends through #3; small TCUs.

Descent: Rappel the route from double-bolts.

MILLION DOLLAR BASH I, 5.10c, 1 pitch, 150 feet (46m), ★★★

First Ascent: *Mike Friedrichs*, Gene Roush, 1991.

Location and Access: *Million Dollar Bash* is left of *Idiot Wind*, around a prow. Climb a left-facing dihedral to rappel slings visible at a hanging belay on the right wall.

Paraphernalia: Friends #1 through #4; stoppers for the top.

Descent: Rappel the route from double-anchors.

MIGHTY QUINN (Quinn the Eskimo) I, 5.12a, 2 pitches, 160 feet (49m), ★★★★

First Ascent: Mike Friedrichs, Gene Roush, 1992. Second ascent: Seth Shaw.

Location and Access: *Mighty Quinn* begins up the left (5.9 off-width) or right side of a 50-foot (15m) light-colored tower obvious left of *Million Dollar Bash*. Pitch 2 climbs from the top of the tower up a left-facing corner of dark varnished rock to rappel slings visible from below.

Paraphernalia: A selection of camming devices; (6) or more blue #1 TCUs.

Descent: Rappel the route from double-anchors.

ALL ALONG THE WATCH TOWER II, 5.10d, 2 pitches, 255 feet (78m), ★★★★★

First Ascent: Mike Friedrichs, solo, 1991.

Location and Access: *All Along the Watch Tower* climbs the left-facing dihedral that composes the left side of an obvious tower (The Watchtower). The crux is a 6-inch crack (15cm) at the roof near the top of the tower.

Pitch 1: Climb to a belay from double-bolts at a small stance, 155 feet (47m).

Pitch 2: Continue past a bolt to the top of the tower and triple-rappel anchors, 100 feet (30m).

Paraphernalia: Friends #1 through #6; TCUs; (1) quickdraw.

Descent: Two rappels down the route.

DON'T THINK TWICE, IT'S ALL RIGHT I, 5.11b, 1 pitch, 80 feet (24m), ★★★

First Ascent: Mike Friedrichs, Anne Yeagle, 1995.

Location and Access: One crack left of *All Along the Watch Tower*. Climb past six bolts to double-rappel anchors on the left wall.

Paraphernalia: Small to medium Friends; (6) quickdraws.

Descent: Rappel the route.

KNOCKIN' ON HEAVEN'S DOOR I, 5.10b, 1 pitch, 60 feet (18m), ★

First Ascent: Will Hair.

Location and Access: One crack left of *Don't Think Twice, It's All Right*. Climb past one bolt to triple-rappel anchors.

Paraphernalia: Friends; (1) quickdraw.

Descent: Rappel the route.

PLANET WAVES I, 5.11a, 1 pitch, 100 feet (30m), ★★★★★

First Ascent: Mike Friedrichs, Mary Ellen Gage, 1991.

Location and Access: *Planet Waves* is one crack left of *Knockin' on Heaven's Door*. Climb a thin crack up a left-facing dihedral past a fixed bolt with the crux low on the route. Continue to a ledge with rappel anchors visible from below.

Paraphernalia: One set of Friends; stoppers; hexes; (1) quickdraw.

Descent: Rappel the route.

Photo: Eric Bjørnstad

Dylan Wall, from left to right: *Planet Waves, Knocking on Heaven's Door, Don't Think Twice It's All Right, All Along the Watchtower, Mighty Quinn, Million Dollar Bash, Idiot Wind, Blowin' in the Wind, Blood on the Tracks.*

CHANGING OF THE GUARD I, 5.8, 1 pitch, 120 feet (37m), ★★★★

First Ascent: Mike Friedrichs, solo, 1992.

Location and Access: Climb past seven bolts up the arête of an obvious fallen tower left of *Planet Waves.*

Paraphernalia: Seven quickdraws.

Descent: Rappel to the west.

BUCKHORN SKYLINE RAG I, 5.11c, 45 feet (14m), ★★

First Ascent: Mike Friedrichs, Mary Ellen Gage, 1991.

Location and Access: *Buckhorn Skyline Rag* is one crack left of *Changing of the Guard* and directly above a stock corral in view next to the cliff in the valley below. The route climbs a fingertip crack up the right side of a corner to a ledge with anchors visible from below.

Paraphernalia: Friends through #2.5; TCUs.

Descent: Rappel the route from obvious anchors.

Photo: Eric Bjørnstad

Dylan Wall, from left to right: *Every Grain of Sand, Buckhorn Skyline Rag, Changing of the Guard, Planet Waves* (around corner).

EVERY GRAIN OF SAND I, 5.11d, 1 pitch, 110 feet (34m), ★★

First Ascent: Mike Friedrichs and party, 1991.

Location and Access: *Every Grain of Sand* is several yards left of *Buckhorn Skyline Rag* and one crack right of an obvious free standing tower. The route ascends a 1.5-inch (4cm) left-facing, then right-facing corner to anchors visible from below.

Paraphernalia: Many #1.5 Friends; kneepads helpful.

Descent: Rappel the route.

TANGLED UP IN BLUE I, 5.11a, 1 pitch, 110 feet (34m), ★★★★

First Ascent: Keith Royster, George Jamison, Mike Friedrichs, 1991.

Location and Access: Far left of *Every Grain of Sand*. Mike Friedrichs: "Wide crack splitter with a horribly awkward crux through a bulge to aesthetic stacking above."

Paraphernalia: Many #4, #5 Friends.

Descent: Rappel the route from double-anchors visible from below.

Stock Exchange Wall

Stock Exchange Wall is the Wingate buttress east of Dylan Wall. Approach from the parking area for Dylan Wall or from Mexican Mountain Road beyond the drainage separating Dylan from Stock Exchange. Routes are listed left to right and are left of a large, light-colored arch-in the-making (blind arch) except for *Selling Short* which is right of the arch.

Photo: Eric Bjørnstad

Stock Exchange Wall

ONCE UPON A TIME IN THE WEST I, 5.10d, 1 pitch, 100 feet (30m), ★★★★★

First Ascent: Mike Friedrichs, Gene Roush, 1992.

Location and Access: *Once Upon a Time in the West* is at the far left side of the wall, faces west, and ascends a handcrack up a splitter crack to a ledge with rappel slings visible from below. The crack narrows from 1¼ to 1⅛-inches (3-7cm).

Paraphernalia: Many #1.5 through #2.5 Friends.

Descent: Rappel the route.

MUTUAL FUN I, 5.10d, 1 pitch, 65 feet (20m), ★★★

First Ascent: James Garrett, Dave Anderson, 1992.

Location and Access: *Mutual Fun* faces west and climbs a right-leaning crack system to a hanging belay at the far left side of Stock Exchange Wall. Rappel slings are visible on the smooth light-colored wall the route ascends.

Paraphernalia: Medium-sized Friends; many TCUs.

Descent: Rappel the route.

BULL MARKET I, 5.11b, 1 pitch, 70 feet (21m), ★★★★

First Ascent: Dave Anderson, James Garrett, 1992.

Location and Access: *Bull Market* faces west and ascends a right-leaning, left-facing corner 20 feet right (6m) of *Mutual Fun*. Begin with #1.5 Friends and end with TCUs.

Paraphernalia: Friends through #1.5; (1.5) sets of TCUs.

Descent: Rappel the route.

HIGH DIVIDEND YIELD I, 5.10a/b, 1 pitch, 80 feet (24m), ★★★★

First Ascent: James Garrett, Dave Anderson, 1992.

Location and Access: *High Dividend Yield* is approximately 200 feet right (61m) of *Bull Market*, on the south-facing Stock Exchange Wall, left of a prominent rectangular block projecting out from the wall. Climb a thin right-leaning, left-facing crack system. Rappel slings are visible from below.

Paraphernalia: Several #0 TCUs to large cams.

Descent: Rappel the route.

SELLING SHORT I, 5.10b, 1 pitch, 60 feet (18m), ★★

First Ascent: James Garrett, Dave Anderson, 1992.

Location and Access: *Selling Short* climbs a handcrack 300 feet right (91m) of *High Dividend Yield*, right of a light-colored blind arch.

Paraphernalia: Friends #2, #3.

Descent: Rappel the route.

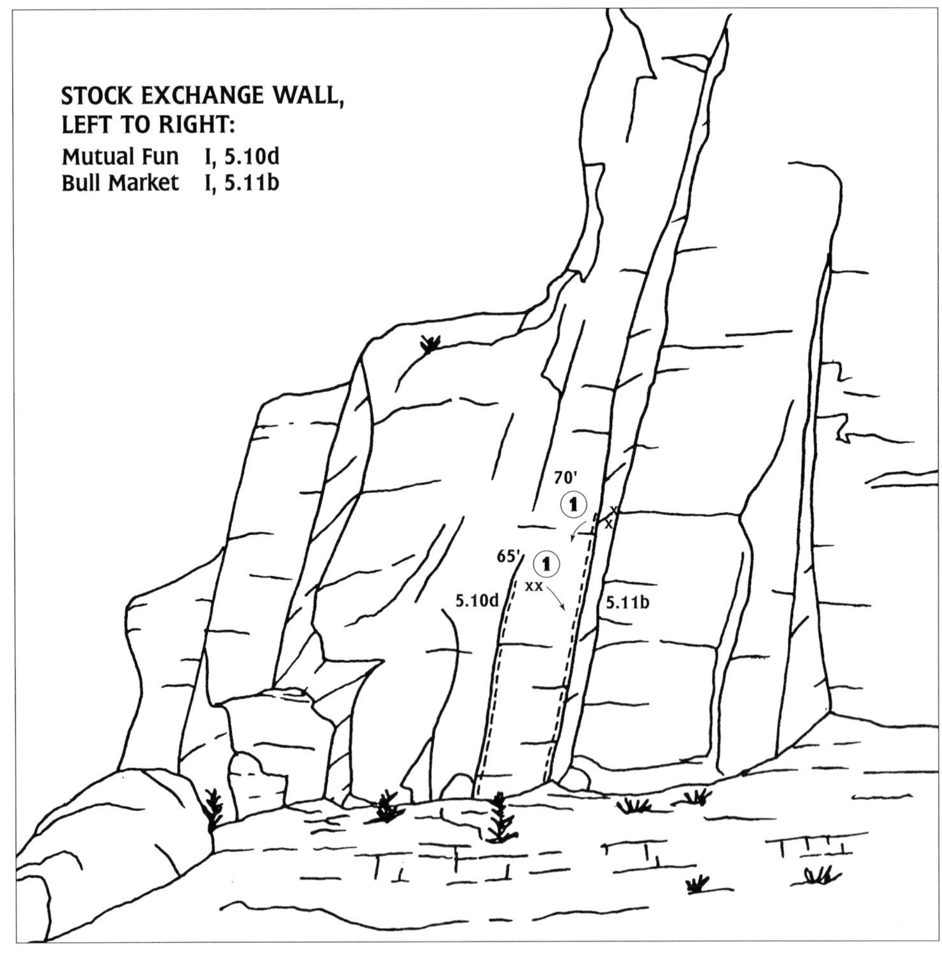

Red Canyon, Emotional Wall

Red Canyon is east of Stock Exchange Wall. To reach, drive 4.6 miles (7.4km) down Mexican Mountain Road from its beginning at the San Rafael River bridge.

Emotional Wall is the buttress left (west) of Red Canyon. The first three routes face Mexican Mountain Road, the last two are on the west wall (east facing) just within Red Canyon. Hike to the wall from Mexican Mountain Road, then traverse right to the climbs, or drive a short distance upcanyon and scramble west to the wall. Both approaches are approximately an hour from the car. Routes are listed left to right.

ANGST CRACK I, 5.11d, 1 pitch, 60 feet (18m), ★★★★★

First Ascent: Mike Friedrichs, Joe Cupps, 1993.

Location and Access: *Angst Crack* ascends a splitter crack left of *Slow Emotion Replay*. Begin up the splitter, then traverse left, and continue up a left-facing corner to rappel slings visible from below. Friedrichs: "A Yosemite-like splitter."

Paraphernalia: Friends through #2; TCUs, stoppers for the traverse.

Descent: Rappel the route.

SLOW EMOTION REPLAY I, 5.11a, 2 pitches, 220 feet (67m), ★★★

First Ascent: Mike Friedrichs, Joe Cupps, 1993.

Location and Access: Right of *Angst Crack*.

Pitch 1: Climb a right-facing dihedral up a 1-1.5-inch crack (2.5–3.8cm) to a belay ledge with double-anchors, 150 feet (46m).

Pitch 2: Continue up a #0.75 TCU crack to double-rappel anchors, 70 feet (21m).

Paraphernalia: Many #1, #1.5 Friends; several #0.75 TCUs; #4 Camalot.

Descent: Two rappels down the route.

AUTOMATIC FOR THE PEOPLE I, 5.11a, 1 pitch, 130 feet (40m), ★★★★

First Ascent: Mike Friedrichs, Todd Leeds, 1994.

Location and Access: *Automatic for the People* is between *Slow Emotion Replay* and *Desolation Row*. Begin up an awkward start through a wide slot that leads to a long lieback. When the crack becomes very small, clip a bolt on the face and traverse to the left crack.

Paraphernalia: Standard desert rack; (1) quickdraw.

Descent: Rappel the route.

DESOLATION ROW I, 5.11d, 1 pitch, 82 feet (25m), ★★★★★

First Ascent: Mike Friedrichs, Joe Cupps, 1993.

Location and Access: *Desolation Row* is right of *Slow Emotion Replay*. Start up a left, then right-facing corner to a 2-inch (5cm) splitter crack which narrows as it climbs. Mike Friedrichs: "*Desolation Row* is the most difficult splitter on the wall." The climb may be top-roped with one rope.

Paraphernalia: Friends through #2; stoppers.

Descent: Rappel the route from double-anchors visible from below.

NEW MOON, EMPTY HEART I, 5.11c, 1 pitch, 110 feet (34m), ★★★★★

First Ascent: Mike Friedrichs, Joe Cupps, 1993.

Location and Access: *New Moon, Empty Heart* is right of *Desolation Row*. Climb a splitter crack to its end, then move left to a crack which curves right at its top. The crux is up a 1.5-inch (5cm) section. Rappel slings are not visible from below.

Paraphernalia: Friends; TCUs.

Descent: Rappel the route from double-anchors.

Red Canyon, Spaghetti Western Wall

Spaghetti Western Wall is on the west side of Red Canyon. To reach, continue upcanyon past Emotional Wall to where rappel slings are visible. Hike to the Wingate buttress between *The Bad, the Good, and the Ugly* and *High Plains Drifter* (a splitter crack up dark varnished rock). Climbs are listed left to right.

FOR A FEW DOLLARS MORE I, 5.11c, 1 pitch, 130 feet (49m), ★★★★

First Ascent: Mike Friedrichs, Will Gilmer, 1992.

Location and Access: Climb a strenuous lieback in the obtuse right-facing corner of dark varnished rock, left of *The Bad, the Good, and the Ugly*.

Paraphernalia: Many #1 through #2 Friends.

Descent: Rappel the route from triple anchors.

THE BAD, THE GOOD, AND THE UGLY I, 5.10b, 1 pitch, 130 feet (49m), ★★

First Ascent: Will Gilmer, Mike Friedrichs, 1992.

Location and Access: *The Bad, the Good, and the Ugly* is left of the approach hike and right of *For a Few Dollars More*. Mike Friedrichs: "A weird start through slightly loose rock (the Bad) just left of cave leads to a really nice handcrack (the Good, #2.5s) and finally to a squeeze chimney (you guessed it, the Ugly) to an anchor on top of a block."

Paraphernalia: Large cams.

Descent: Rappel the route from double anchors.

HIGH PLAINS DRIFTER I, 5.11a, 1 pitch, 140 feet (43m), ★★★★★

First Ascent: Mike Friedrichs, Mary Ellen Gage, 1992.

Location and Access: Climb a left-facing corner between *The Bad, the Good, and the Ugly* and *Angel Eyes*. Mike Friedrichs: "Cruxy start through switching corner to beautiful long handcrack, classic."

Paraphernalia: Friends #2 through #4.

Descent: Rappel the route from a good ledge.

ANGEL EYES I, 5.10, 1 pitch, 140 feet (43m)

First Ascent: Mary Ellen Gage, Mike Friedrichs, 1992.

Location and Access: *Angel Eyes* is right of *The Bad, the Good, and the Ugly*. Begin up a right-facing, right-leaning crack to the top of a column. Continue up a flared left-facing loose and dirty crack system to anchors visible from below.

Paraphernalia: Selection of Friends.

Descent: Rappel from double anchors left of the crack system.

Mexican Mountain Area

Mexican Mountain Area is at the eastern end of Mexican Mountain Road. From Mile Post 137 on I-70 (left to right), Triple Towers, Peak 6333, and Lone Rock are in view. Mexican Mountain, to the right, is the highest landform and has a flat "hat box" summit. The rest area on I-70 (east bound lane) between Mile Post 140 and 141 offers excellent views of the area and the San Rafael Desert south and east. To reach Mexican Mountain area from the San Rafael River bridge, cross the river going north and turn right (east) onto Mexican Mountain Road. Continue approximately 13.8 miles (22.2km) to a wire fence which is the boundary of the Mexican Mountain Wilderness Study Area.

Lone Rock

Lone Rock is a Wingate Sandstone peak with a Kayenta caprock, designated 6145 on the USGS Mexican Mountain quadrangle (7.5 minute topographic series). It is the obvious lone peak at the end (north) of Mexican Mountain Road. From this point, far to the east, the LaSal Mountains are in view east of Moab. The previously unnamed peak was dubbed Lone Rock by Michael Kelseyin his book *Hiking Utah's San Rafael Swell*. Begin the one-hour approach (with heavy packs) below the east face of Lone Rock where Mexican Mountain Road crosses an obvious wash. Follow the wash to an old mining road, then hike it to a prominent bench at the top of the Moenkopi Formation. Complicated route finding is required to work through bands of rock to the base of Lone Rock.

WEST RIDGE II, 5.8, 3 pitches, 350 feet (107m)

First Ascent: Paul Horton, Hal Gribble, Steve Walker, 27 February 1988.

Location and Access: Approach by scrambling up the north side of the west ridge (which leads to the steep summit cone).

Pitch 1: Ascend the crest of the ridge, then make a long traverse left across the face to a large chimney, 5.7.

Pitch 2: Climb the chimney to a large balcony ledge, 5.0.

Pitch 3: A short crack followed by face moves attains the summit, 5.8.

Paraphernalia: One set of Friends.

Descent: Downclimb 15 feet (5m) into a chimney splitting the summit. A chockstone serves as the anchor for a double-rope rappel down the northwest face to easy ground.

OWL'S EYES II, 5.11c, 4 pitches, 400 feet (122m), ★★★★★

First Ascent: James Garrett, solo, 3 October 1992, 5.10, A1. Second ascent: Lorne Glick, Dave Medara, with a variation to pitches 2 and 3. First free ascent: Mike Friedrichs

Location and Access: *Owl's Eyes* climbs to the lower south summit by the east face, then traverses to the higher north summit. A register was left on the first ascent.

Pitch 1: Climb hands-to-thin-hands up a right-leaning splitter crack to a ledge and 2-bolt belay, 5.11c.

Pitch 2: Chimney up and left to face climbing. Pass bolts and continue up a crack to a ledge and 2-bolt belay, 5.10+.

Pitch 3: Continue straight up and left to a belay on the south face under the summit caprock, 5.9.

Pitch 4: Climb a short face past two bolts to the summit.

Paraphernalia: Two set of Friends; Camalots #0.5 through #4 with extra #1.5, #2, #2.5; quickdraws.

Descent: Downclimb the west ridge to the top of Pitch 3, then rappel 165 feet (50m) to the west and continue 3rd class to the ground.

Peak 6333

Peak 6333 is the next landform west of Lone Rock and is designated on the USGS Devils Hole Quadrangle (7.5 minute topographic series).

SKAREN KAREN I, 5.10+/5.11a, 1 pitch, ★★★

First Ascent: Tim Coats, Todd Leeds, Karen Coats.

Location and Access: A one pitch splitter crack (not to summit). Rappel slings are visible on the right side of the tower through binoculars from the Lone Rock approach wash at Mexican Mountain Road.

Paraphernalia: Friends (2–3) sets; extra #2's.

Descent: Rappel the route.

MR. EGYPTIAN 5.9+,

First Ascent: Todd Leeds, Karen Coats, Tim Coats

Location and Access: The corner system right of Skaren Karen.

Descent: Double set of TCU's; Friends

Triple Towers

Triple Towers are in Sulphur Canyon, approximately one mile (1.6km) west of Lone Rock. The spires are in view north of I-70 east of Mile Post 138 (when lighting is favorable). Approach takes 1 to 1-1.5 hours from Mexican Mountain Road. Begin below the east face of Lone Rock where Mexican Mountain Road crosses an obvious wash. Hike the wash to a mining road. Follow the road over a pass and descend a talus slope following the left side of a major drainage, then climb steep talus on the left to a prominent juniper tree. At the tree you are on a rim of rock and can contour right to the towers. Only two of the Triple Towers have been climbed. Thin Man Pinnacle was named by Steve Allen in his excellent book, *Canyoneering: The San Rafael Swell.*

THIN MAN PINNACLE II, 5.9, A1, 2 pitches, 175 feet (53m), ★★★

First Ascent: Steve Walker, Bert Stolt, Hal Gribble, Joe Demarsh, 1988. Second ascent: James Garrett, Ron George, 12 June 1993.

Location and Access: *Thin Man Pinnacle* is the far eastern tower of the Triple Towers. The route begins at the southwest corner of the spire.

Paraphernalia: (1) full set Friends; quickdraws.

Descent: One long rappel down the route.

MIDDLE TOWER—ANALOG CRACK I, 5.10, A1, 2 pitches, 140 feet (43m), ★★

First Ascent: James Garrett, Franziska Garrett, 1 March 1994.

Location and Access: Begin up a large chimney on the north side of the tower. Continue through to the south side, then climb a wide crack to the top where a register was left on the first ascent.

Paraphernalia: Friends through #4 with (1) #5, #6.

Descent: One rope rappel will reach the ground on the south side of the spire.

Mexican Mountain

Mexican Mountain is designated on the USGS Mexican Mountain Quadrangle (7.5 minute topographic series). To approach, drive east from the bridge over the San Rafael River, approximately 13.8 miles (22.2km) to the end of Mexican Mountain Road.

MEXICAN MOUNTAIN IV, 5.0, 6 miles (9.6km), 1800 (549m), ★★★★★

First Ascent: Unknown.

Location and Access: The summit of Mexican Mountain is 6393 feet in elevation (1949m). From the trailhead at the eastern end of Mexican Mountain Road hike approximately one mile (1.6km) to the first point where the dirt track comes close to the river. Ford the San Rafael and continue south toward the mountain, heading for a triangular-shaped slope of the maroon-colored Moenkopi Formation. At its top climb through Chinle cliffs, 5.0, 30 feet (9m), then continue to the base of the Wingate. Traverse east (left), then southwest as the wall curves right. Watch for a U-shaped slickrock gully that may be climbed to the band of rock above. Continue south on a good ledge and at a cairn go west up steep slickrock to a white cliff band. If the ledge widens and large white boulders are found, the cairn has been missed and one should backtrack. Proceed 4th class past several cairns, then traverse around the mountain's summit to the north and a point where cairns lead to the top. This last section is approximately 40 feet (12m) of 4th class scrambling.

Paraphernalia: A short rope and plenty of water.

Descent: Reverse the ascent.

River Bridge West

River Bridge West is west of the campground and the bridge over the San Rafael River.

Trojan Man Wall

Trojan Man Wall is upriver (west) from the bridge over the San Rafael River. To reach, drive 0.4 mile south (0.6km) from the river and turn west and continue approximately one mile (1.6km) to where the road ends at a stock corral near the river. Please leave gates as you find them, open or closed. Trojan Man Wall is high above to the west. Scramble west to break through the Chinle cliffs, then traverse east to the base of the southeast-facing buttress. Routes are listed left to right.

AGAMEMNON I, 5.10d, 1 pitch, 140 feet (43m), ★★★★

First Ascent: Mike Friedrichs, Gene Roush, 1992.

Location and Access: *Agamemnon* begins up a left-facing corner, then climbs a long right-facing dihedral.

Paraphernalia: Wide variety of units.

Descent: Rappel the route.

HELEN OF TROY I, 5.12a, 1 pitch, 120 feet (37m), ★★★★

First Ascent: Mike Friedrichs, Gene Roush, 1992.

Location and Access: *Helen of Troy* is right of *Agamemnon*, and climbs a 0.75-inch (1.9cm) crack system up a smooth left-facing corner through a roof.

Paraphernalia: Friends #1.5; TCUs #0.75.

Descent: Rappel the route

ZEUS I, 5.10b, 1 pitch, 130 feet (49m), ★★★

First Ascent: Gene Roush, Mike Friedrichs, 1992.

Location and Access: Climb a thin handcrack passing a large block on its right. Continue to a ledge with rappel slings visible from below.

Paraphernalia: Protection for hands-to-thin-hands.

Descent: Rappel from double-anchors on the left wall.

Sand Worm Buttress, Petrified Wood Tower

Drive to the parking area for Trojan Man Wall, then hike west along the path on the south side of the San Rafael River for about one hour or approximately three miles (4.8km). Petrified Wood Tower will become obvious on the west (left) side of the river. It is between contour lines 5200 and 5800 below the word "RIVER" on the USGS Bottleneck Peak Quadrangle (7.5 minute topographic series). Sand Worm Buttress is a north-facing wall approximately three-fourths of the way to Petrified Wood Tower.

SAND WORM BUTTRESS—PAJAMA PEOPLE I, 5.10, A2, 2 pitches, 200 feet (61m), ★★

First Ascent: Jon Allen, Doug Byerly, 1995.

Location and Access: *Pajama People* climbs the north-facing buttress before the only major canyon entering the San Rafael River drainage from the west.

Pitch 1: Climb 5.8 loose rock to belay bolts.

Pitch 2: Continue with thin aid to a fingercrack widening to hands, 5.10, A2.

Paraphernalia: Finger-to-handsize protection.

Descent: Rappel the route.

PETRIFIED WOOD TOWER—THE BLACK COW IV, 5.10, A3, 3 pitches, 395 feet (120m)

First Ascent: Lorne Glick, James Garrett, 15 March 1995.

Location and Access: Begin at the middle of the north wall. Bolts were placed only at belay stations.

Pitch 1: Climb a right-facing, left-leaning thin crack, then angle back right up steep rock to a double-anchor belay, 150 feet (46m), A3.

Pitch 2: Climb A2 up a thin to 1-inch crack (2.5cm) to a double-anchor belay, 80 feet (24m).

Pitch 3: Continue up a thin A3 crack ending with 5.10 fist at a 3-drilled-piton belay/rappel station, 165 feet (50m).

Paraphernalia: Friends (2-3) sets; (2) sets of nuts; (3) Bird Beaks; RPs; RURPs; knifeblades; Lost Arrows; assorted angles and Z-pitons.

Descent: Three rappel down the route.

PETRIFIED WOOD TOWER—AWEFUL WIDTH CRACK DIRECT III, 5.10+, A2, 4 pitches, 395 feet (120m)

First Ascent: Kim Csizmazia, James Funsten, 15 November 1995.

Location and Access: The route climbs a crack system on the southeast side of the tower with dark varnish on the left and light varnish on the right.

Pitch 1: Begin 5.10– up a right-facing corner. Tunnel inside the tower and place a #5 Camalot to protect the crux. Continue 5.10+ to a double-anchor belay below a roof, 150 feet (46m).

Pitch 2: Pass the roof on the right side with an awkward A2 move, then back clean. Continue 5.10 past "Laundry Shoot Roof" up a right-facing corner. Pass a chimney on its left and climb 5.10+ to a double-anchor belay station, 150 feet (46m).

Pitch 3: Climb 5.10 to an overhang. Tunnel inside the tower again and place a #3 and #4 Big Bro with a 10-foot sling. Pass the overhang and continue 5.10 to a prominent belay ledge with double-anchors, 80 feet (24m).

Pitch 4: Continue to the summit, 5.2, 15 feet (4.5m).

Paraphernalia: One set of finger-to-handsize units; Camalots (2) #4, (4) #5; Big Bros (2) #3, (4-6) #4; stoppers (3).

Descent: Rappel the route.

Halloween Wall

Halloween Wall is the Wingate buttress west of Bottleneck Peak. Either approach by traversing west from the base of Bottleneck Peak or drive up the road as for the Trojan Man Wall approach. From the end of the road hike up a wash, first west, then south, then scramble up broken Chinle cliffs at the north end of the Halloween Wall buttress. All routes face east and are listed left to right.

SCARY MONSTERS I, 5.12–, 1 pitch, 130 feet (40m), ★★★★★

First Ascent: Dave Medara, Lorne Glick, 1992. On sight by Jose Perada, May 1997.

Location and Access: *Scary Monsters* is one crack left of *Herman Munster*, a little left of center on the buttress. Technical moves in a corner bring one to a ledge and the base of a perfect splitter crack. Continue up an overhanging handcrack to a stance, then climb a narrowing crack to rappel slings (visible from below) on the left wall. Dave Medara: "This monster will eat you."

Paraphernalia: Protection for 0.5- through 3-inch crack system (1.2–7.6cm).

Descent: Rappel the route.

HERMAN MUNSTER TOTAL BODY WORKOUT I, 5.11c, 1 pitch, 110 feet (34m), ★★★

First Ascent: Dave Medara, Steve "Bucky" Bullock, May 1994.

Location and Access: *Herman Munster Total Body Workout* is one crack right of *Scary Monsters* and three cracks left of *The Treat*. Climb a prominent right-facing dihedral

Photo: Eric Bjørnstad

Halloween Buttress

beginning with a lieback up a large light-colored boulder, then continue (with jamming) to rappel anchors visible from below on the left wall. Dave Medara: "This one will get you pumping."

Paraphernalia: An assortment of #0.5 through #4 cams.

Descent: Rappel the route from double-anchors.

THE TREAT I, 5.10+, 1 pitch, 100 feet (30m), ★★★★★

First Ascent: Lorne Glick, Dave Medara, 31 October (Halloween) 1992.

Location and Access: *The Treat* was the first route established on the buttress and was climbed on Halloween Day, giving the buttress its name. Begin up a tall light-colored block right of *Herman Munster*. From the top of the block continue up a left-facing, left-sloping dihedral with prominent light-colored water streaks on its smooth right wall. The route climbs from a 1.5-inch (3.8cm) to an overhanging hand-to-fist crack. Rappel anchors are visible from below. Dave Medara: "Killer!"

Paraphernalia: Camalots #1.5 through #4.

Descent: Rappel the route.

SUPERSTITION I, 5.11+, 1 pitch, 80 feet (24m), ★★★

First Ascent: Dave Medara, Steve "Bucky" Bullock, May 1994.

Location and Access: *Superstition* is two cracks left of *Nightmare on Choss Street*. Begin behind a tall juniper tree near the base of the rock. Climb past four bolts through an overhang to rappel slings visible from below. Dave Medara: "Very technical."

Paraphernalia: A selection of small gear; (4) quickdraws.

Descent: Rappel the route.

NIGHTMARE ON CHOSS STREET I, 5.10+, 1 pitch, 80 feet (24m)

First Ascent: Dave Medara, Linus Platt, March 1994.

Photo: Eric Bjørnstad

Halloween Wall, from left to right: *Scary Monster, Herman Munster Total Body Workout, The Treat, Superstition, Nightmare on Choss Street.*

Location and Access: *Nightmare on Choss Street* is two crack systems right of *Superstition* and two cracks left of the right (north) prow of the buttress. The route starts small and widens to 4-inches (10cm). There is a large block projecting from the wall above the route. Rappel anchors are visible below the block between two horizontal bedding seams. Dave Medara: "Worthless."

Paraphernalia: Friends #1 through #4.

Descent: Rappel the route from a single anchor.

Road Draw, Oil Well Flat Road

Road Draw and Oil Well Flat Road is the region east and west of Cottonwood Wash Road, from Bottleneck Peak to Pinnacle. Approach from the San Rafael River Bridge (north) or I-70 Exit 129 (south).

Bottleneck Peak

Bottleneck Peak is the commanding landform 6235 feet in elevation (1900m) to the right of the road when viewing south from the San Rafael River. Two miles south (3.2km) from the river the peak is identified by a sign and is obvious to the west. Bottleneck Peak is mislocated on the USGS Bottleneck Peak Quadrangle (7.5 minute topographic series). Its true location is designated 6235 on the map. Routes are listed left to right.

WOODY'S ROOFS (Northeast Prow) IV, 5.10+, A2, 4 pitches, 575 feet (175m), ★★★★

First Ascent: James Garrett, Dave Medara, 18 November 1992. Second ascent: Carol Ciliberti, Mary Ellen Gage, 1994.

Location and Access: Locate *Woody's Roofs* by finding a splitter crack in the left margin of the desert-varnished north face (in view from the San Rafael River Bridge). *Woody's Roofs* is on the northeast prow and faces the approach road north from the river. It is approximately 80 feet (24m) left (around the corner) from the original *Langdon Route*. Look for a bolt about 40 feet high (12m) on Pitch 1 and for roofs. The crack system followed gets progressively wider. All belays have some fixed gear and there is a register on the summit. Madera is Spanish for wood, and Medara's excitement for the lead gave the route its name.

Pitch 1: Begin in an easy right-facing corner and climb to a ledge at the base of a left-trending splitter crack. Aid the crack to an optional belay or continue until it widens enough to accept gear. Aid through a roof to a 2-bolt belay. The pitch begins with thin nailing getting progressively wider to TCU size, A2, 150 feet (46m).

Pitch 2: Continue up a Friend crack (#1 through #3) at A1 with some free climbing (will probably go free at 5.11). Pass another roof and end on a comfortable stance below a crack/chimney system, 150 feet (46m).

Pitch 3: Climb an offwidth crack and chimney, 5.10+, 200 feet (61m).

Pitch 4: Chimney 5.9, 75 feet (23m).

NOTE: Doug Hall's topo lists only three pitches, not including the 75-foot (23m) 3rd class summit pitch.

Paraphernalia: Two sets of Friends with (1) #5, #6, #7; (2) sets of TCUs; (1) set of nuts; (1) set of RPs; (4) 0.5" angles; a selection of knifeblades and Lost Arrows; Bird Beaks; 200-foot ropes (60m); quickdraws.

Descent: Three double-rope rappels down *Langdon Route (Northwest Face)*.

TIPPIN' THE BOTTLE IV, 5.11+, 4 pitches, 575 feet (175m), ★★★★★

First Ascent: Mike Pennings, Doug Hall, 20 November 1993. Second ascent: Dave Madera, Ralph Ferrarr, 19 April 1997.

Location and Access: *Tippin' the Bottle* follows a prominent crack and upper corner on the north face of Bottleneck Peak approximately 50 feet (15m) right of *Woody's Roofs* and 30 feet (9m) left of *Langdon Route*. There is no fixed gear left at belays or on the pitches.

Pitch 1: Climb a corner past blocks to a thin handcrack splitting a roof, 5.11–. Continue up "Banana Splitter" and lieback left around a second roof, 5.10–. Belay from a right-angling crack system, 150 feet (46m).

Pitch 2: Ascend a right-angling crack. Pull through an awkward V-slot bulge (5.10+) to a steep fingertip crack that leads to hands and the crux (5.11+) and on to a large belay ledge, 120 feet (37m).

Pitch 3: Pull an awkward thin move over a step and into a cave, 5.10. Climb through the roof of the cave up a fistcrack, 5.11–. Continue up an obvious flake (5.8), then steeper rock (5.9) through blocks to easier ground, 150 feet (46m). The pitch is the original Pitch 3 of *Langdon Route* and is the logical (direct) finish for *Tippin' the Bottle*.

Pitch 4: Scramble 4th class to the summit, 75 feet (23m).

NOTE: Doug Hall's topo lists only three pitches, not showing the 4th class scramble to the summit.

Paraphernalia: Two sets of Friends; (1) #3, #4 Camalot; TCUs #0 through #4. Medium to large nuts.

Descent: Three rappels down the *Langdon Route (Northwest Face).*

LANGDON ROUTE (Northwest Face) IV, 5.10, A2, 4 pitches, 650 feet (198m)

First Ascent: Jim Langdon, solo, 23 June 1973, 5.7, A3. Second ascent: Steve Walker, Bert Stolp, March 1985.

Location and Access: *Langdon Route* is two dihedrals right of *Woody's Roofs.*

Paraphernalia: One set of Friends.

Descent: Three double-rope rappels down the route.

Photo: Jim Langdon

Bottleneck Peak seen from the north.

ZOOMERANG (North Face) IV, 5.11–, 4 pitches, 575 feet (175m), ★★★★

First Ascent: Mike Pennings, Jeff Hollenbaugh, 28 March 1993.

Location and Access: *Zoomerang* ascends the right-facing corner on the right side of the pillar *Langdon Route* climbs the left side of.

Pitch 1: Begin up a left-facing fistcrack until it switches to a right-facing corner, then belay, 5.10.

Pitch 2: Continue up a right-facing corner with a handcrack until it progressively gets wider and requires strenuous wide crack climbing to the top of a pillar, 5.10+.

Pitch 3: Traverse left across the top of the pillar and join *Tippin' the Bottle.* Pull an awkward thin move over a step and into a cave, 5.10. Climb through the roof of the cave with a fistcrack, 5.11–. Continue up an obvious flake (5.8), then up steeper rock (5.9) through blocks to easier ground, 150 feet (46m).

Pitch 4: Scramble 4th class to the summit, 75 feet (23m).

NOTE: Doug Hall's topo combines Pitches 3 and 4 and thus gives the climb only three pitches.

Paraphernalia: Two sets of Friends; (2) #4 Camalots; (1) set of nuts;

Descent: Rappel *Langdon Route.*

BOTTLENECK PEAK:

A. Woody's Roofs (Northeast Prow) IV, 5.10+, A2
B. Tippin' the Bottle IV, 5.11+
C. Langdon Route (Northwest Face) IV, 5.7, A3
D. Zoomerang (North Face) IV, 5,11–
E. Johannis Offwidth (North Face) III, 5.10+

Topo: Doug Hall

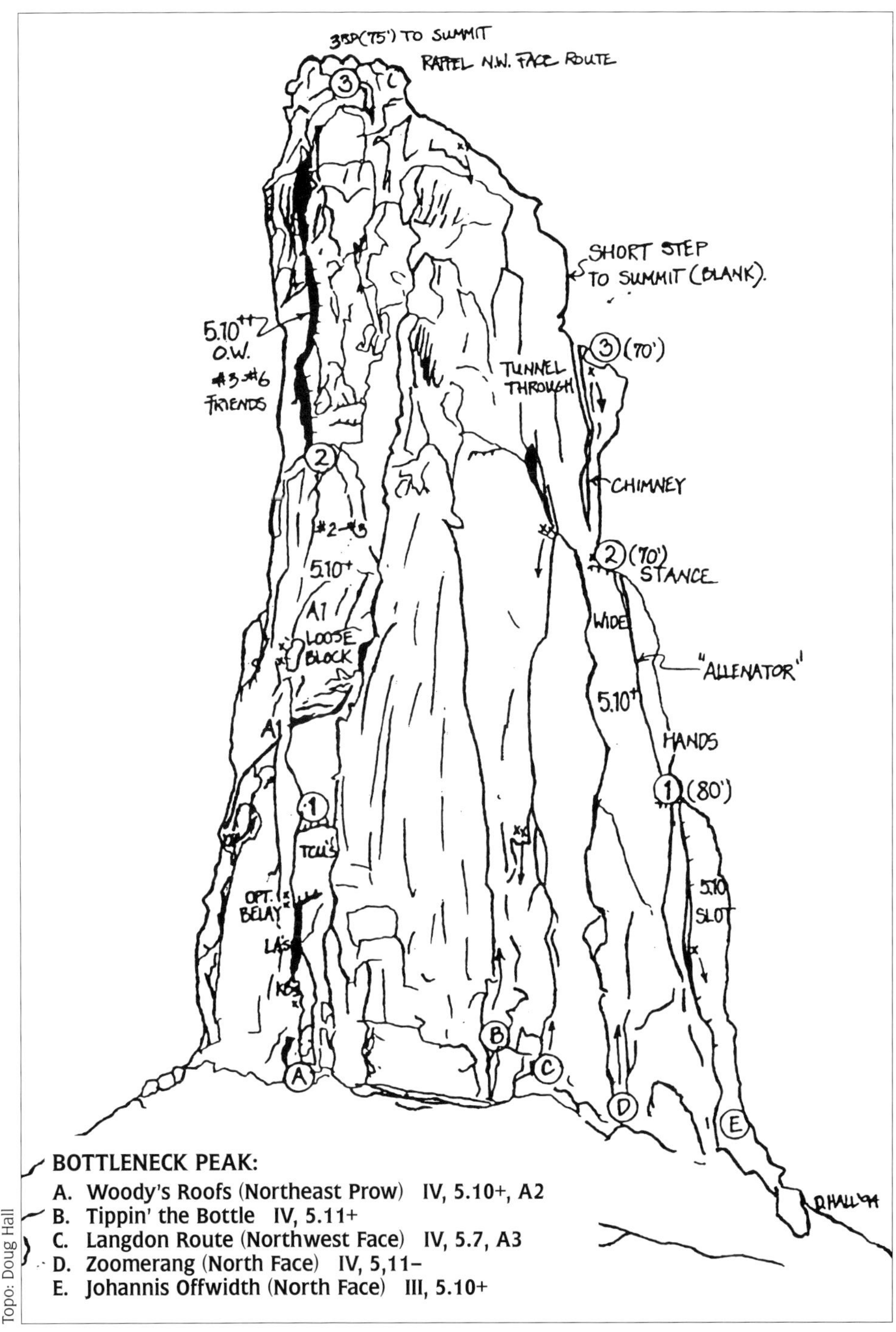

BOTTLENECK PEAK:

A. Woody's Roofs (Northeast Prow) IV, 5.10+, A2
B. Tippin' the Bottle IV, 5.11+
C. Langdon Route (Northwest Face) IV, 5.7, A3
D. Zoomerang (North Face) IV, 5,11–
E. Johannis Offwidth (North Face) III, 5.10+

Topo: Doug Hall

FUMBLING TOWARD ECSTASY III, 5.10, 4 pitches, 225 feet (69m), ★★★★★

First Ascent: Dougald MacDonald, Laura Zaruba, 12 October 1996.

Location and Access: Left of *Johannis Offwidth*. Climb a right-facing corner system on the right side of the north face. A rappel anchor is visible in a chimney approximately 60 feet (18m) up the route. The climb ends at a blank headwall atop the west peak. To reach the higher summit would require a long bolt ladder.

Paraphernalia: Standard desert rack.

Descent: Rappel the route.

JOHANNIS OFFWIDTH (North Face) III, 5.10+, 3 pitches, 220 feet (67m), ★★

First Ascent: James Funsten, Jon Allen, 28 March 1993.

Location and Access: *Johannis Offwidth* begins at the far west end of the north face, approximately 150-200 feet (46-61m) right of *Langdon Route*.

Pitch 1: Climb a left-facing corner to a slot where the first ascent party found a ⅜-inch bolt and "bail-biner." Continue to a belay ledge, 5.10, 80 feet (24m).

Pitch 2: Begin up a perfect handcrack, then climb a steep/wide crack to a belay stance at a drilled angle piton, 5.10+, 70 feet (21m).

Pitch 3: Continue up a chimney and eventually tunnel through to a belay ledge and another drilled angle, 70 feet (21m). Above is a 35-foot (11m) blank wall leading to the summit. The first ascent team chose to rappel the route rather than put up a perfunctory bolt ladder to the top. Please do the same.

Paraphernalia: Two sets of Friends #1 through #4 with #6 and #7 useful; (1) set of TCUs #0.4 through #0.75; (1) set of nuts; quickdraws.

Descent: Rappel *Langdon Route*.

Assembly Hall Peak (Northwest Face)

Assembly Hall Peak is 6395 feet in elevation (1949m) and dominates the view left of the road when looking due south from the San Rafael River Bridge, the vantage from which routes on the Northwest Face are most easily scoped-out. The landform is designated Assembly Hall Peak on the USGS Bottleneck Peak Quadrangle (7.5 minute topographic series).

NOTE: Scott Carson has established routes on the south face with one rated 5.12+. No further information is available at the time of this writing.

HEAVY METAL II, 5.10, A0, 3 pitches, 600 feet (183m), ★★★

First Ascent: James Garrett, Franziska Garrett, 22 October 1992.

Location and Access: There are three cracks sloping left at the band of rock below the obvious bowl on the northwest side of Assembly Hall Peak. Climb a handcrack in a corner at the far right to two bolts placed by an unknown party. Continue 4th class for 250 feet (76m) up the bowl to steep rock, then continue up a left-facing crack system past a number of bolts to the summit. The name *Heavy Metal* refers to the large number of bolts placed on the climb.

Paraphernalia: One set of Friends; quickdraws.

Descent: Rappel an unknown route to the far right (right of three cracks). This unknown route climbs a left-facing dihedral one crack left of *Heavy Metal* before crossing it in the bowl.

ARTHRITIC ANGST I, 5.10a, 1 pitch, 60 feet (18m), ★★★★

First Ascent: James Garrett, Franziska Garrett, 22 October 1992.

Location and Access: *Arthritic Angst* climbs the right side of a leaning pillar left of *Heavy Metal.* Left of the route is a prominent left-facing dihedral and left again, 20 feet (6m) is a splitter handcrack. The route is named for how it cranks on fingers.

Paraphernalia: Small Friends and TCUs. Thin protection.

Descent: Rappel the route.

HAND ASSEMBLY I, 5.10a, 1 pitch, 90 feet (27m), ★★★★

First Ascent: James Garrett, Franziska Garrett, 23 March 1993.

Location and Access: *Hand Assembly* is left of the leaning pillar *Arthritic Angst* climbs. Ascend a 2- to 2.5-inch crack (5–6.3cm) ending up a 1.5-inch crack (3.8cm) to a double-anchor rappel station.

Paraphernalia: Protection for 1-2.5" (2.5–6.3cm) crack.

Descent: Rappel the route from a double-anchor.

LACTIC STACKIDOSIS I, 5.10+, 1 pitch, 80 feet (24m), ★★★★★

First Ascent: James Garrett, Franziska Garrett, 23 March 1993.

Location and Access: *Lactic Stackidosis* is approximately one hundred feet left (43m) of *Hand Assembly.* Climb a right-facing dihedral on the left side of Assembly Hall Peak when viewed from the San Rafael River Bridge. There is a left-facing dihedral, a smooth wall, and farther left a right-facing dihedral. Climb a crack on the right of the wall, close to a left-facing strenuous dihedral. *Lactic Stackidosis* is named for the stacking techniques needed on the route.

Paraphernalia: Offwidth protection.

Descent: Rappel the route from double-bolt anchors.

Window Blind Peak

Window Blind Peak is the major landform 1.5 miles (2.4km) due south of Assembly Hall Peak on the same (east) side of the road when traveling south from the bridge over the San Rafael River. It is 7030 feet in elevation (2143m) and is designated Window Blind Peak on the USGS Bottleneck Peak Quadrangle (7.5 minute topographic series).

WEST FACE IV, 5.9, 5 pitches, 700 feet (213m), ★★

First Ascent: Jim Langdon, Dale Black, Dave Paler, 22–23 September 1973.

Location and Access: *West Face* ascends a crack system right of the center of the west face. Black and Paler were 14 years old when they made the first ascent with Jim Langdon.

Pitch 1: Climb the lower rock band beginning with a 5.9 crack, then continue up a chimney ending with face climbing, 100 feet (30m).

Pitch 2: Climb 4th class to the base of the third rock band, 100 feet (30m).

Pitch 3–5: Climb a chimney and face to the summit, 500 feet (152m).

Paraphernalia: One set of Friends.

Descent: One double-rope rappel, then two short rappels down the southwest ridge.

NORTH RIB II, 5.7, 4 pitches, 700 feet (213m), ★★★

First Ascent: Hal Gribble, Paul Horton, Renny Jackson, Roger Jackson, Guy Toombes, Cindy Wilbur, 19 February 1977.

Location and Access: *North Rib* ascends the rib separating the windows on the North Face of Window Blind Peak.

Pitch 1: Attain a notch low on the rib by climbing chimneys either from the east (slightly easier) or west, 5.5.

Pitch 2: Ascend the rib with face climbing and discontinuous cracks, 5.7.

Pitch 3: Follow a shallow groove to a broken bushy area, 5.5.

Pitch 4: Obvious ramps leading right are easily scrambled to the summit.

Paraphernalia: One set of Friends.

Descent: Rappel the route.

Mother Hubbard's Shoe

The landform is designated 6365 on the USGS Bottleneck Peak Quadrangle (7.5 minute topographic series). It is 0.5 mile north (0.8km) of Window Blind Peak and is the only tower between Window Blind and Assembly Hall Peaks.

SOUTH RIDGE II, 5.8, 3 pitches, 200 feet (61m), ★★

First Ascent: James Garrett, Lorne Glick, 16 March 1995.

Location and Access: Approach as for Window Blind Peak, then gain access to the prominent bench leading to the south ridge tower. Route find through cliff bands as approaching Window Blind, then traverse on a high rim to gain access to the south ridge of the tower. Climb the line of least resistance on the south ridge.

Paraphernalia: One set of Friends; (2) Lost Arrows.

Descent: Rappel to the northwest from slings around a horn, then off a tree, then a sling through an hourglass section of the wall. Make a final rappel to the lower drainage over the rim of the approach.

Weasel, Breezeway, Pinnacle

Pinnacle is designated on the USGS Wickiup Quadrangle as elevation 7010 (7.5 minute topographic series). There is a USGS benchmark on top dating from 1937. To reach, drive 2.2 miles south (3.5km) from the San Rafael River Bridge. Turn west (right) on Oil Well Flat Road and continue (over a cattle guard) 1 mile (1.6km) to a "Y." Keep left and drive 2.5 miles farther (4km). Hike due north to the obvious towers. Approach all three landforms from the left side of the mesa (¾–1 hour). Once at the base of the Wingate Sandstone, reach *Weasel* by traversing to the north face of the tower (the largest on the west end of the mesa). *Breezeway* is also climbed from the north side and is the fin-shaped tower between *Weasel* and *Pinnacle*.

WEASEL—WEASEL ON THE RUN III, 5.11c, 4 pitches, 360 feet (110m), ★★★

First Ascent: James Garrett, Franziska Garrett, 5.10, A0, 24 October 1995. First Free Ascent: Seth Shaw, Beth Malloy, March 1996.

Photo: Frosty Weller

Weasel (south side)

Location and Access: *Weasel on the Run* begins up a left-facing dihedral at the apex of the talus cone on the north side of the landform.

Pitch 1: Climb a 3–5-inch (7.6–13cm) left-facing dihedral to a 2-bolt belay at Alcove Ledge, 5.10, 80 feet (24m).

Pitch 2: Continue with hands up a left-facing corner 2–3-inch (5–7.6cm) to a second 2-bolt belay, 140 feet (43m), 5.11c.

Pitch 3: Climb a 5.8 crack (just in from the right corner of the wall) to a good ledge, 40 feet (12m).

Pitch 4: Scramble 4th class up and right to a 5.7 crack system and a 2-bolt belay/rappel station, 100 feet (30m).

Paraphernalia: Two sets of Friends with extra #1.5, #2, #2.5; (1) set of TCUs; (1) set of nuts.

Descent: Rappel the route.

BREEZEWAY—WEST FACE (aka Tibia Tower) I, 5.9, 2 pitches, 150 feet (46m)

First Ascent: Jim Howe, Tommie Howe, March 1996.

Location and Access: Begin in a handcrack on the north face, move left to another crack and continue to a ledge on the west face. Above is a narrow low-angle face. Continue past drilled pitons to below the summit block and belay. Climb right to the south face and the final moves to the summit.

Paraphernalia: A light standard desert rack to a #4 Friend.

Descent: One 150-foot rappel (46m) down the steep south face.

PINNACLE—GENERIC ROUTE II, 4th class, 370 feet (113m)

First Ascent: Unknown.

Location and Access: Pinnacle is the eastmost of the tower group (designated as Pinnacle on the Wickiup USGS map). Approach from Oil Well Flat Road south of the landform. Scramble to a point directly beneath the summit. Move east, then north and finally south where there are several ponderosa pines. Continue from behind a large boulder and climb a series of steep ledges, then move left to the summit. Steve Allen: "Plan on spending a little time on the marvelous summit platform."

Paraphernalia: Belay rope.

Descent: Reverse the route.

PINNACLE—SOUTH FACE III, 5.11, A0, 5 pitches, 370 feet (113m)

First Ascent: James Garrett, Jim Howe, with Franziska Garrett on Pitches 1 and 2, 17 March 1996.

Location and Access: *South Face* climbs the large obvious left-facing dihedral on the south side of the landform.

Pitch 1: James Garrett: "Climb nice hands until the rock gets a little chossy in the dihedral and another crack appears on the left wall. Go up a right-facing little crack 50 feet until it ends and a short bolt ladder allows access to the main dihedral again. Continue up the wide crack (all #4 Camalot size) to a 2-bolt belay under a small roof," A0, 90 feet (27m).

Pitch 2: Continue over the small roof past a bolt (up and right) placed due to expanding rock. Climb steep 3-3.5-inch crack (7.6–9cm) to a belay in an alcove, 5.10c, 80 feet (24m).

Pitch 3: Traverse right past a bolt and around a corner, then continue up easy face moves to a 2-bolt belay, 5.6, 50 feet (15m).

Pitch 4: Face climb right to a short 2-inch crack (5cm) to a leftward ramp which climbs above a large arch. Continue straight up a steep face past 1-bolt, a hole, and 2 more bolts to a good ledge and a 2-bolt belay, 5.11, 130 feet (40m).

Pitch 5: Veer right and continue through easy 5th class climbing to the top.

Paraphernalia: Standard desert rack with extra #3.5, #4 Friends; many #4 Camalots for Pitch 1; quickdraws.

Descent: Walk-off to the north.

Devils Monument, Phred Phlinstone

Devils Monument is designated on the USGS Devils Monument Quadrangle (7.5 minute topographic series). It is approximately 7 miles (11.2km) north of I-70, west of Saddle Horse Canyon. It may be approached with route finding from I-70 between Mile Post 122 and 123. See Chimney Rock, page 233. To reach from Cottonwood Wash Road, see approach to Pinnacle, page 230. Past Pinnacle continue south on Oil Well Flat Road for 3.2 miles (5km). Ascend a hill to a junction with Cane Wash, 1 mile (1.6km). Continue on Oil Well Flat Road, up Cane Wash 1.6 miles (2.5km) to caves obvious on the right of the wash. One hundred yards (91m) past the caves, exit the wash to the right on a hard-to-see trail. Seventy yards (64m) farther veer right at a "Y." Gain a pass at 2.5 miles (4km) with views to Devils Monument to the northwest. Continue up Saddle Horse Canyon to the east approach to Devils Monument. To reach *Phred Phlinstone*, exit I-70 at Mile Post 129. Drive south on a dirt road 3.3 miles (5.3km) to a cattle guard. At 5.7 miles (9km) go through an I-70 underpass (north). Turn left at mile 6.8 (11km) at an intersection. Continue through a fence gate at mile 7.7 (12km). At mile 8.3 (14km) there is an intersection with the right branch ending in 0.3 mile (0.4km) at a pictograph panel. The *Phred Phlinstone* tower is obvious from this vantage.

PHRED PHLINSTONE II, 5.7, C2+, 2 pitches, 220 feet (67m), ★★★

First Ascent: Dave Gloudemans, solo, 15 May 1997.

Location and Access: The route climbs a large left-facing corner on the south face of a spire slightly detached (and right of) the butte with Barrier Canyon style pictographs (badly vandalized). The location is approximately 200 yards (183m) north of I-70.

Pitch 1: Aid up a crack to loose blocks, 65 feet (20m). Move right (C2+) into a crack with stoppers for protection. The system quickly grows to 3-inches (7.6cm) and continues the same size for 60 feet (18m) before widening (#5 Camalot helpful). Move through a slight overhang onto a ramp (not visible from below). Belay on nuts and small cams at a good stance.

Pitch 2: Free or aid up a left trending ramp (nuts) to an obvious overhanging crack. Aid (C1) through this section and gain a stance above, then avoid rotten rock by traversing left on a sloping shelf (5.7, nuts). Pull up on a large ledge at head height, and wander to the top. A register was left hidden on the summit.

Paraphernalia: One set of Friends with extra 3-4 #2.5, #3, #3.5; two sets of stoppers; Tri-cams; hexes; #5 Camalot.

Descent: Rappel the route or the shorter back side of the spire.

DEVIL'S DOG II, 5.9, 4 pitches, 270 feet (82m)

First Ascent: Billy Roos, Patrick Morrow, 24 April 1995.

Location and Access: *Devil's Dog* climbs the crack system on the southeast corner of Devils Monument. No fixed anchors are in place on the route.

Pitch 1: Begin up 20 feet (6m) of offwidth and climb to a ledge, 5.8. Protect with a large hex and #3 Camalot.

Pitch 2: Continue up a loose left-facing corner with hands/fingers, 5.9, 80 feet (24m). Protect with #2 and #3 Camalots.

Pitch 3: Chimney 5.8 for 130 feet (40m) with an optional belay at the chockstones encountered part of the way up the pitch. Protect with large cams.

Pitch 4: Climb 4th class 40 feet (12m) to the summit.

Paraphernalia: Standard desert rack with extra #3 and #4 cams.

Descent: Rappel the route.

Head of Sinbad North, Eagle Canyon Area

Climbs at Head of Sinbad North are in the central San Rafael Swell and are reached from I-70 between Mile Post 122-123. Drive south through a wire gate, then north under the Interstate. West-bound traffic may access by crossing the median on a dirt road opposite the wire gate. Eagle Canyon Area climbs are in the region of Eagle Canyon Bridge between Mile Post 117-118 on I-70.

Chimney Rock

Chimney Rock is a large dome north of I-70 (northwest of the exit between Mile Post 122-123). To reach, exit I-70 between Mile Post 122-123 and drive south through a wire gate, then north under the Interstate and continue straight (right fork goes to Sandcastle).

CHIMNEY ROCK II, 5.3

First Ascent: Unknown.

Location and Access: Chimney Rock is 7406 feet in elevation (2253m). From the north climb a steep gully 100 feet (30m) to a ledge and move left (east). Pass a narrow point (with exposure), then ascend a gully to a slot. Continue to the top. The crux is the first 15 feet (4.6m) protected with a sling through a hole, 5.3.

Paraphernalia: Belay rope; slings.

Descent: Reverse the route.

NOTE: Steve Allen in *Canyoneering, San Rafael Swell*: "Rock climbers note: The 175-foot-tall Golden Gate Pinnacles have potential for several fine climbs. Elevation 7079 has two moderate routes on the southeast side that are destined to become classics (see San Rafael Knob USGS topo)."

Scallywag Point, Mustard Jar, Twin Raven

Twin Raven is the most prominent of these landforms and is in view 0.75 mile (1.2km) north of I-70 from Mile Post 123. To reach, exit between Mile Post 122-123, go south through a wire gate, north under the Interstate, then straight to the entrance of a small canyon with Twin Raven obvious at its far end. Near the entrance to the canyon, park at a fork coming from the right (east). Scallywag Point is to the northeast. North from Scallywag Point, at the end of a small canyon, is a 100-foot (30m) "jump" or drop. Mustard Jar can be seen in the middle of Cane Wash from this lookout, and to the right 100 yards away (91m) is Twin Raven. Rappel the jump (leaving a fixed rope for the return), then ridgewalk to Mustard Jar.

NOTE: Fremont Indian petroglyphs are located through the tunnel under the Interstate and to the right.

Photo: Randall Weekley

Scallywag Point, *Plank Walk*

SCALLYWAG POINT—PLANK WALK I, 5.10-, 1 pitch, 160 feet (49m)

First Ascent: Frosty Weller, Randall Weekley, 10 October 1992.

Location and Access: *Plank Walk* climbs the northwest face of the tower.

Paraphernalia: Standard desert rack; (1) 6" Tube Chock; (2) long Lost Arrows.

Descent: One double-rope rappel down the route.

MUSTARD JAR—MEAN MR. MUSTARD I, 5.10+, 1 pitch, 80 feet (24m)

First Ascent: Keen Butterworth, Frosty Weller, Fall 1992.

Location and Access: *Mean Mr. Mustard* is left of *Mustard Jam* on the west face of the landform.

Paraphernalia: One set of Friends.

Descent: One simultaneous rappel, then ascend the fixed rope to exit Cane Wash.

Photo: Frosty Weller

Mustard Jar* and *Twin Raven

MUSTARD JAR—MUSTARD JAM I, 5.10+, 1 pitch, 80 feet (24m)

First Ascent: Frosty Weller, Keen Butterworth, Fall 1992.

Location and Access: *Mustard Jam* climbs the west face right of *Mean Mr. Mustard.*

Paraphernalia: Protection for off-hands-to-fist.

Descent: One simultaneous rappel, then ascend the fixed rope to exit Cane Wash.

TWIN RAVEN—DIVIDE AND CONQUER II, 5.8 R, C2, 2 pitches, 180 feet (55m)

First Ascent: Frosty Weller, Jonathan Auerbach, 30 September 1995.

Location and Access: *Divide and Conquer* climbs the opposite side of the tower (northeast) from its approach view.

Pitch 1: Begin up a right-facing corner C1, then C2 protected with Big Dudes. Climb a 5.7 chimney to a belay ledge, 120 feet (37m).

Pitch 2: Ascend a 5.8 R chimney (with no protection) 60 feet (18m). A register was left on the summit by the first ascent team. Frosty Weller: "Last pitch is a wild chimney/stem with great views out both sides of the spire."

Paraphernalia: Two sets of Friends with extra large sizes; Tri-cams; (3) or more Big Dudes 6–7"; quickdraws.

Descent: One double-rope rappel to the east.

Sandcastle, Outpost, Secret Pillar

Sandcastle and Outpost are on a ridge between Cane Wash and Oil Well Flat. To reach, exit I-70 between Mile Post 122-123. Drive south through a wire gate, then north under the freeway, and take the east (right) fork. Continue around cliffs, through a gate, and over a large open meadow. Go left at a "Y" in the meadow and continue northwest. When the road begins to drop into the Cane Wash drainage it becomes 4-wheel-drive only. Go northeast on the rim road approximately 1.6 miles (2.6km). Sandcastle and Outpost landforms will be obvious.

Secret Pillar is approached as for Sandcastle and Outpost. Before the road begins to drop into Cane Wash, Secret Pillar will reveal itself directly to the east against the cliffs. The view of Secret Pillar from this point is impressive. It is free standing yet never separate from the wall behind it by more than 10 feet (3m). The pillar can be seen from I-70 before Mile Post 123 westbound. It blends in with the cliffs behind, hence the name.

NOTE: Fremont Indian petroglyphs are through the tunnel under I-70 and to the right, on the approach to Sandcastle.

Photo: Frosty Weller

Outpost* and *Sandcastle

SANDCASTLE (Northwest Face) III, 5.10–, A2, 4 pitches, 300 feet (91m)

First Ascent: Frosty Weller, Randall Weekley, 11 October 1992.

Location and Access: *Sandcastle* climbs the center of the northwest face, right of a prominent chimney. The last pitch traverses right.

Paraphernalia: Standard desert rack; (1) #7 Tri-cam; (1) baby angle, (5) ¾", (1) 1" through 1.5"; (1) long thick knifeblade.

Descent: Two double-rope rappels down the route.

SANDCASTLE (Southwest Face) III, 5.8, A2, 3 pitches, 300 feet (91m)

First Ascent: Randall Weekley, Frosty Weller, 2-3 April 1994.

Location and Access: Climb to a 7-inch pod (18m) with a fixed anchor in the center of the southwest face and continue up a 2- to 3-inch (5–7.6cm) crack system to a belay stance 80 feet (24m) up the route. From the top of Pitch 2 climb to a fixed anchor, then make a right traverse around the corner and up to the summit, 5.8.

Paraphernalia: Standard desert rack; Friends (3) #0.5 through #3, (2) #3.5, (2) #4; (2) #5 Camalots; (2) sets of Tri-cams through #3; (1) #7 Big Dude; (1) #2 Big Bro; (10) pitons, knifeblades through 1"; (3) Lost Arrows; (3) baby angles; (2) quickdraws.

Descent: Two rappels down the north face.

OUTPOST II, 5.8+, 3 pitches, 250 feet (76m)

First Ascent: Frosty Weller, Randall Weekley, 12 October 1992.

Location and Access: *Outpost* is climbed by the east ridge of the tower. The step below the top of Pitch 1 is reached with a scramble from the north. Pitch 2 is a traverse along the north side of the formation.

Paraphernalia: One set of Friends; (1) 6" Tube Chock.

Descent: Reverse Pitch 2, then rappel from a block at the top of Pitch 1.

Photo: Randall Weekley

Sandcastle (view from the northwest)

SECRET PILLAR—SKELETON IN THE CLOSET II, 5.10a, C1, 2 pitches, 190 feet (58m)

First Ascent: Frosty Weller, Jonathan Auerbach, 1 October 1995.

Location and Access: Begin on the south face up a right-facing dihedral with 5.10a hands. Continue C1 angling right and up rotten rock to a stance and a belay at the beginning of a chimney. Protect with two #5 Camalots and a Big Bro. The second pitch follows a chimney (The Closet) with 5.8 climbing up a 5 to 12-inch crack system (12.7-30cm). There is a register in a hole a few feet off the summit.

Paraphernalia: Friends (2) #1.5, (1) #2, (2) #2.5, (3) #3, (4) #3.5, (2) #4; a selection of Tri-cams and nuts; quickdraws.

Descent: One double-rope rappel down the backside of the pillar from double-anchors.

Photo: Frosty Weller

Secret Pillar

White Knight, Mother Goose

White Knight is approximately 1 mile (1.6km) north of I-70. The landform may be identified by a small tree at the center of its summit and a cairn on the west edge. To view from westbound lanes it is necessary to pull off I-70 and look back to the northeast. It is more easily in view from eastbound lanes to the northeast (below the skyline) just past Mile Post 116. There is a median cross-over west of Mile Post 116 and a view of White Knight east of Mile Post 116. To reach, drive just east of Mile Post 118 where there is a locked gate with a sign reading "authorized personnel only" and a road leading to a highway maintenance shed. Hike the road into Eagle Canyon, then scramble to White Knight.

Mother Goose is a "pointy" formation beside the Interstate (north) on the approach to White Knight and is visible from I-70 east of Eagle Canyon. It is the obvious landform in front of a long outcrop of rock blocking the view of White Night from points east of Eagle Canyon.

WHITE KNIGHT—EAST RIDGE II, 5.9, 2 pitches, 180 feet (55m)

First Ascent: George Hurley, Bill Forrest, 29 November 1977.

Location and Access: The route is obvious on the east side of the tower.

Pitch 1: Climb 5.9, 130 feet (40m).

Pitch 2: Climb 5.7, 50 feet (15m).

Paraphernalia: One set of Friends.

Descent: Rappel 165 feet (50m) down the north face.

WHITE KNIGHT—WEST FACE II, 5.9, A2, 2 pitches, 175 feet (53m)

First Ascent: James Garrett, Allan Murphy, 9 November 1991.

Location and Access: *West Face* was the second ascent of White Knight. Climb the opposite side of the tower from the first ascent line.

Paraphernalia: Climb with clean aid except for (1) knifeblade placed low on the tower.

Descent: Rappel 165 feet (50m) down the north face.

MOTHER GOOSE—NURSERY RHYMES I, 5.6, 1 pitch, 80 feet (24m)

First Ascent: Keen Butterworth Jr., Keen Butterworth, 2 August 1992.

Location and Access: *Nursery Rhymes* ascends the northeast face of the landform.

Paraphernalia: A small selection of Friends.

Descent: Rappel the East Face.

SAN RAFAEL SOUTH

I am not sure whether anyone who has wandered (the canyon country) and looked upon the wonders that nature has wrought-its gorges, its canyons, its mountains and its painted rocks and upon its ancient stone city, and the cliff dwellings of its canyons-is ever afterward quite sane.

Colonel Charles D. Poston, 1920

[T]he least inhabited, least inhibited, least developed, least improved, least civilized, most arid, most hostile, most lonesome, most grim bleak barren desolate and savage quarter of the state of Utah-the best part by far.

Edward Abbey, Desert Solitaire

San Rafael South is the region south of I-70. Many routes are reached from Ranch Exit 129 (same exit for San Rafael North) 29 miles west (47km) of Green River. The south exit begins a loop road which will exit the Swell at Temple Mountain Junction on State Highway 24, a point 25 miles south (40km) of I-70 and 20 miles north (32km) of Hanksville. For further information and maps on San Rafael Swell South, visit the Hanksville BLM office at 406 South 100 West, (801) 542-3461.

San Rafael Knob Area

The San Rafael Knob Area is the south central region of the Swell south of I-70. Access from Exit 114.

Phantom Spire, San Rafael Knob

The Phantom Spire is beside Copper Globe Road in the west-central region of the Swell. It is visible from eastbound lanes south of I-70 just past Mile Post 115. To reach, drive 44 miles west (71km) of Green River on I-70 to Exit 114. The exit is the Moore Cutoff Road, and an Interstate designated "View Area" with restrooms. To the east, White Knight is in view, although it is difficult to distinguish without binoculars. Cross the Interstate south and follow a paved frontage road east to the dirt Copper Globe Road. Justensen Flats is reached in 2 miles (3km) and offers good camping. Copper Globe Road is 1.5 miles farther (2.4km). The spire is beyond Devils Canyon Wash 3 miles (5.6km) from the Interstate and is reached at the bottom of a steep hill that may require 4-wheel drive beyond the junction. Phantom Spire and I-70 may also be reached from Utah 10 (driving south from Price) at a turn on the Moore Cutoff Road.

San Rafael Knob is the highest point in the San Rafael Swell. It is named and designated 7921 on the San Rafael Knob USGS topographic quadrangle (7.5 minute series). Steve Allen in *Canyoneering, San Rafael Swell*: "If you do only one hike in the San Rafael Swell, this should be it. Be forewarned, it is like eating Almond Roca; once you are on top of the knob and can see the whole swell and what it has to offer, you will keep coming back! Guaranteed... To

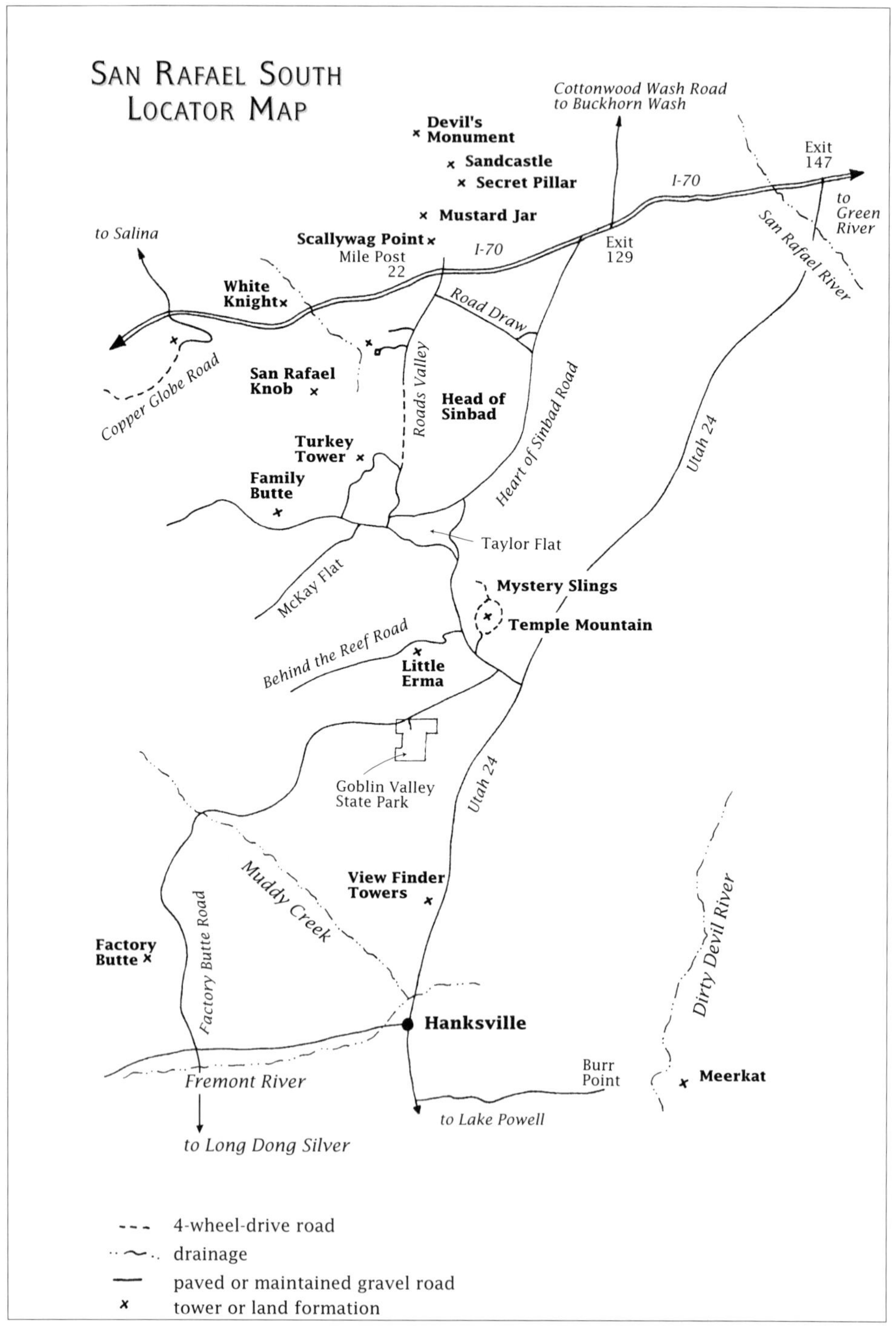
SAN RAFAEL SOUTH
LOCATOR MAP
Cottonwood Wash Road
to Buckhorn Wash
Devil's Monument
Sandcastle
Secret Pillar
Mustard Jar
Scallywag Point
Mile Post 22
I-70
Exit 147
to Green River
Exit 129
to Salina
White Knight
Road Draw
San Rafael River
Copper Globe Road
San Rafael Knob
Roads Valley
Head of Sinbad
Heart of Sinbad Road
Utah 24
Turkey Tower
Family Butte
Taylor Flat
McKay Flat
Mystery Slings
Temple Mountain
Behind the Reef Road
Little Erma
Goblin Valley State Park
Muddy Creek
View Finder Towers
Factory Butte
Factory Butte Road
Dirty Devil River
Hanksville
Burr Point
Meerkat
Fremont River
to Lake Powell
to Long Dong Silver
4-wheel-drive road
drainage
paved or maintained gravel road
tower or land formation

keep you from being confused, there are many slickrock knobs in the area. The San Rafael Knob is not one of them. It is the peak-like monolith seen to the southeast as you go down Copper Globe Road."

PHANTOM SPIRE I, 5.9, 1 pitch, 80 feet (24m)

First Ascent: Keen Butterworth, Frosty Weller, Fall 1992.

Location and Access: *Phantom Spire* climbs the north side of the tower beginning up a right-facing dihedral before continuing up an arête.

Paraphernalia: Friends (1) set with doubles on medium to large sizes; a small selection of nuts.

Descent: Rappel the route.

SAN RAFAEL KNOB 5th class

First Ascent: Unknown.

Location and Access: To reach, see approach to Phantom, page 239. Where the road crosses Devils Canyon, hike east into the canyon, then upcanyon passing several steps by scrambling up steep slopes on their side. After passing each step return to the canyon floor. At each "Y" take the right fork. Note the arch on the left just past the first step. After approximately two hours the knob comes into view to the south. Hike to its north side. Climb a series of steep slabs and ledges. Near the top traverse to the south side and continue up slabs to the summit. Chimney Rock is the largest and nearest landform north of I-70. Beyond to the right is Window Blind Peak. Also in view is Pinnacle and Devils Monument. Far to the east are the LaSal Mountains (east of Moab) and southeast is Temple Mountain. Nearer, Turkey Tower and Family Butte are in view. Beyond Family Butte is Factory Butte and farther south the Henry Mountains.

Paraphernalia: None required.

Descent: Reverse the route. To make the hike a loop, hike the track visible to the southwest, continuing west, then north as the track joins Copper Globe Road.

Head of Sinbad South

Head of Sinbad South is the region from I-70 to Family Butte. To reach, take Exit 129 south from I-70, the Heart of Sinbad Road. A sign reads: "Utah 24, 29 (miles), Goblin Valley 30, Temple Mountain" with arrows pointing south.

Broken Cross, Turkey Tower, Family Butte (aka Seven Sisters)

Broken Cross is the tower behind the historic Swasey Cabin. To reach, take Exit 129 and go south under the Interstate. The road travels west at the beginning, crosses a cattle guard, then 1.8 miles farther (2.9km) turns south. At a "T" take the branch to the right (west) and continue for 1.1 miles (1.7km), then turn right and drive northwest for approximately 4 miles (6.4km). At this point I-70 will be only 0.3 mile north (0.4km). Drive south for 2 miles (3.2km) and turn right. Swasey's Cabin is reached in approximately 0.6 mile (0.9km).

An alternate approach to Broken Cross is to drive 35.5 miles (57km) west from Green River on I-70 to a point 0.5 mile (0.8km) past Mile Post 123. Turn south through an underpass (difficult to see and accessible from eastbound lanes only). Continue through a gate, then

Photo: Frosty Weller

Family Butte, southeast face

follow Road Draw west 0.3 mile (0.5km) and turn right at an intersection, always following the most used road. There is a corral at 0.9 mile (1.4km), a gate at 1.1 miles (1.8km), and a "T" in the road at 1.6 miles (2.5km). Make a left turn. At 2.3 miles (3.7km) keep right (west). Broken Cross is 0.8 mile farther (1.3km).

The cabin was built in 1921 by the Swaseys, a Mormon pioneer family who came to the Swell in the 1870s. Their name for the shelter was Cliff Dweller Cabin. There is a spring with fresh water behind the cabin and a BLM-maintained outhouse east of the cabin. (The USGS topo map misspells Swasey designating it "Swazy".) The area is 7218 feet (2200m) in elevation and a good place to camp in the hot San Rafael summer.

Turkey Tower is named by Steve Allen in his book, *Canyoneering, The San Rafael Swell*. It is shown as Peak 7601 on the USGS San Rafael Knob Quadrangle (7.5 minute topographic series). To approach Turkey Tower, take Exit 129 from I-70 and go south under the freeway. The road travels west at the beginning, crosses a cattle guard, then 1.8 miles farther (2.9km) turns south. Keep left at a "T" 3.8 miles (6km) beyond the cattle guard. At another junction keep left

Photo: Frosty Weller

Turkey Tower, from left to right: *Swiss Gentlemen*, South Face.

(south). At the next junction (9.9 miles, 16km from the cattle guard) turn right (southwest). In the distant west Family Butte comes into view, with Turkey Tower prominent to the right of the butte.

Family Butte is in the center of San Rafael Swell South at an elevation of 6575 feet (2004). To reach, follow directions to Temple Mountain, page 246. Continue past Temple Mountain and Flat Top Mesa. The road eventually leads to Tan Seep intersection which has a sign to I-70. Continue west toward Reds Canyon, passing the road to McKay Flats on the left (south). The six pinnacles of Family Butte (the seventh has fallen) will be obvious atop the mesa on the right (north) side of the road. The easiest approach to the butte is from the southeast. Park along the road west of a poorer road on the right leading to Green Vein Mesa. Scramble up the steep, loose slopes of the mesa to the north. The south faces are 200–350 feet in height (61-107m). The north faces are 30–50 feet (9–15m) in height.

BROKEN CROSS I, 5.10+ S, 1 pitch, 140 feet (43m), ★★★

First Ascent: James Garrett, Michael Franklin, 1991. Second ascent: Frosty Weller, Randall Weekley, 12 June 1993.

Location and Access: *Broken Cross* climbs the rightmost crack system when viewed from Swasey Cabin.

Paraphernalia: Two sets of Friends; hooks for bolt holes at the start of the route.

Descent: Rappel left when viewing from Swasey Cabin.

TURKEY TOWER—MR. TAMBOURINE MAN III, 5.11, C1, 3 pitch, 320 feet (98m), ★★★★★

First Ascent: Mike Friedrichs, James Garrett, Winter 1990.

Location and Access: Turkey Tower is shown as Peak 7601 on the USGS map and is north of and visible from Family Butte. *Mr. Tambourine Man* climbs a left-facing dihedral with a hand-to-fingercrack up three pitches on the west face of the tower. There is a summit register left by the first ascent party.

Pitch 1: Climb a right-facing dihedral (5.9) to a short rotten band protected by a bolt, then climb a 5.11 left-facing dihedral to a 3-bolt hanging belay under a roof, 165 feet (50m). James Garrett: "Great 5-star pitch."

Photo: James Garrett

Turkey Tower, *Mr. Tambourine Man*

Pitch 2: Continue left through a roof, following a thin right-facing dihedral to a traverse, and right past 2 bolts to a belay ledge.

Pitch 3: A short pitch which ascends an easy, then steep bolt ladder to the top.

Paraphernalia: Three sets of Friends; TCUs; quickdraws.

Descent: Rappel the south face.

TURKEY TOWER—SWISS GENTLEMAN II, 5.8, A2, 2 pitches, 250 feet (76m), ★★★

First Ascent: Seth "ST" Shaw, James Garrett, 19 November 1990.

Location and Access: Turkey Tower is point 7108 on the USGS map. *Swiss Gentleman* ascends the second summit by its northeast corner. A 20-foot (6m) cleft divides the summit.

Paraphernalia: One set of Friends with extra #2 through #3; a selection of pitons.

Descent: Rappel the route.

TURKEY TOWER—SOUTH FACE II, 5.11a/b, 2 pitches, 250 feet (76m), ★★★★

First Ascent: James Garrett, Annette Keller, 21 April 1991.

Location and Access: The route climbs the middle of the south face. Two drilled angles with rappel slings were found at the top of Pitch 1, placed by an unknown party.

Pitch 1: Climb a splitter crack up the center aspect of the south face.

Pitch 2: Continue up and left through a rotten chimney to better rock, with face climbing to the south summit of *Swiss Gentleman*.

Paraphernalia: Friends (3) #1 through #3.5; Camalots #4 or #5 for Pitch 2 and the bottom of Pitch 1.

Descent: Traverse to the top of *Swiss Gentleman*, then make three rappels.

SOUTH TOWER—ALIEN CHILD III, 5.10, A2, 3 pitches, 250 feet (76m)

First Ascent: James Garrett, Mike Friedrichs, 3 November 1990.

Photo: Randall Weekley

First pitch variation on second ascent of *Alien Child*.

Photo: B. Baett

Bicker Sucker Crack.

Location and Access: *Alien Child* climbs the right side of the south face, and was established during the first ascent of South Tower of the Family Butte spires.

Pitch 1: Begin with a 5.10 squeeze chimney and continue to a 2-bolt anchor.

Pitch 2: Work left and up past bolts and a thin crack to a sloping ledge.

Pitch 3: Follow a 20-foot (6m) bolt ladder to the top. Pitches 2 and 3 may be combined.

Paraphernalia: Standard desert rack with a selection of pitons; knifeblades up to 2" plus offwidth-size protection; quickdraws.

Descent: Rappel to the north from 2 bolts.

SOUTH TOWER—ALIEN CHILD VARIATION III, 5.9, A2, 2 pitches, 200 feet (61m)

First Ascent: Randall Weekley, Frosty Weller, 14 November 1992.

Location and Access: The variation begins 15 feet (5m) left of *Alien Child*, bypassing an unappealing squeeze chimney. Pitch 1 climbs 100 feet (30m) to join Pitch 2 of *Alien Child*. The climb was the third ascent of South Tower.

Paraphernalia: Standard desert rack with a selection of pitons; knifeblades up to 2"; quickdraws.

Descent: Rappel to the north.

SOUTH TOWER—BICKER SUCKER CRACK I, 5.8, 1 pitch, 50 feet (15m)

First Ascent: Benny Bach, Kelly McMenamen, March 1991.

Location and Access: *Bicker Sucker Crack* climbs the South Tower from its southeast corner. Climb the crack system behind the left side of a prominent flake. The route was established and summit register placed during the second ascent of South Tower.

Paraphernalia: Friends #2, #3.

Descent: Rappel the north face.

MIDDLE TOWER—DAUGHTER III, 5.11b, 3 pitches, 350 feet (107m), ★★★★

First Ascent: James Garrett, Allan Murphy, 5.10, A1, 29 October 1990. First free ascent: Mike Friedrichs, Gene Roush.

Location and Access: Middle Tower is the third spire of the Family Butte group counting from the left. *Daughter* climbs the Middle Tower from the south (left) side. Begin at a point directly below the second tower from the left. After a short climb the route angles right to eventually top-out up a crack system in the center of Middle Tower.

Paraphernalia: Two set of Friends.

Descent: Rappel the north side.

NORTH TOWER—SON OF PUTTERMAN I, A0+, 1 pitch, 150 feet (46m)

First Ascent: Benny Bach, Charles Martin, Cameron Burns, 13 March 1993.

Location and Access: *Son of Putterman* climbs the northernmost of the Family Butte towers by a 17-bolt ladder. The route faces south and has a 4th class approach.

Paraphernalia: Three-eighths-inch bolts and hangers.

Descent: Rappel the route.

Temple Mountain

Temple Mountain Area includes Temple Mountain, Mystery Slings (near it) and Little Erma (southwest of Temple Mountain).

Temple Mountain, Mystery Slings Variation, Little Erma

Temple Mountain is 6772 feet (2064m) in elevation and is approximately halfway between Hanksville and I-70. It is designated on the USGS Temple Mountain Quadrangle (7.5 minute topographic series). To reach from Green River, drive west on I-70 to State Highway 24 (Exit 147), then 25 miles south (40km) to the Goblin Valley State Park Road which is also Temple Mountain Junction, between Mile Post 136-137. This is a point 20 miles north (32km) of Hanksville, nearest town to the Temple Mountain Area of the Swell. From the east the massive butte is visible above the San Rafael Reef for many miles. Temple Mountain has been mined for vanadium and uranium since the turn of the century. The area is littered with mining debris and pockmarked by dangerous drifts and shafts containing radioactive gases, unstable rock, rotten timber, and explosives.

Mystery Slings Variation climbs a large wall across a dry creek bed on the south side of the road as one travels west around Temple Mountain. This is a point where the road levels after climbing past Temple Mountain. Old mining debris is obvious beside the road.

Little Erma is a tower south and above Little Erma Uranium Mine at the top of Chute Canyon. Approach is from Behind the Reef Road, which begins 7.2 miles (11.5km) down Temple Mountain Road from State Highway 24. Chute Canyon is a left (south) turn from Behind the Reef Road. Little Erma is obvious above the mine.

NOTE: Chute Buttress is the highest point in the southern portion of the San Rafael Reef at 6508 feet (1984m) in elevation. A USGS benchmark is anchored to its summit.

TEMPLE MOUNTAIN—NORTH FACE 4th-5th class with 50 feet (15m) of vertical climbing

First Ascent: Unknown. A USGS benchmark shares the summit with a wooden survey stake with carved names and dates as early as the 1930s.

Location and Access: An obvious weakness on the north face leads to the ridge between the summit and the northeast peak.

Paraphernalia: Drinking water; rope optional.

Descent: Reverse the ascent by downclimbing or rappelling.

MYSTERY SLINGS VARIATION III, 5.10b, 3 pitches, 340 feet (104m)

First Ascent: James Garrett, Franziska Garrett, 1993.

Location and Access: *Mystery Slings Variation* is along the road south of Temple Mountain. Begin in a crack 30 feet (9m) right of unknown mystery slings.

Pitch 1: Climb a right-trending crack, 5.9+, 120 feet (37m)

Pitch 2: Ascend a splitter crack, 5.10a, 110 feet (34m).

Pitch 3: One move of 5.10b, 110 feet (34m).

Paraphernalia: Standard desert rack with mostly 1" through 2.5" pieces.

Descent: Move 100 feet (30m) left, then make two rappels from double-anchors visible from below.

LITTLE ERMA I, 5.9, 2 pitches, 120 feet (37m)

First Ascent: Keen Butterworth, Mike Bryan, Spring 1992.

Location and Access: *Little Erma* ascends the east face of the landform.

Pitch 1: Climb 5.8, then tunnel through a chimney to a belay ledge.

Pitch 2: Angle left on 5.9 face to a handcrack leading to the summit.

Paraphernalia: Standard desert rack.

Descent: One double-rope rappel down the route.

Factory Butte Area

Factory Butte Area is the southern region of the San Rafael Swell west of Utah 24. Hanksville is the nearest town with gas, food, water, motels, a BLM and San Rafael Swell information office but with few other amenities. Climbs in the area are Factory Butte, Long Dong Silver, and View Finder Towers.

Factory Butte

Factory Butte is 6358 feet (1938m) in elevation and a prominent landmark in San Rafael Swell South, visible for many miles from all directions. To reach, drive 10.5 miles (17km) west of Hanksville on Utah 24 (toward Capitol Reef National Park). Hanksville is approximately 45 miles (72km) south of I-70. Turn north onto Factory Butte Road (unmarked) but with a stop sign for vehicles entering Utah 24. Due east of the butte, park and hike west on a 4-wheel-drive road. In approximately 0.5 mile (0.8km) a small knoll is reached. From the knoll continue west about 1 mile (1.6km), hiking along ridge tops of cascading dirt piles, to a steep gully on the southeast end of the butte.

SCHOOL FOR ADVANCED SUFFERING IV, 5.9+, 11 pitches, 1800 feet (549m)

First Ascent: Tony Calderone, on-sight free solo, 22 December 1994.

Location and Access: Begin up a steep dirt gully on the southeast end of the butte.

Pitch 1: Climb a "scary" dirt face, 5.9, 150 feet (46m).

Pitch 2: Continue up a "scary" loose chimney, 5.9+, 150 feet (46m).

Pitch 3: Chimney past large blocks, 5.7, 150 feet (46m).

Pitch 4 and 5: Climb loose dirt, 5.5, 300 feet (91m).

Photo: Tom Till

Factory Butte

Pitch 6: Continue up loose dirt, 5.5, 150 feet (46m).

Pitch 7: 4th class to a large ledge, 300 feet (91m).

Pitch 8: Ascend a chimney with large blocks in it, 5.7, 150 feet (46m).

Pitch 9: Continue over very exposed rock, 5.8, 150 feet (46m).

Pitch 10: More exposure, 5.4, 150 feet (46m).

Pitch 11: Climb to the summit, 5.4, 150 feet (46m).

Paraphernalia: Pitches 1–7 are up very loose dirt and protectable with thin ice equipment (e.g. Archeopteryx or Black Diamond Spectre). Pitches 8–11 are on more stable sandstone and protected with (2) full sets of cams; 3- to 4-foot-long (7.6–10cm) 2x4s; long slings.

Descent: Rappel the route from long 2x4s jammed in chimneys.

Photo: Matt Moore

Long Dong Silver

Long Dong Silver

Long Dong Silver is approximately 2 miles south (3.2km) of Utah 24. To reach, drive 10 miles west (16km) of Hanksville on Utah 24. Just before an abandoned brick building (on the left) turn south on a dirt road and continue up Town Wash into Blue Hills Valley. Hike to the spire when it comes into view, approximately 0.3 mile ahead (0.48km).

LONG DONG SILVER I, 5.9, A3, 1 pitch, 100 feet (30m)

First Ascent: Matt Moore, Josh Blumental, February 1993.

Location and Access: Long Dong Silver is climbed from its east side.

Paraphernalia: Toucans; Auks; soft (aluminum) Arrows w/ small RP's; very long slings.

Descent: Downclimb 10 feet below summit to rap slings.

View Finder Towers

View Finder Towers are hoodoo-like spires approximately 10 miles north (16km) of Hanksville at a pullout on the west side of Utah 24. Sighting pipes and name signs are obvious at the pullout.

SANDY DUNCAN I, 5.8+, 1 pitch, 75 feet (23m)

First Ascent: Keen Butterworth, Jonathan Averbach, 30 October 1993.

Location and Access: *Sandy Duncan* is northwest of *Prairie Dog* and *Space Baby*. The route ascends the west face.

Paraphernalia: One set of Friends.

Descent: One simultaneous rappel.

PRAIRIE DOG I, A3, 1 pitch, 80 feet (24m)

First Ascent: Keen Butterworth, solo, 10 October 1993.

Location and Access: *Prairie Dog* climbs the west face to a stance and a bolt, then continues up a north-facing crack system to the top.

Paraphernalia: Selection of Friends; nuts; pitons; (1) quickdraw.

Descent: One simultaneous rappel.

SPACE BABY I, 5.10–, 1 pitch, 35 feet (11m)

First Ascent: Keen Butterworth, Jonathan Averbach, 30 October 1993.

Location and Access: *Space Baby* is northeast of *Prairie Dog*. The route climbs the west face.

Paraphernalia: Friends (1) #1.5, #2, #2.5, #3.

Descent: One simultaneous rappel.

Photo: Jonathan Averbach

Meerkat Spire

Dirty Devil River Gorge

Meerkat Spire is at the southern edge of the San Rafael Desert in the Dirty Devil River Gorge and is included in this chapter for its geographic proximity to the San Rafael Swell. To reach, drive south of Hanksville on State Highway 95 approximately 15 miles (24km) to a dirt turn to the east. Drive approximately 10 miles (16km) to Burr Point Overlook and park. From the Overlook it is approximately 4 miles (6.4km) and a 1500 foot (457m) elevation loss to Meerkat Spire. Hike the Burr Trail (which proceeds generally north along Kayenta benches) to the northeast-facing gully across from the mouth of Twin Corral Box Canyon. Descend, then cross the Dirty Devil River (which is seldom more than knee-deep). Meerkat Spire is first observed about halfway down the descent gully on the ridge that separates Twin Corral Box Canyon and the Dirty Devil River.

MEERKAT SPIRE—THE POWER AND THE GLORY I, 5.10b R, A1 (or 5.11+ C1), 3 pitches, 160 feet (49m)

First Ascent: Frosty Weller, Jonathan Auerbach, 6 April 1996.

Location and Access: *The Power and the Glory* ascends the northwest face of the Wingate spire named for the small African desert animal which stands erect when alerted. A summit register was left in a hole at the second belay station.

Pitch 1: Climb a 5.9 slot, pass a small overhang on its left, then continue up a left-facing corner with thin hands (5.10b), and finally 5.9 hands to a belay station.

Pitch 2: Climb a 5.9 chimney and on to 5.9 hands. Continue up a left-facing corner at 5.11+, C1 with thin hands/fingers, then easy hands past a 5.9 offwidth and a 5.8 squeeze to a belay ledge where a register was left on the first ascent.

Pitch 3: Climb loose rock at 5.8 R, then A1 ending with 5.8 R and the summit.

Paraphernalia: Friends (1) #0, #0.5, (2) #1, #1.5, (3) #2, #2.5, #3, (2) #3.5, #4; Camalots #5 optional; Tri-cams #0.5 through #3; (1) set of nuts.

Descent: One rappel north to obvious blocks, then downclimb 4th class to the ground.

The pleasure of risk is in the control needed to ride it with assurance so that what appears dangerous to the outsider is, to the participant, simply a matter of intelligence, skill, intuition, coordination–in a word, experience.

A. Alvarez

On, under, and around these red-and-tan sandstone towers moves a private, sometimes bewildering subculture of climbs. It has its own idioms, taboos, and personalities, its own literature, history, and language.

Jeff Long

ERIC BJØRNSTAD
A Climbing Life

Eric Bjørnstad is perhaps best known as a pioneer of desert towers during the incredible early years when those phenomenal spires were first being climbed. Indeed, many of us climbing his routes today would shudder at the idea of doing them in the 1960s and early '70s with the available gear and lack of information. Certainly Eric's name is indelibly etched in the rich lore of desert climbing. But a broader look also reveals a life of great variety and interest, both within and outside the climbing world.

From the start, Eric engaged himself in a wide range of endeavors. Raised in California, his early passions included poetry writing, chess, speed typing, classical music, and playing both the piano and oboe. He also sought physical challenges such as boxing, in which he excelled. Eric began camping early, with numerous trips to the High Sierra, and like many climbers then and now, a great love of high places was kindled.

Eric's first job was as a Gandy Dancer on the narrow gauge railroad near Lone Pine, California. This began a working life of incredible variety; over the years he worked as a draftsman, piano salesman, photo processor, gardener, bartender, dump truck driver, tree topper, and handyman at a sorority traded for a place to live, to name only a sampling. His life apart from work was no less interesting. He married three times (to a Hungarian beauty queen, an art student, and the daughter of a major American business mogul), divorced three times, and fathered four children (David, Heather, Mara, and Eigerwand). He practiced Theravada Buddhism in Berkeley in the '50s, partied with the likes of Alan Watts, Jack Kerouac, and Ferlingetti and took up spelunking. In the late 1950s he moved to Seattle and began a long career in alpine mountaineering. He amassed an impressive list of climbs and first ascents: Zodiac Wall, the first grade VI on the Squamish Chief, the North Face of Mount Howser in the Bugaboos, first winter ascent of Mt. Robson, first ascent of the North Face of Mt. Slesse, seventh ascent of Liberty Ridge on Mt. Rainier, Mt. Seattle in the St. Elias Range in Alaska, second ascent of the West Peak of the Moose's Tooth, and many others. He also taught climbing for the Seattle Mountaineers, served on the Seattle Mountain Rescue team for

eight years, and represented American climbers during the Seattle World's Fair French-American climbing week. It was also during this time that Eric began to write about climbing, in both magazines and books. He co-authored the *Climber's Guide to Leavenworth Climbing Areas* with Fred Beckey and wrote the "Pitoncraft" chapter for the second edition of the classic text, *Mountaineering, Freedom of the Hills.*

From the 1960s on, Eric moved often and lived in cities across the country. He added weaving and three dimensional stained glass to his professional repertoire, as well as proprietorships of five restaurants/coffee houses. He also developed a passion for climbing in the mysterious landscape of the Southwest desert. The routes that he and other desert pioneers established on these spooky towers tested the limits of existing equipment and techniques as well as their nerves. First ascents in the '60s included Echo Tower in the Fisher Towers, the Beckey Buttress on Shiprock (20 days), Middle Sister and Jacobs Ladder in Monument Valley, Chinle Spire, and the 574th overall ascent of Devil's Tower when he and Fred Beckey put up the popular *El Matador* route.

During these years, Eric climbed with such well-known figures as Ed Cooper, Alex Bertulis, Don Claunch, Harvey T. Carter, Yvon Chouinard and Galen Rowell. He also developed an intense relationship with Fred Beckey–the two would share many first ascents over the years.

In 1970 he opened his famous Teahouse Tamarisk (24 page menu). In 1975 he began a ten year period as a researcher investigating the effects of air pollution on lung health for the Harvard School of Public Health, which kept him traveling extensively. He returned to the desert time and again during this period, establishing first ascents such as Eagle Rock Spire in Monument Valley (another 16-day marathon), and Zeus and Moses in Canyonlands. He also did the 5th ascent of the incredible Totem Pole in Monument Valley, during the making of the film *The Eiger Sanction.*

In 1985 Eric finally made Moab his permanent home and made the 600th ascent of Castleton Tower, the first ascent of the 1000 foot El Piñon Blanca in Mexico, and participated in the first ascents of such well-known climbs as *Zenyata Entrada* in Arches. He also undertook the phenomenal researching and writing task of authoring *Desert Rock*, the only comprehensive guide to desert climbs.

Eric now guides hikes in Arches, works with Canyonlands Natural History Association, drives four-wheel desert tours, produces and sells Desert Glass Light Catchers, etched glass window hangings of anasazi rock art, and is completing an expanded four-volume guide to technical rock climbs on the sandstone walls of the southwest desert, the only comprehensive climbing guide to the Colorado Plateau.

Eric has truly lived a climbing life–in the high mountains, on rock walls, and in the desert Southwest. He has lived a well rounded life as well, full of rich and enviable experiences. He loves the company of climbers, and will spend hours telling and listening to stories or pressing for information. His home is like a climbing museum. Yet, just as easily, he will revel in an opera or classical orchestral piece, or spend an evening preparing a fine dinner.

These guides are a tribute to Eric's life as a climber–and to his love for this desert land.

Jeff Widen
November 1995

INDEX

Bolded numbers refer to topos or photos of the feature or route. Formations and areas are in all capitals.

C

N

Q

R

Notes

Notes

Notes

ACCESS: It's every climber's concern

The Access Fund, a national, non-profit climbers organization, works to keep climbing areas open and to conserve the climbing environment. Need help with closures? land acquisition? legal or land management issues? funding for trails and other projects? starting a local climbers' group? CALL US!

Climbers can help preserve access by being committed to Leave No Trace (minimum-impact) practices. Here are some simple guidelines:

• **ASPIRE TO "LEAVE NO TRACE"** especially in environmentally sensitive areas like caves. Chalk can be a significant impact on dark and porous rock – don't use it around historic rock art. Pick up litter, and leave trees and plants intact.

• **DISPOSE OF HUMAN WASTE PROPERLY** Use toilets whenever possible. If toilets are not available, dig a "cat hole" at least six inches deep and 200 feet from any water, trails, campsites, or the base of climbs. *Always pack out toilet paper.* On big wall routes, use a "poop tube" and carry waste up and off with you (the old "bag toss" is now illegal in many areas).

• **USE EXISTING TRAILS** Cutting switchbacks causes erosion. When walking off-trail, tread lightly, especially in the desert where cryptogamic soils (usually a dark crust) take thousands of years to form and are easily damaged. Be aware that "rim ecologies" (the clifftop) are often highly sensitive to disturbance.

• **BE DISCRETE WITH FIXED ANCHORS** *Bolts are controversial and are not a convenience*—don't place 'em unless they are *really* necessary. Camouflage all anchors. Remove unsightly slings from rappel stations (better to use steel chain or welded cold shuts). Bolts sometimes can be used proactively to protect fragile resources—consult with your local land manager.

• **RESPECT THE RULES** and speak up when other climbers don't. Expect restrictions in designated wilderness areas, rock art sites, caves, and to protect wildlife, especially nesting birds of prey. *Power drills are illegal in wilderness and all national parks.*

• **PARK AND CAMP IN DESIGNATED AREAS** Some climbing areas require a permit for overnight camping.

• **MAINTAIN A LOW PROFILE** Leave the boom box and day-glo clothing at home—the less climbers are heard and seen, the better.

• **RESPECT PRIVATE PROPERTY** Be courteous to land owners. Don't climb where you're not wanted.

• **JOIN THE ACCESS FUND** Become a member! Make a tax-deductible donation of $25.

The Access Fund

Preserving America's Diverse Climbing Resources

PO Box 17010
Boulder, CO 80308
303.545.6772 • www.accessfund.org